ENGLISH
FOLK
POETRY

Publications of the American Folklore Society
New Series
General Editor, Marta Weigle
Volume 2

ROGER deV. RENWICK

ENGLISH
FOLK
POETRY

Structure
and
Meaning

UNIVERSITY OF PENNSYLVANIA PRESS
1980

Library of Congress Cataloging in Publication Data

Renwick, Roger deV   1941–
  English folk poetry, structure and meaning.

  (Publications of the American Folklore Society :
New series ; v. 2)
  Bibliography: p. 259
  Includes index.
    1. Folk-poetry, English—History and criticism.
I. Title.   II. Series: American Folklore Society.
Publications of the American Folklore Society : New
series ; v. 2.
PR976.R4   398.2'0941   79–5260
ISBN 0–8122–7777–5

CONTENTS

ACKNOWLEDGMENTS

A doctoral grant from the Canada Council and a stipend from the University of Pennsylvania permitted the 1973 fieldwork on which chapters 4 and 5 of this book are based. During the same period, the library research that provided the raw data for chapter 3 was conducted. Other institutional aid has come from the University Research Institute of the University of Texas, Austin; their Summer Research Award in 1976 made possible the writing of the first drafts of chapters 1 and 2, while their Special Research Award in 1979 paid for typing expenses.

I solicited critical comments from several colleagues at the University of Texas during various stages of the writing. My thanks in this regard go to Roger D. Abrahams, Richard Bauman, Larry Carver, John P. Farrell, and Archie Green. An indebtedness of a more encompassing sort I owe to two in particular of my mentors: D. K. Wilgus, who taught me so much about folksong and who more than anyone is responsible for whatever may be praiseworthy in chapters 1, 2, and 3; and Kenneth S. Goldstein, not only for his role as teacher but also for encouraging my plunge into a relatively unexplored subject matter, modern-day working-class poetry.

As for individuals who for the most part are not connected with the academy, foremost among these are, of course, the Yorkshire poets responsible for the work analyzed in chapters 4 and 5 who kindly gave me permission to print their poems. Many gave freely as well of their time and hospitality in interviews. In this book these poets are faithfully identified by their real names: Mr. Roy Blakeley of Ravensthorpe, Mr. Walter Greaves of Keighley, Mr. Danny Hampsey of Laughton Common, Mrs. Mavis Walsh Proud of Thorp, and Mrs. Margaret Watford of West Ardsley. I owe especial gratitude to yet another Yorkshire poet, "Martha Bairstow," to whom I have assigned a pseudonym, as I have to her places of residence, "West Hartford" and "Millington." My fieldwork in Yorkshire was also aided immeasurably by the friendship and hospitality of Bill and Wendy Price of Dewsbury and their many friends, and by the collegiality of A. E. Green of the University of Leeds.

For permission to reproduce published material my thanks go to Mr. Ephraim Mugglestone of Langold, Nottinghamshire, and to Mr. George Wainwright of Holbeck, Leeds. Photographs of the broadsides on which their poems were first printed appear in chapter 5. The editor of Leeds's *Evening Post*, Mr. Malcolm G. Barker, allowed the quoting of a short news item and its accompanying poem, the poet being one of the newspaper's own reporters, Mr. Gordon Pickles. The director of the Institute of Dialect and Folk Life Studies at the University of Leeds, Stewart F. Sanderson, not only made the Institute's archives available to me during 1973 but also permitted reproduction of items from the archives appearing in chapter 3. From quite a bit further south, Peter Kennedy, director of the Centre for Oral Traditions, Harberton, Totnes, Devon, gave permission to reprint several excerpts from his *Folksongs of Britain and Ireland* (London: Cassell, 1975). Finally, the National Museum of Man, National Museums of Canada, allowed the quoting of selections from Kenneth Peacock's *Songs of the Newfoundland Outports* (Ottawa: National Museum of Canada, 1965); Oxford University Press from *Cecil Sharp's Collection of English Folk Songs*, edited by Maud Karpeles (London: Oxford University Press, 1974) and from *Lark Rise to Candleford*, by Flora Thompson (London: Oxford University Press, 1954).

PREFACE

This is a book about a certain kind of subject matter, English folk poetry. It is not a book about a theory, or about a method, or even, for that matter, about a segment and period of English culture. Although I welcome readers of all interests and persuasions, I have written these studies with a distinct audience in mind: collectors, analysts, and lovers of folk poetry.

The primary goal of the studies is to discover implicit meanings in texts. The result is a set of interpretations not generally part of scholars' current stock of knowledge and understanding of the genre English folk poetry. Thus they are, in a sense, revelations. Since there are in the study of folk poetry no well-established and systematic procedures, analytical constructs, or terminologies for the enterprise in which I engage, I have taken the liberty of drawing ideas and materials from a wide range of scholarly sources. By "drawing from" I do not mean that I have adhered to any one existing system of inquiry or, indeed, to any one epistemology; I mean only that I have used the results of what some serious but quite selective reading in a number of fields has, over the past eight years, planted in my mind (and sometimes quite subliminally at that)— results that I can best describe as bits of notions, perspectives, *ways of thinking* about folk poetry. But the subject matter of that folk poetry is the only thing that has been truly constant in my thoughts and purposes throughout the period.

The study of folklore is the one discipline in which I can claim expertise and thoroughness, and it is in this field of study that my work is firmly grounded. The discipline has provided me with a feeling for the kinds of stylized expressions that are an integral part of a social group's everyday resources; with a knowledge of seminal works, critical, bibliographical, and substantive, on the relevant subject; with a basic terminology of words like *traditional, version, motif,* and so forth, that folklorists use with a shared understanding; and with an allegiance to a comparative approach, practiced within regional limits. The study of folklore, in short, is generative of my thinking.

Two other disciplines that have contributed are cultural anthropology and social history. The first has influenced me not only in that so many of the *interpretive* studies of quotidian cultural products have come from practitioners of that scholarly craft, but also in that it has stimulated me to seek the relationships of folklore products to their cultural contexts, an attention that one may call— using the terms nontechnically—structural and functional. My debt to social history is a more topical and materialist one, brought about by my need for information on the cultural background to traditional folksong. I have no lengthy acquaintance with this field, and must confess to at times plundering it for my special needs. I hope the social historian will not feel ill used by, for instance, my citing of E. Royston Pike's convenient but highly selective anthology, *"Hard times": Human Documents of the Industrial Revolution,* to amplify a brief characterization of life in northern industrial towns that I make in chapter 3. I *have* read a bit more widely than that, but not—as a true historian would—the original documents themselves in all their fullness and complexity.

Three other contributing fields of study—but ones whose boundaries are almost impossible to define—may be called, respectively, phenomenological approaches to culture, studies in communication, and general systems theory. The attenuated influence of the first can be seen in my consistent stress on the cognitive, on typified models of experience as they are mapped into poetic texts, and especially on the familiarity or unfamiliarity of the topics of poetry in the real everyday experiences of its makers and users. Studies in communication and in general systems—insofar as they apply not to the physical and natural sciences but to the cultural— have influenced me, particularly in my emphasis on the interrelationship among phenomena as a primary analytical construct. I have also taken the liberty of borrowing some terminology from these fields—four terms in particular. Two of these, *information* and *code,* are important because they not only highlight the cognitive, the meaningful, the optional, the "signifying" in folk poetry (as contrasted with the merely mechanical, the rote, the obligatory, the "formulaic"), but also remind us that the producing and exchanging of meaning is governed by socially constructed rules. The two other terms of note, *negative feedback* and *positive feedback,* are a little less necessary to the logic of my analyses; they convey, however, the important notions not merely of interrelationships but of dynamic, processual ones, notions that possible alternatives like *adaptation* or *cooperation* on the one hand and *conflict* or *antagonism* on the other do not quite capture. But I use the relatively unfamiliar terms in such specific contexts and so consciously as part of the analytical apparatus that the reader will have no difficulty in following their intended meanings. The use of all such borrowed terminology truly reflects the sources of my "way of thinking." To translate them would be, in effect, to mask my true indebtedness.

As far as distinct methods go, other than those common in the study of folklore, my major influence has come from the kind of Structuralism and its close relation, semiology, associated with a large number of European scholars, the best known of whom is Claude Lévi-Strauss. But once again the influence—especially the semiological—is only partial and is highly selective. The reader will not, for instance, encounter in this work many of the catchwords that are almost inseparable from Structuralist endeavors, words like *syntagmatic* and *parole,* since my analyses had no particular need of them. But he or she will encounter words like *image* and *semantic domain* that are not normally part of the Structuralist lexicon. Moreover, I make free to borrow Structuralist/semiological terms and adapt their meanings to suit my own ends: most noticeably, the word *signifier,* as I use it, denotes simply a textual element that has a connotative property and a capacity to affect the context of its occurrence (as in idiomatic English, "it doesn't signify"), as opposed to a *sign,* which, as I use it, refers simply to a text's denotative quality. In Structuralism proper, however, the construct *sign* is of a different order—the combination of a *signifier* and a *signified.* I also employ *transformation* in a sense different from— and more specific than—its normal use in Structuralism, as will become clear.

Finally, I owe a debt to many critics of literary texts, not only for their terminology—though such terminology, because of the long-established, highly regarded, and pervasive role of literary studies in our general fund of scholarly knowledge, will be quite familiar and apparent to the reader—but also for an awareness, an understanding that all expressive materials carry much more meaning than a superficial scanning will allow, and that all one's perceptiveness and disciplined imagination is needed to do them justice. My debt here, while not explicitly acknowledged, will be apparent throughout.

All these and more have contributed, a little here and a little there, to my "way of thinking" about English folk poetry. This perspective, while it cannot be perfectly matched up with any one of the systems of inquiry that represent the sources of my ideas, is still, I like to think, consistent and systematic on its own terms and in its elucidating of the data—which is the goal I have striven for. I am not and do not wish to be associated with any particular "school," "method," "theory," "approach," or even social group ("Young turks," for example) other than that of scholars and lovers of my chosen subject matter. For it is that subject matter which this book is *about*: English folk poetry.

ENGLISH
FOLK
POETRY

Some
Assumptions

Cecil J. Sharp was England's most prolific collector of folksong. He was also her most ambitious theorist, attempting to discover typologies of folk music as well as laws of folksong's behavior. His contribution as a collector is undisputed; indeed, without the recent publication of so much of Sharp's field collection in *Cecil Sharp's Collection of English Folk Songs* the first two chapters of this present work could hardly have been written.[1] As for his theories, while our debt to this side of Sharp's work, as embodied in his *English Folk Song: Some Conclusions,* is today relatively slight, his example of boldly assaying generalizations about English folksong remains a shining one.[2] Thus the similarity of this introduction's title to that of Sharp's major theoretical work is an intentional tribute to our great progenitor.

Were Cecil Sharp alive today, perhaps he might admire my boldness in seeking regularities in a sizable corpus of English folk poetry. It is not so certain, though, that he would have smiled upon the data I have chosen as subject matter for analysis and interpretation. Since part of these data may also initially trouble some contemporary readers, I should give "some assumptions" that have guided their choice. It is well known, for instance, that despite

Sharp's assertion that "the folk-singer attaches far more importance to the words of his song than to its tune," the great collector himself paid more attention to the music than to the poetry of English traditional song both in his collecting and in his theorizing.[3] This book, on the other hand, treats only the words of folksong when song is the subject matter at hand. There is ample precedent for doing this; but the major assumption justifying the treatment of song poetry divorced from its accompanying melodies is chiefly a function of the kinds of questions my analyses are designed to answer—questions of meanings that could hypothetically have been intellectualized and communicated discursively by the folk themselves. I have seen no evidence that music is so coded; music's "meaning" appears to be textural and affective and of quite a different order from meaning in a poetic text. In truth, I suspect that when we do evolve an analytical system for interpreting musical meaning we may find such meaning redundant in affect with cognition's world view; for the moment, however, folk musicology's analytical instruments are able to identify primarily genetic relationships among its materials, not semantic ones.

Sharp might also have thought much of the data analyzed in the following essays tangential to his own notion of *folk* poetry. Chapter 3, for instance, examines local songs, songs with particularistic topics from the immediate environments of their composers. Such songs usually have a short life in tradition, are seldom learned by singers from outside the song-topic's sphere of relevance, and are often associated in public recognition with their known composers. Sharp would have been dubious about designating such songs "folk," as he would have been about the data of chapters 4 and 5, whose subject matter is even further removed from conventional notions of folk poetry. These chapters examine poetry for recitation or reading, not singing, that dates from the 1960s and 1970s. The composers are almost always known, are all molded by the industrial experience, and are all of the urban working class, save for three poets in chapter 5 who are quite removed from even a workable notion of "folk," but who provide interesting comparisons with working-class poets.

At one level, therefore, there are at least three distinct kinds of "folk" poetry treated at some length in this work. Chapters 1 and 2 deal with the poetry of those largely traditional, anonymously created, orally disseminated, and widely popular songs that Sharp and his contemporaries collected so vigorously, chiefly from the rural working class, over the latter years of the last century and up to the 1920s, and that others have continued to collect since, though not in such profusion. Such songs need no justification for the designation "folk," since they are the very standard against which any song one wishes to so call is usually measured.

The case is not so clear-cut, however, with the second kind of material, local songs. Less easily generalized than traditional songs from person to person and from place to place because of the relative concreteness and topicality of their subject matter, local songs may enter equally local tradition but only for a short while; their content and language will be less formulaic and predictable; and renditions of the same song by two or more singers will show relatively little variation in text and music. So many descriptive and analytical studies of local songs, as well as of their makers, have appeared in folklore scholarship over the past twenty years or so that the treatment of such songs as "folk" poetry would seem to be established by precedent—though it is true that many analysts of the genre themselves often go to considerable lengths to establish the customary criteria of "oral transmission" and "variation" as these apply to their particular examples.[4] But to my way of thinking, there are two criteria that argue more powerfully for a "folk" designation for local songs. First, like traditional and anonymous folksongs, local songs do not attempt to disguise their conventionality, and go to great efforts to familiarize and to legitimize their topics and messages by placing these within well-known frames of reference of both culturally normative content and culturally normative ethos. Traditional songs exhibit similar familiarization and legitimization motives, though their techniques—given their more easily generalized subject matter—are not quite the same in kind or degree: traditional songs are subject to such operations as localization, sentimentalization, moralization, and others, as well as to drawing again and again upon the same familiar stanzaic forms, story-types, language formulas, and themes.[5]

The second characteristic of "folk" poetry that local songs display is that in their topics, messages, composition, and performance they are intimately related to ongoing social life. Local songs are seldom made primarily for personal material gain or for individual aggrandizement, whether it be the raising unilaterally of one's social status vis-à-vis one's peers, or the attaining of personal and subjective insight, or even, for that matter, the achieving of psychological "release." As is the case with traditional folksinging as an activity, motives for the composition and performance of local songs are in very important measure social ones: the songs are intended to inform, to persuade, to manipulate, or to affirm the relationship of *communitas* with and among Significant Others in one's primary social and cultural networks—those Others who are structurally, functionally, or affectively linked in a direct way with one's life within a family, an occupational group, or a community.

Wherever a nonindividualistic, community-oriented pragmatic and ethic appear particularly strong, therefore, it seems useful to examine the relevant item as a "folk" phenomenon.[6] One consequence of this social pragmatic in folk poetry for my analyses is that, in the studies to follow, levels from which depth psychology draws its constructs—like "collective unconscious," say, or motivations that stem from the most covert of sexual anxieties—are not addressed. Thus in chapter 2, for instance, in which I talk of themes of love and death, I do not tie these to Freud's Eros and Thanatos and to theories of aggression, nor do I link certain poetic representations in both chapters 2 and 3 to sexual referents with which they are clearly not incompatible. The studies in this book seek to illuminate the implicit and the tacit, not the unconscious.

Similar criteria justify the study as "folk" poetry of our third major genre, local poetry for recitation or reading, not singing, made by contemporary working-class men and women whose primary social identities are as father, miner, Robinson, longtime Smithsville resident, wife, neighbor, or whatever, not as poets. Such local working-class poetry is a genre so minimally studied that I cannot appeal to scholarly precedent to any significant extent.[7] Certainly, if nothing else, one may advance the claim that local poetry is the modern-day substitute for older traditional and local song, since there is little doubt that songmaking and singing in the context of ongoing community life is not a flourishing activity in England today, whereas local poetry making and "performing" is. One can only speculate on the reasons for this: perhaps the pervasiveness of print and the concomitant national literacy has in recent times so collapsed the two genres of song and poetry that the musical side of amateur poetic expression has simply lost importance; or perhaps music as a general expressive skill has been so coopted by the readily-available-to-all talents of professionals that the amateur has bowed out; or perhaps the milieux for amateur song performance are not as favorable today as they formerly were; or perhaps, indeed, local poetry making and performing has *never* been strictly separated by the practitioners themselves from songmaking and singing, for it has long been the case that the same verses were regarded as equally appropriate for both singing and reciting and that commonplace books freely intermixed "song" poems with "poem" poems. Whatever the reasons, there is little doubt that songmaking or even just singing as a community activity—as a mode of processing and communicating information expressively about *ourselves*—is not nearly as common today as it once was, whereas the making and disseminating of poetry is still an extremely common and vigorous everyday social activity.

Since scholarly attention to this genre has been so minimal, let me describe it from a folklorist's perspective sharpened by eight months of fieldwork in Yorkshire's Industrial West Riding during 1973. Working-class folk poetry differs from traditional song poetry in that—like local songs—its topics and sentiments are far more explicitly situated in the poet's bounded and knowable world, whether that world be confined to the narrow matrix of a family, a friendship or occupational group, a small-town community, a district, or, at probably the widest level, a culture region like a county. National or international events, cultural universals divorced from an actual occurrence (a poem on the topic of nostalgia, say, or the delights of love), or even fictional events—these are seldom treated in modern-day working-class folk poetry. At the other end of the spectrum, highly personal and individualistic matters are seldom treated either, unless they can be generalized and legitimized to close Social Others. Real happenings in the immediate cultural contexts of maker and audience are by far the preferred topics of working-class folk poetry.

Consequently, only rarely and only for a very particular class of topics will working-class poetry, *like* traditional and local song, use stylized tropes like irony or even metaphor that challenge normative perceptions. Nor will such poetry often employ prosodic devices that similarly deflect audience attention away from the referential and conative (or persuasive) functions of the verse by means of such unconventional features as variable meter and non-rhyme.[8] Thus the language of working-class poetry, while not as formulaic in its materials as is traditional song, which depends so much more on oral and aural channels in composition and performance, is closer to the language—if not prosody—of conversational discourse than is traditional (or for that matter, elite) poetry. In fact, one very important subgenre of local folk poetry, "dialect verse," strives intentionally to reproduce the culture-specific language of regional everyday speech.

The communication of modern-day folk poetry takes place in contexts perhaps not terribly dissimilar to those that characterized the older patterns of folksinging. Composers share their context-specific poems in one-to-one exchanges; in one-to-kin at domestic gatherings on festive occasions like birthdays and family reunions; in one-to-a-homogeneous-few at the pub, the workplace, the working men's club, or the woman's institute meeting; or in one-to-a-homo-geneous-many through such channels as the "Letters" section of the local newspaper.[9] This last, the network of one-to-a-homogeneous-many, depends never on recitation but always on print, the trait that most strikingly distinguishes the performance of modern folk poetry from traditional rural folksinging. True, pre-nineteenth-century traditional song as well as nineteenth-century local song depended significantly on print for both their composition and their dissemination, in broadsides, chapbooks, the later penny song-books, and—in the case of rural local songs particularly—handwrit-ten copies. But modern folk poetry is not only kept alive almost entirely by print but also communicated to district-wide audiences through local newspapers and to smaller group audiences through, for example, parish church newsletters and other such quotidian magazines.[10] Other common methods of communication are through a single handwritten copy which may be circulated among friends and workmates; through lending one's commonplace book to friends; or, in interpersonal contacts, through the medium of a letter. Very occasionally, and under very special circumstances, a local poem may be printed on a broadside to be given away or sold; the reader will meet examples of this rare occurrence in chapter 5. In general, the smaller and more homogeneous the group contain-ing the poet and his audience, the better the chance of oral per-formance; the larger the group and the more casual the links among its members, the more likely communication through print. But poet and audience, even at the widest level, are extremely delimited, culturally and geographically.

Finally, present-day local poetry differs radically from tradi-tional folksong, though somewhat less from local song, in two nota-ble characteristics. First, a poem's performance is invariably lim-ited to the known composer; second, a poem's popularity over time and space is severely restricted (though it may be preserved in the composer's memory or commonplace book, and may in fact be reconstituted at a later date as a vitally relevant social statement if events similar to the poem's topic recur). Songs and poems—particu-larly the former—that do enter modern oral tradition to enjoy wide and lengthy popularity are primarily national ones, learned ori-ginally in primary school or during wartime, like "Jerusalem," "There'll Always Be an England," and "Pack Up Your Troubles in Your Old Kit Bag," or even transatlantic hits from the record indus-try. Such songs appeal primarily to nostalgic, vicarious, or escapist sentiments and do not reveal much to us about a culture-specific ethos, however much they may tell us about modernization or about

6

psychology. Local working-class poetry, on the other hand, tells us much about what it means to the maker-performer and his audience to be "folk."

In short, contemporary working-class folk poetry is to local folk songs as local folk songs are to traditional folksongs. Though it may get weaker as we move from traditional, anonymous, and orally circulated song to present-day local verse, the thread linking these three major genres of act and expression within the same field of folk poetry is their delimited, publicly performed, and socially relevant content, ethos, and pragmatic. For all folk poetry is in some important measure a message about, and is designed to influence, human relationships among Significant Others and between Self and those Others in a way intimately linked with everyday living, much as were and are such traditional folk genres as proverbs, legends, and mummers' plays. People change, their environments change, their expressive forms and contents change; but *meanings* in a folk's lore remain remarkably stable, as do the structure and behavior of the interrelationships among the three subsystems of people, environment, and lore. And of these three the one that has perhaps changed most noticeably between the England of the eighteenth century and the England of today is the living and working environment of most of her subjects.

In its fundamentals, this change has been from the smaller and less complex world of rural village life (which the majority of the population enjoyed two centuries ago) to the larger and more complex environment of industrial urban life, the milieu of most today.[11] The older world held far fewer amounts and kinds of information, and fewer resources for generating, storing, retrieving, and disseminating it. Taking for example that minirepertoire of one kind of information, the culture's inventory of popular ballads, we may say that in preindustrial England there were few alternatives in, for instance, a love relationship. If the lovers failed to gain a successful union in marriage, then the reason probably was one parent's opposition to the match on the grounds of extreme differences in the lovers' kinship affiliations or social statuses. And in their failure, one or both lovers would probably die. If the lovers succeeded, they were aided either by existing social equality or by the inferior's raising of his or her official status through sudden acquisition of wealth.[12] In other words, the rightness or wrongness of the existing social order itself was not questioned; one could only manipulate the *means* of satisfying that order. Folk ballads of the later eighteenth and earlier nineteenth centuries provided more alternatives: poor girls could marry rich men without having to prove themselves social equals, though they did have to display other skills—exceptionally quick wit, for example. To some extent, the social order was manipulable; ground rules, rather than simply the mechanics of the play, could on occasion be challenged successfully. Later on, particularly after 1850, we find the very ground rules being questioned, competing ideologies and interests battling for supremacy—as in poor boy marrying rich girl despite parental opposition, or, in the occupational sphere, battles between management and workers that cannot be easily resolved by mediation. The difference between the older and the newer repertoires is not necessarily that one preference replaces another but that the *amount* of choices increases, providing for greater heterogeneity in the available inventory of choices. Thus we find in older, traditional folk poetry far more redundancy not only of poetic language, forms, topics, and themes but also of fundamental ethic and world view. Generally, the newer the poetry, the less redundant it is in all these aspects in relation to the popular repertoire that is coeval with it.

The increasing heterogeneity of English life took a large leap over the latter eighteenth and earlier nineteenth centuries. Similar accelerated rates of change and internal diversification would come again from the First World War to the 1920s, and yet again after the Second World War. But the Industrial Revolution coincided with the most strikingly radical changes in demography, culture, and landscape that the country as a whole had experienced since, perhaps, the period following the Norman Conquest. In brief, the experience of the majority of its population, and especially of the working classes, changed ever more quickly after 1750 from one of a shared, knowable, and not-widely-questioned environment to one of distributed knowledge; of much in one's environment that was not knowable because of its rate of change, its amount, and its complexity; and of increasingly competing definitions of norms. Not all the English experienced these changes equally, of course. The older patterns of an agricultural society with its small communities; multiple smallholders; living-in help; women and children as well as men working in the fields; everyday contact between residents in the exchange of labor, goods, and services; lack of a sharp delineation between work and leisure; nonseparation of living place from working place—all these existed in much of rural Yorkshire, for instance, while between classes the traditional reciprocity of deference and patronage still obtained, as elsewhere, in certain parts of East Anglia.[13] Even today we find some of these patterns in the heart of industrial milieux—in some coal mining communities, for instance.

A consequence of the relative noncomplexity of the older rural life is that one may with some justification treat a population of traditional songs, their singers, and their audiences as a unity. The relative heterogeneity of industrial life, on the other hand, which allows its participants greater freedom of choice in poetic topics, expressive modes, and ideologies, demands more finely drawn categories for truly meaningful insights into the data. But since the study of contemporary working-class folk poetry is in such an embryonic stage, for the moment we are stuck at levels too fine—those of the individual poet or, in rare instances, of a common topic. These are the levels at which I work in chapters 4 and 5. I do, however, at least tentatively suggest how the individuals and their poems may be deemed representative of more encompassing categories, though not quite as encompassing as categories like "countryman," or "villager," or "songs of love relationships," or "story-types," or even poetic "formulas" that we can more justifiably use when analyzing traditional folksongs.

Yet another reason for the different foci—a population on the one hand, an individual on the other—is historical accident. When the great field collections of English traditional song were being made, fieldworkers did not think it necessary to collect other cultural data as well. In part, their rationale for this lacuna (which is how we conceive of it today) may have been an extreme version of the homogeneity-and-consequent-redundancy notion advanced above: thus any part of the culture—like folksong—could stand for the whole. But in yet greater part, their reason must have been that *even then*, around the turn of this century, the most vital and natural context for the kinds of songs they were collecting was no longer common in England. David Harker has shown, for instance, that many of Sharp's major informants lived in towns and had little primary connection with agricultural life.[14] As a result, the collectors felt that they were collecting survivals, memorial traces that had outlived their natural contexts of composition, communication, and use; it made little sense to collect the available "contextual" information. Consequently, in analyzing such traditional folksong today, we have no hard data about "native speakers" on which to draw, nor any of their exegeses containing explicit or implicit knowledge—exegeses we could use to generate research questions and to check results our own analyses reveal. In contrast, the student of working-class poetry, a currently vital and flourishing culture form, is potentially blessed with many available native speakers to aid interpretation.[15] In a sense, therefore, we have little choice but to organize our analyses around texts when the subject is traditional folksong, around the individual poet when our subject is working-class verse, because of the nature of the data presently available on each genre. However, while the future of discovering more significant categories for the study of the latter is bright (we just need to collect much more data), the possibility of refining our analytical categories of traditional folksong is dim, since we have little opportunity nowadays to gather much more relevant information about meaning and use of folksong in a community setting.

Still, all roads need not be closed to the scholar of English traditional song. For one reason, preindustrial village life was, as I have said, a relatively noncomplex and internally nondifferentiated one. Thus we can to some extent draw upon other documentation, like local histories and autobiographies, to construct an idea of what typical village life before as well as outside the domination of the Industrial Revolution was like—a village life that many assume, and that I assume here, to have been the most vital context of meaning and use of the popular song repertoire Sharp and others collected before World War I. And for another reason, we should not be too reticent in asserting a certain "native competence" ourselves, for in contrast with many anthropologists, say, who may lament the lack of native speakers of their chosen cultural data, Anglo-American scholars do themselves, after all, share the same basic language and even in some measure the world view and value system of their departed rural ancestors. To be sure, we will never know with any degree of certainty whether our preserved stock of traditional song was the specialty of a particular social or even occupational class; which songs were appropriate to men, which to women, or indeed whether that was an applicable distinction in the first place; whether any particular age—under twenty? over forty?—or social identity—unmarried? married? mothers? fathers?—was most appropriate for singing itself or for singing certain types of songs; what were the most common singing occasions and milieux; and so on.[16] We will never know for sure the answers to these questions. But we have simply too much textual data to let go to waste, and must proceed with interpretation; in chapters 1 and 2 especially I will not only proceed boldly but will even, in fact, attempt to deduce answers to some of the above questions, despite the paucity of cultural data and the impossibility of strong confirmation of the answers' correctness.

All of these matters are relevant to the question of just how valid the results of the analyses in this book are, especially those of the folksong studies. The argument I would advance in their favor rests on the assumption that the singers of traditional folksongs and the makers of local songs as well as of working-class poetry all sought and saw coherence in their poetic repertoire and in their everyday life. Thus, the validity of an analysis—or as much of it as we can hope for—is gained if that analysis reveals coherence in the materials. As far as possible, (1) nothing in the poem text should contradict the revealed interpretation; (2) the interpretation should be applicable to other texts manifestly of the same type or from the same source, since they are presumably generated by the same code; and (3) the interpretation should be logically related to other aspects of the culture within which the item flourished as well as to the life experiences of the individual poet, if known.[17] In short, pattern, order, and logical interrelationships are strong criteria for validity. The analyses of English folk poetry in the chapters to follow all strive to achieve, as far as possible, "validity" in this sense.

Each analysis also possesses a further quality, a quality which has largely determined its presence in this volume: surprise value. In other words, the results of each study either go against or add significantly to our widely accepted understandings of folk poetry; in addition, none of the results could have been predicted, I think, before the analysis applied here had been attempted. Chapter 1, for instance, shows that a frequently sung folk ballad, "The Bold Fisherman" (Laws O24), is not necessarily the mysterious and unique piece we have often thought it to be, but is instead squarely in the tradition of that most common of folksong story-types, the returned-unrecognized-lover, and thus is a song of love relationships.[18] I proceed to place the traditional imagery and language of this song within the semantic field of other popular English traditional songs possessing the same features, and reveal that they all share a thematic concern with notions of life and death. The analysis moves on to suggest that those same common language "formulas" may not be just the mechanical memory aids we have so often taken them for, but may be in fact highly symbolic. I then relate these folksong-expressed notions of life, death, and love to the extra-folksong (or what I call "pragmatic") world view with which they would have been most meaningfully linked, as well as with even larger environmental conditions of agricultural working-class life which would most logically have sustained such a twice-removed folksong world view; in the case of "The Bold Fisherman," these larger conditions turn out to be the social realities of a class living at a level of bare economic subsistence. These results all satisfy the criterion of surprise value; the criterion of validity is satisfied by the revealing of coherence both within the traditional song repertoire popular in nineteenth-century rural communities and between the message of songs on love relationships and their cultural environment, the assumed context of the songs, as flourishing and vital items.

This synopsis of chapter 1 may serve as a paradigm for synopses of the other four studies. Each takes as its point of departure a clearly interrelated assortment of folk poetry, though the nature of the first-order interrelatedness is not always the same: in chapter 1, it is a common thread of shared language and associated imagery; in chapter 2, a topic, sexual liaisons; in chapter 3, a topic and a culture region. A poet provides the link among the data in chapter 4, while the topic does so in chapter 5. These broad categories are broken down further in each study, depending on the data and the surprise value of the results obtained. In each study, the validity criterion is applied, first of all, by subjecting to analysis *all* the items found belonging to the data-type under investigation in a reasonably large sample. For instance, in chapter 2 the analysis accounts for songs on sexual liaisons taken from most of the largest published repositories of English folksong. The total sample runs to over 150 songs; the analysis accounts for them all. Chapter 3's sample is much more modest: some fifty local songs from Yorkshire. (Most of these I originally gathered for their regional value only, with no particular analytical purpose in mind.) Chapter 4, which takes as its subject a contemporary working-class poet, includes in its analysis her entire poetic production known to me. And so on. One consequence of these attempts at exhaustiveness is a plethora of illustrations; I ask the reader to bear with this profusion—though, mind you, each illustration is interesting in itself—in deference to the criterion of validity-in-coherence.

After first revealing coherence of meaning in its corpus of texts, the analysis in each chapter then goes on to search for logical interconnections between that meaning and the poetry's cultural matrix —as in the paradigmatic example of chapter 1. I have much less confidence in these results than I do in the textual analyses, since the ethnographic data are so spotty, especially in the folksong chapters; still, I do not hesitate to make hypothetical but informed inferences when I lack relevant data. In no instance does my argument rest on positing a simple semantic relationship (for instance, that the poetic world view "reflects" the pragmatic world view) or a simple functional one (that the poems functioned, for instance, as entertainment, as validations of pragmatic world view, as escape mechanisms, or as agents of socialization).[19] In each case I try to go as far as possible beyond these valuable but overly fundamental insights into the folklore/culture nexus.

The second quality I have striven for, surprise value, is particularly strong, I think, in the folksong chapters (1–3). I say so in part because studies of British folksong as poetry have been predominantly limited to the data of song texts themselves, with the result that we know very little about possible text/context interdependencies, while this volume does address such matters and so at the very least fills a void.[20] But I for one also consider the textual analyses in each of the chapters that follow to have more surprise value in their own right than the cultural analyses that accompany them—and I think this despite the fact that textual analysis is something folksong scholars are extremely competent at. My reason is simple and is, in fact, incorporated into the subtitle of this book: these studies are interpretive, which is to say that their analytical goal is to discover abstract *meanings* and that such meanings have to be actively sought by a method of textual decoding. Interpretive studies of this sort in British and Anglo-American folksong scholarship are rare, to say the least.[21] Even one of the most satisfying analyses of implicit meaning in traditional folksong texts that I am aware of appears in but one chapter of a full-length work devoted primarily to exploring a quite different question—the historic/geographic dissemination of a text-type.[22] And, in general, when our analyses of British and Anglo-American folk poetry do emphasize interpretation as a *raison d'être,* the interpretation is invariably governed by two major premises: first, that meaning is to be sought in the environment of the textual element's supposed *date of origin* (an illustration of this kind of premise is given in chapter 1); and second, that the textual element to be interpreted will be a literal, denotative index of that older historical phenomenon.

Valuable studies emerge from these forays into interpretation of traditional British folksong texts, certainly. Yet the assumption that the "real" or "best" or "correct" or even "most interesting" meaning is in the original utterance and that its semantic status becomes less relevant as the original grows farther away in time begs the question of why the utterance should continue to enjoy a life in memory and performance. The other assumption, that meaning in folksong is literal and denotative, runs counter to the assumption (more acceptable to my way of thinking) that folklore of any sort—and particularly folk poetry—requires skill and effort to compose, learn, remember, and perform, and that consequently it would make little sense to expend such effort if the product were simply a verbal equivalent of the referent itself. If the purpose were primarily to record and inform, the rural working class has had available many genres more suitable for "reflecting" experience or ideas denotatively—anecdotes, legends, genealogies, histories, even journals, diaries, and biographies.

In some studies based on these two assumptions of original and denotative meaning, the analyst is unable to find a shared coherence among texts that are clearly related in topic or language. Instead of challenging the assumptions, however, the usual reaction is to throw out data that do not fit the interpretation—even though such data are manifestly of the same sort as those that are retained—on the grounds that the singer was "mistaken" or suffering from faulty memory or whatever (examples are given in chapters 1 and 2). There is no doubt that in some cases these assumptions are correct. But if another set of assumptions and a different analytical procedure can account for a greater proportion of the same textual population, then they are to be preferred—according, that is, to the widely accepted principle that the fewer the hypotheses that account for the greater amount of data, the better those hypotheses are (another version of the validity criterion advanced earlier).

My own assumption is that coherence should obtain among members of a clearly related textual corpus: in particular, the coherence of a unified system of meanings informing those texts. Finding the code to this coherent system requires analytical instruments of some sensitivity, an "apparatus" that in our case has built into it another of my assumptions: that folk poetry—like any other kind of literature, I am sure[23]—exhibits levels of signification that range from straightforward denotative "reflection" to profoundly connotative symbolization. Denotative signs in a folk poem's text do not require interpretation, only identification, since no code of poetic conception interposes between the referent as conventionally perceived and its textual image. But as rules for imaginatively rearticulating subject matter into poetic expression are applied, so that the topic becomes increasingly distant from the constraints of its conventional and singular reality in the process of being expressed in a textual *signifier,* then the more the text will "refer" to concepts and values rather than to empirically knowable "things." The most connotative of images are symbols; symbols "refer" far more to culturally marked abstractions than they do to "things," or indeed to referents in general that may, in the pragmatic perception of routine life, be of entirely separate orders. That is one reason why we often speak of the "ambiguity" or the "paradoxical" nature of symbols.

The point here is that folk poetry often contains signifiers that have to be decoded if the poetry's meaning is to be revealed, not

14

simply identified and matched up one-to-one with equivalents in the empirical or conventionally defined world. Often, even after we have succeeded in decoding textual signifiers, our task is not complete, for we still cannot simply match the revealed meaning with an existing reality in the environment. This is because the referents revealed by cracking the folksong code are often themselves abstract ideas and themselves coded in relation to the wider reality of life's empirical conditions. But this second code of the pragmatic world view is easier to crack than is the poetic code, since its status is closer to denotation.

If these assertions seem to suggest the claim that folk poetry is almost nothing *but* signifiers that must be subjected to ingenious analysis in order to be understood, let me quickly declare that such is not at all the case. In fact, one of the notable properties of *folk* poetry is that it does have a substantially literal quality, maintains a close and practical link with the real world. I am proposing only that we have taken the implications of this feature to extremes and too often assumed that our inability to make sense of many folksong texts stemmed from our not knowing the poetry's "original" referents, or from some flaw in those who provided us with the texts. The truth lies somewhere between these two extremes: most folk poetry exhibits both conventional, uncoded, denotative signs and poetic, connotative, coded signifiers. It depends on the subgenre and on the topic. By too often disregarding signification in our scholarship, however, we may not only have failed to find "sense" but also have unwittingly ignored the very quality that defines folk poetry as folk *poetry*. It is the signifiers that are peculiar to the genre, not the denotative signs determined by other requirements, like the need to be easily comprehended, to be useful, to be credible, or to be persuasive, signs shared with other culture forms, from conversational speech to folktales. Such qualities of the literal and the instrumental may distinguish folk poetry from elite poetry, and may *link* folk poetry with other folklore; but folk poetry's signifiers *distinguish* it from other folk phenomena. As chapter 1 will argue, it is those very signifying motifs and language units that we have long recognized as special to folk poetry but have hastily dubbed "cliches," and as a result thought to be the most utilitarian of crutches, that may constitute the "deepest language" of the genre and carry implicitly the most significant meanings.

The reader will have surmised by now that the analytical perspective that most informs the studies in this book is a Structuralist one.[24] Structuralism is appropriate because its most basic analytic construct is predicated on meaning-in-context rather than on simply the presence of an image or its formal grammatical function. This meaning-in-context can be defined (to borrow a phrase Gregory Bateson uses for another purpose) as "a difference that makes a difference."[25] So, for instance, a "white lie" as an element of meaning-in-context performs its significant semantic function in its difference from a "lie," since that difference will "make a difference" to the set of circumstances in which the white lie occurs (whereas, in contrast, "lie" in its difference from "truth" would "make a difference" of quite another sort). In a poetic text, such a difference (that makes a difference) is simply another word for a signifier, since it has a causal effect on its context (thus "signifies"), as opposed to a *sign*, which simply denotes a singular, objective referent that means intrinsically rather than in its relationship of difference from some other object (though, of course, very few representations are wholly one or the other but possess varying degrees of singularity and relationality—or denotativeness and connotativeness, as I call these two characteristics).

Structuralism's basic operational constructs, therefore, are always relationships: "a difference" (a relationship) that "makes a difference" (another relationship). It is how relationships at various levels are conceptualized and manipulated within the imaginative world of a poem's text that provides us with the key knowledge of the poem's signification, or what I shall simply call its meaning— the text's major premises, the world view built on those premises, and the specific messages thus generated. The common-denominator relationship is the first "difference" in the above definition, a relationship to which Structuralism gives a single term, *opposition*, regardless of whether the difference, by evaluative standards, is minimal (as in the "truth"/"white lie" contrast) or maximal (as in the antithesis between "truth" and "lie"). A signifier is always manifested in such an oppositional relationship.

Other kinds of relationships the reader will meet frequently in the analyses to follow—all of which are manifestations of the relationship a signifier may bear to its contextual Others (the second "difference" in the definition)—may be characterized briefly here. The first is analogy (the key relationship in a model of interparticipation that I shall later call, in a more technical application, *match*). As an illustration of analogy, suppose that two pairs of oppositions appear in the same setting—for instance, the opposition between "truth" and "lie" on the one hand and that between "labor" and "management" on the other; we can easily conceive of an analogy being made in the text between "truth" and "labor" or between "lie" and "management." Closely akin to analogy is homology, a formal similarity between two pairs of oppositions. A homologous relationship would be of the following sort: "truth" is to "labor" as "lie" is to "management," which means that the structure of the relationship between the first two is very much like the structure of the relationship between the second two.

Another kind of prominent relationship between a signifier and its contextual Others is the dialectical kind, which is not a two-term but a three-term structure in which each member of an oppositional pair contributes properties to a third variable, which then resolves the original difference into a unity. Thus a "white lie" synthesizes the opposing pair "lie" and "truth." Similar to dialectic is transformation, also a three-term structure; but the third term is taken not from selected properties of the two opposing elements (as in the dialectic), but from a different frame of reference (or "province of meaning"), thus changing the very definitions and values of the opposing pair so that the two are transformed into something significantly different. For instance, the opposition between "truth" and "lie" may be transformed by redefining the pronouncements of a charismatic cult leader in terms of a visionary experience; thus the opposition between "truth" and "lie" in their conventional frame of reference, the secular, is transformed by being placed into a sacred frame of reference where the two become a unity of "prophetic vision" or whatever. This is an example of a kind of transformation we may call "transcendence" (a raising of value in "quality space"); its opposite, "debasement" (a lowering of value in quality space), is also possible, though rare in English folk poetry.[26] Symbolization relies heavily on transformational relationships of the "transcendence" sort.

Two final kinds of relationships that the reader will meet often in this book are more processual than the above ones and usually appear in a narrative text, such as a ballad. The first is a negative feedback relationship between two elements "in opposition"; in negative feedback one element's properties are manipulated in order to bring about its unity or "fit" with another. In the second, positive feedback, the relationship of opposition itself is stressed and magnified, even to the point of becoming a strongly antithetical difference that cannot be resolved. It is as if, for example, there were no such construct as "white lie" to mediate "lie" and "truth"; the two are inalterably opposed and in continuous, increasing conflict. Hypothetically, the logical end of a positive feedback relationship over time would be either the removal from the universe of action, or the destruction, of one or both of the pair—that is, unless some other mechanism, such as transformation, could be effected.

These are the major kinds of relationships that will appear frequently throughout these studies of English folk poetry. As for actual analysis along Structuralist principles, in its most formalized guise this proceeds according to a fairly well-defined method. A text's provinces of meaning are first isolated—not a difficult task in the case of English folk poetry, since a folk poem invariably deals with a single topic and thus a single province of meaning. Once a province of meaning has been isolated (for example, "political ideology"), the images that *mean*—because in their relationship of opposition they make a difference to their context—are identified. These, of course, are the signifiers, and each oppositional pair of signifiers will occupy a semantic domain: thus the opposition "truth/lie" might belong to the semantic domain of *conduct*; the juxtaposed opposition "labor/management" to *occupational role*. In a fairly simple (and often-found) structure, all the semantic domains within a single province of meaning will be in an homologous relationship and thus constitute a more general opposition between two paradigms, which will usually exhibit opposing values (+ and −) as well. Thus in our ongoing example, "truth" from the *conduct* domain and "labor" from the *occupational role* domain might belong to the larger paradigm of Socialism, say, with a positive value, while "lie" and "management" might belong to the paradigm of Capitalism, with a negative value. Other kinds of relationships, if they obtain, may then be sought—dialectical, transformational, or whatever.[27]

With its basic unit, then, one of meaning rather than simply of text, Structuralism is particularly appropriate for interpretive investigation. Consider, for example, how Structuralism (or its often indistinguishable kin, semiology) would approach an example of folk poetry in contrast with how one of Structuralism's affines, morphological analysis, might analyze the same datum.[28] I will use for illustration that most common of incipits to British traditional ballads on the topic of love relationships, "As I roved out one May morning." Morphological analysis, restricting itself to the manifested text, would probably score this textual element as belonging to the class of action "Journey" or something of that sort, and (since the text would more than likely be a ballad—that is, a narrative song) proceed in the same manner to plot succeeding actions as they unfold—"Meeting," "Courtship Plea," "Courtship Refusal," and so forth. Structuralism, on the other hand, would be alert to at least three signifiers in this line, belonging to the semantic domains of *motion, space,* and *time.* Thus, the "roving" signifier in the *motion* domain implies an opposition between mobile and immobile. "Out" signifies, in the *spatial* domain, a place beyond the boundaries of one's customary context, with which it is in contrast —the village church, cottages, artisans' shops, even the outlying farms and cultivated fields, where one is fixed to one's repetitive daily duties and their concomitant constraints; "out" thus refers to ground where everyday rules do not apply and where one is freed to participate in an unusual adventure—probably an adventure, in fact, that is tabooed by intravillage norms. In the third semantic domain, *time*, "May" might connote an interstice between the just-ended period of in-farm work and the imminent period of heavy field work, thus a time also temporarily free of everyday requirements, a "play-time" in contrast with "work-time." Structuralism would take these basic insights—the oppositional structure between movement and stasis, woods and village, play-time and work-time, whose meanings are generated in their relationships (e.g., of analogy or homology) with each other—and seek their paradigmatic opposition (in this case, perhaps the categorical difference between Nature and Culture, or perhaps Instinct and Law, or Individual and Society, or Id and Superego). Thus would the analysis, using all these kinds of contents in their manifested relationships, seek to crack the code of the world view underlying the poem's chosen province of meaning, love relationships. Finally, Structuralism would display its open-ended quality by looking for similar structures in cultural activities, beliefs, and conditions other than folk poetry in order to discern patterned relationships, coherence, between the poetry's meaning and its cultural ground.[29]

This method of analysis, then, characterizes a Structuralist approach at its relatively noncomplex and most formalized level of application. These conceptual tools guide my thinking in the majority of the studies in this book. I must caution, however, that this sketch does not represent *the* discovery procedure one can simply map whole-cloth onto any text of folk poetry to emerge with revealing results.[30] First of all, it would be an impossibly long and tedious task to analyze all textual signifiers and their structural array in a data sample of any meaningful size; second, much in folk poetry texts is not significantly structured and not highly connotative; third, Structuralism and semiology at their present state of development are as much *ways* of thinking about cultural products as they are formalized analytical methods; and fourth, in the humanities it is primarily by the results of an inquiry—foremost of all, by its surprise value—that we customarily measure the inquiry's significant worth, not by its methodology. Thus, in each study to follow, the criteria of surprise value and coherence are what chiefly determine the particular type and method of analysis employed. Consequently, chapter 1, in its focus on individual signifiers, is more semiological than structural, the structural approach emphasizing relationships among signifiers. Chapter 2 is the most structural (and Structuralist) of all, as well as semiological. Chapter 3, which deals with the semitraditional local song, is predominantly structural, though not terribly Structuralist. Chapters 4 and 5 are both structural and semiological in their textual analyses, depending on the individual datum. The common subject matter of these last two chapters is poetry on local topics made by working-class men and women, though chapter 5 goes farther and extends the historical evolutionary line from agricultural working class through industrial blue-collar working class to include the white-collar middle class by comparing working-class folk poetry with middle-class poetry on the same topic, a local mine disaster.

1

"THE BOLD FISHERMAN"

Symbolism
in
English
Traditional
Folksong

Whenever we are confronted with a song that was popular in rural English tradition, we may reasonably hypothesize that it had a viable place in the culture's network of meanings. Should we meet a folksong that, though popular, does not appear to fit the general repertoire but that instead seems highly individualistic or even unique, we should ask ourselves whether we have interpreted it correctly, for often we are prone to regard a song as unique if no obvious analogies to its surface content come readily to mind. Take the English ballad "The Bold Fisherman" (Laws O24), for instance. At the very least, the frequency of its collection attests to its popularity, for Cecil Sharp alone noted fifteen renditions (*CSCEFS*, 1: 222–29, 721), while several other field collectors of English rural traditions have found the song at least once (*EC*, pp. 60–61; *ECS*, p. 110; *EFSD*, p. 3; *EHFS*, pp. 113–14; *JFSS* 1 [1901]: 138; *JFSS* 7 [1922]: 21–22; *JFSS* 7 [1923]: 36–37; *MB*, p. 3; *SC*, pp. 18–19; *SES*, pp. 254–55).[1] "The Bold Fisherman" also appeared on English broadsides.[2] Gavin Greig found one version in Scottish tradition (*FSNE*, no. 179), and, more recently, several texts have been noted from North American folksingers (*BMNE*, pp. 218–19; *SNO*, 2: 603–4; *TSNS*, pp. 113–14). Like folksongs of any age, "The Bold

Fisherman" differs in minor detail from text to text, but the great majority of its available texts exhibit a consistent enough narrative. Strolling by a riverside, a maid sees a fisherman approaching on the tide. She asks what brings him here. He replies that he has come for her sake. He moors his boat, takes her by the hand, and removes his "morning gown," whereupon she spies gold chains hanging from his neck. She forthwith falls on her knees, begging his pardon for mistakenly thinking him a fisherman (often adding, "instead of some lord"). He bids her rise, saying he is not offended, and announces that he will take her to her father's house, where they will be married.

Since on the surface there is much in this ballad that is unusual for British folksong, Lucy Broadwood was moved to argue that "The Bold Fisherman" may be "a vulgar and secularized transmutation of a medieval allegorical original." In her fascinating analysis, Broadwood links several elements in the ballad with similar elements in ancient Gnostic symbolism: "To students of Gnostic and Early Christian mystic literature, the River, the Sea, the royal Fisher, the three Vestures of Light (or Robes of Glory), the Recognition and Adoration by the illuminated humble Soul, the free Pardon, the mystical Union of the Bride to the Bridegroom in the House of the Father (or Father-House) are familiar elements, and we can find them all, certainly, among the variants of this ballad."[3] Scholarly reaction to Broadwood's thesis has ranged from acceptance, through cautious neutrality on the issue, to skepticism about its validity.[4] But at the very least, there does seem to be widespread agreement that the ballad is a fairly old one and that, had he known of its existence, Francis James Child would have included it in his canon of early British balladry, even though we have no versions from before the nineteenth century, and even though the ballad in its known form displays a broadside style that suggests an eighteenth-century origin.[5]

My purpose is neither to disprove nor to affirm Broadwood's thesis, but rather to use it as an illustration of one implicit conception of "meaning": the notion that meaning is best found in the environment of a text's first emergence. But the song's continued popularity in nineteenth- and even twentieth-century rural tradition suggests that to those who could perform "The Bold Fisherman" for collectors something in the ballad must have signified more than trivially. Surely English country singers in the nineteenth century—much less the twentieth, and much less in North America —knew nothing about Gnosticism; thus the song's significance to the folk must have lain elsewhere. I propose that we seek this "elsewhere" not in the remote past—thus looking to the song's uniqueness, to its difference from other popular folksongs—but in the contemporary folksong universe, in "The Bold Fisherman's" similarity to other traditional songs popular at the same period.

Of course most scholars who countenance the interpretation of the ballad's "original" meaning recognize that its familiar form has similarities to the existing folksong repertoire, even if only to deprecate, however gently, that similarity. Iolo A. Williams, for instance, observes that "the original meaning has been entirely forgotten, and all that is left is an apparently secular, and even unedifying, tale."[6] Reginald Nettel proposes that "the attraction of the song is in its wish-fulfillment, it is in the tradition of many songs wherein the young woman yearns for a perfect, or at any rate socially superior, lover. Thus it is preserved in the folk mind intact, though its inner meaning was forgotten by the singer."[7] Kenneth Peacock remarks, "Nowadays, the ballad has lost all its mystical connotations and survives only as a charming love lyric."[8] Of those analysts who are neutral toward Broadwood's thesis, G. Malcolm Laws's response may be taken as typical. He places "The Bold Fisherman" in his O category ("Ballads of Faithful Lovers") rather than in the Q section ("Humorous and Miscellaneous Ballads"), under which latter rubric, had he been disposed toward the mystical interpretation, he would have listed the ballad, alongside, say, the Masonic "Building of Solomon's Temple" (Laws Q39).

No one to my knowledge, however, has hinted that "The Bold Fisherman" may share thematic elements with yet another of Laws's ballad clusters, his N section of "Lovers' Disguises and Tricks." Of the forty-three British broadside-ballad types in North American tradition Laws lists in this section, no fewer than sixteen (N28–N43) are of the "returned-unrecognized-lover" sort, a story-type very common in British folksong. Its narrative, in skeleton, is as follows. Two plighted lovers who have been parted for many years meet at last, but the maid does not recognize her beloved. This enables him to test her fidelity by such means as wooing her in the guise of a stranger. She passes the test admirably by forthrightly refusing the suit, whereupon the young man reveals his true identity as her quondam lover finally returned, and the two are happily reunited. When I first began looking closely at "The Bold Fisherman," I was quite struck by the discernible returned-unrecognized-lover pattern lying beneath the text's apparent unusualness: the fisherman, it seems, is the girl's former lover, and the sign indicating to her his true identity is the gold chains that come into view when he removes his "morning gown." She recognizes him, he embraces her, and they are reunited happily, soon to marry.

Assuming that mystical Christian symbolism was not a flourishing element in the knowledge-inventory of turn-of-the-century folksingers; assuming that there are a fairly select and limited number of topics and themes in the popular folksong repertoire of a noncomplex culture; and assuming that if the tradition of a song is widespread and vigorous then it must possess a semantic fit with the rest of the popular repertoire—assuming all these principles, I felt the inference could be made that it was *this* association country singers had in mind as one aspect of the meaning—on a concrete level at least—of "The Bold Fisherman's" story. And in fact two texts support this inference by intimating a prior love relationship between the fisherman and the maid—strangely enough, both the earliest version collected from oral tradition (Hertfordshire, before 1893 [*ECS*, p. 110]) and the latest (Newfoundland, 1960 [*SNO*, 2:603–4]). The Newfoundland text is almost unequivocal on the subject:

> He boldlye stepped up 'long side
> When to his great surprise
> He saw 'twas his true lovyer fair
> Who rung her hands and cried.

We have, therefore, an initial insight: to turn-of-the-century folksingers "The Bold Fisherman" may very well have been a quite secular song of love relationships, belonging, moreover, to the subcategory of the returned-unrecognized-lover story-type. Morphological analysis has given us that initial insight; for an analysis of fuller meaning, however, we must turn to special signifiers in the text. The special signifiers are those that "make a difference" between the poetic universe of *folksong* imagery on the one hand and the nonpoetic signs on the other. The fact that the male protagonist comes "rolling down the tide," for instance, is the result of poetic choice, determined in fair measure by the requirements of folksong meaning, while the maid "spying" the approaching fisherman is demanded by empirical logic, her greeting him with a "good morning" a requirement of similarly nonpoetic, everyday propriety. The poetic imagery signifies and connotes; the nonpoetic indicates and denotes. We can isolate a poetic signifier and seek its range of possible meanings by canvassing the genre for all other manifestations of the same image, the genre in this case being represented by the repertoire of traditional folksong popular in the same cultural milieux and at the same period as "The Bold Fisherman."[9] And if this range of meanings is distinctly finite and distinctly patterned, then we can be sure that we are dealing with an artifacted network of concepts that constitutes a world view specific to folksong. (The relationship of the folksong world view to the pragmatic world view will be considered later.)

Let me discuss these signifying images under four of Kenneth Burke's categories of motivated human action: Act, Scene, Agent, and Agency.[10] Since "The Bold Fisherman" is a ballad, the Act category not surprisingly contains the largest number of signifiers, the first of which appears in the usual opening stanza, as the fisherman comes rolling (or roving or rowing—we can treat these as synonymous) down the river or "tide":

> As I walked out one May morning
> Down by the riverside
> And there I spied a fisherman
> Come rolling down the tide (*CSCEFS*, 1:222).

The signifying quality of this image is the river as a conveyor of one *dramatis persona*. The folksong corpus reveals that, as in "The Bold Fisherman," rivers function to bring potential lovers together: for instance, in "The Baffled Knight" (Child 112) the would-be lover meets his "pretty maid / A-floating by the tide" (*CSCEFS*, 1:135–36), as does the young traveler in "The Maid of Australia" (*FBI*, pp. 412–13).[11] On the other hand, rivers also carry one lover away from the other and thus function to permanently separate them, as in "The Wexford Girl" (Laws P35), where the false lover throws into the river his own sweetheart whom he has just murdered ("Look how she goes, look how she flows / She's a-floating by the tide" [*FBI*, p. 713]). Other appearances of this Act signifier match these two meanings: for instance, in "The Silvery Tide" (Laws O37) the same tide—here the ocean surf rather than a river—both separates the lovers (an unsuccessful rival for the girl's affections drowns her in the tide) and reunites them (the true lover goes in search of the missing girl and eventually finds her body "floating in the rolling tide" [*CSCEFS*, 1:304–5]). Similar is the experience of lovers in "The Constant Farmer's Son" (Laws M33), where the male suitor is killed by the girl's brothers (*CSCEFS*, 1:283–85).[12] Thus the two overarching significations of a tide, whether river or seashore's waves, as human conveyor are clear; it brings lovers together to facilitate mating (a spiritual mating only, if either or both of the lovers are dead) on the one hand, and on the other separates sweethearts irrevocably.

The next signifier in the narrative chronology of "The Bold Fisherman" is the man's taking hold of the maid's "lily-white hand":

> He tied his boat unto a stand
> And to this lady went,
> For to take hold of her lily-white hand
> It was his full intent (*CSCEFS*, 1:228).

Since hand-holding is such a common act in British ballads, I will exemplify its semantic field with references to those cases in which the qualifier "lily-white" is specified.[13] The results of such an analysis are very similar to the case of the first signifier, rolling down the tide. The act can be the immediate prelude to a romantic commitment on the part of the hand-taking male (as in "Poor Nell and the Chimney Sweep," *CSCEFS*, 2:100–102)—especially when the advances of either partner are explicitly sexual (e.g., Child 110 [*JFSS* 3 (1908): 222]; Child 299 (*CL*, pp. 22–23]; Laws P18 [*EC*, pp. 247–48]; "Gathering Rushes" [*EC*, p. 118]; "Low Down in the Broom" [*WS*, p. 70]; and many others). In direct contrast, taking by the lily-white hand may also signal the imminent death of the one whose hand is taken, whether it be murder by the lover (as in "The Wexford Girl" [*FSNE*, nos. 137, 179]) or by a jealous rival whose suitor has slighted her in favor of the victim.[14] In one instance, an interesting reversal of "The Wexford Girl" episode, we have the lover discovering the maid's body floating in the river (she has drowned herself because of his falseness) and taking her lily-white hand—here quite dead—to draw her out ("Floating down the Tide," *FMJ* 1 [1969]: 309–10, 326–27. This song will feature more prominently a little later on in our analysis).

The Act signifier of taking by the lily-white hand, therefore, exhibits a number of possible arrangements in which hand-taking, lovemaking, dying, and even an ambiguous "rescuing" may be integral features. But even though the sex of the various actors and the individual roles may differ, the signifier always clusters at the two poles of unification and separation. An especially intriguing combination is displayed in a few texts of "The Wexford Girl": in almost all the traditional and broadside versions of this ballad with which I am familiar, the false lover's actions on reaching the appointed spot with his unsuspecting sweetheart match his already formulated resolution, and he murders the girl with little ado; in an unusual variation, however, he seems to be ambivalent:

I catched fast hold of her lily-white hands
And I kissed both cheek and chin
And I had no thought of murdering her
And yet she wouldn't give in (*FBI*, p. 713, cf. *GG*, pp. 40–41).

He then proceeds with the customary murder; but it just may be that the taking by the lily-white hand signifier carries so powerfully the two contrasting meanings of *both* mating *and* murder that the young man is unclear, for a brief moment, as to just which of these two polar courses to adopt.

The next Act image in "The Bold Fisherman," the gown removal, exhibits a similar pattern:

Then he pulled off his morning gown, and laid it on the ground. 'Twas then she spied three chains of gold, all round his neck was bound (*JFSS* 7 [1923]: 37).

Gown removing is common in ballads where the act is integral to the uniting of lovers in their "true" guise: the returned-unrecognized-lover "Hind Horn" (Child 17), for instance, removes his beggar's disguise to reveal his real identity to the patient heroine who has so long endured his absence (*TTCB*, 1:255, no. 2); in "The Bailiff's Daughter of Islington" (Child 105) it is the girl who removes her disguise, to the delight of the lover from whom she had been parted (*TTCB*, 2:521, no. 12) ; and in the runaway-wife tale of "The Gypsy Laddie" (Child 200) the noble lady discards her fine clothing in favor of an ill-fared blanket, as she forsakes her unloved lord for a new and true gypsy lover (*CSCEFS*, 1:168–69). As for the opposite pole of motivated separation of lovers, gown removal is central both to the hugely popular "Lady Isabel and the Elf-Knight" (Child 4), in which the false-lover orders the maid to disrobe before he kills her (*GG*, pp. 50–51), and to a native Newfoundland murdered-sweetheart ballad, "Fair Eleanor" (*SNO*, 2:608–9), where the murderer's demands are the same (though he is successful in his attempt, whereas Lady Isabel, as is well known, turns the tables on her potential slayer with a neat bit of trickery and a pair of exceptionally strong arms).

Almost all versions of "The Bold Fisherman" call the fisherman's cloak a "morning gown," and this qualification may be as important semantically as the "lily-whiteness" property of hands appears to be. It is difficult to be sure on this point, since gowns specified to be of the morning variety appear very seldom in British folksong. Certainly, daytime is a common feature of sexual intercourse in British folk ballads, and perhaps the "morning" qualifier stresses this aspect of the fisherman's meeting with the maid, over and above the occasional quite overt statement about his erotic intentions.[15] Yet even if we restrict our signifier to "morning" gowns, its three appearances also follow a pattern of opposition. In "Gathering Rushes," the maid is persuaded to remove her morning gown and spread it on the grass so that she and her young wooer can make love undiscomfited by the remnants of night's dewfall (*EC*, p. 118). In "Easter Snow" the man proposes to the maid he meets in the fields to "roll you in my morning cloak and bring you home to Easter Snow," a proposal she quite sensibly refuses, though without any apparent acrimony on either side (*FBI*, p. 304; *MFS*, p. 43). The morning gown's third appearance (though as Agency rather than Act) is in a Berkshire version of "The Banks of Dundee" (Laws M25) and involves—no surprise by now—the separation of potential lovers by murder. The squire, who has been instrumental in the pressing to sea of Mary's true ploughboy lover, attempts to over-power and seduce the now-unprotected lass; but in the throes of their struggle she draws the pistols that show in the waistband beneath his morning gown and fatally shoots him (*ECS*, p. 117).

One appearance in the sample of gown removal (though not of the morning variety, if that *is* significant) does not fall into either of the two contrasting sets, lovers uniting and lovers separating; in "Willie o' Winsbury" (Child 100) an unmarried girl removes her gown to reveal to her father that she is, as he had suspected, pregnant (*CSCEFS*, 1:122–24). Since this is the only appearance of such an act/meaning association, and since the act-sign is such an empirical indicator of its referent, we may safely consider this to be not a signifier but a denotative sign. We face a similar case in considering the next Act signifier of "The Bold Fisherman"—the falling on bending knees and the crying for pardon or mercy (the kneeling and the importuning always appear together and thus seem to constitute a single signifier):

> Then on her bended knees she fell
> "Pray, sir, pray pardon me
> For calling you a fisherman
> And a rover down the sea!" (*JFSS* 5 [1915]: 132).

We find this act in several ballads where it is not immediately relevant to love relationships, indicating that the kneeler, in a subordinate role (and usually a transgressor to boot), is requesting a boon of someone in a dominant, authoritarian role. So, for instance, does the kneeling "Councillor's Daughter" (Laws N26) beg her father's blessing on the marriage she has contracted knowingly against his wishes (*CSCEFS,* 2:104–5). So does the wife of "Geordie" (Child 209) kneel to beg the court's mercy on her convicted husband (*CSCEFS,* 1:174–80). And so does the unwed mother of "The Forsaken Mother and Child" (Laws P20) kneel to ask God's mercy just before she and her child perish from exposure to the wintry outdoors (*FBI,* p. 354). These are all conventional images of supplication to authority, and thus once again closer to denotative signs than to signifiers. But the other examples of this Act, in which the interchange is between two lovers, encompass the above meanings and more, and thus seem to have a greater signifying function. For instance, in both Laws K38, "The Saucy Sailor" (*CSCEFS,* 2:311) and Laws P12, "Nancy" (II) (*FD,* p. 76) a maid who has refused someone she considered an inferior suitor kneels and begs pardon of the slighted man when it turns out that their positions are in fact reversed—that he is a better match than she, a set of circumstances quite close to the overt case in "The Bold Fisherman." Unlike the pleas of the maid in our ballad, however, those of the girls in "The Saucy Sailor" and "Nancy" (II), who have *explicitly* transgressed, are unsuccessful, and the lovers are parted forever. An even more definitive parting is displayed once again in a host of murdered-sweetheart ballads, several of which have already illustrated other Act signifiers: "Mary Thompson" (*FMJ* 2 [1974]: 349–50), "The Wexford Girl" (*JFSS* 7 [1922]: 23), "Fair Eleanor" (*SNO,* 2:608–9), "James MacDonald" (Laws P38; *FSNE,* no. 137), and "The Murder of Betsy Smith" all have the girl kneeling to beg for mercy or pardon after her false lover has declared his intent to murder her, as does the murdered-girl ballad "The Folkestone Murder" (*JFSS* 5 [1915]: 138–39; *FBI,* p. 703).[16] In a final instance of kneeling that signifies the pole of the tragic, the separation of lovers, we find the maid of "Scarboro Sand" (Laws K18) falling to her knees in grief on discovering her drowned lover's body washed up by the tide (*CSCEFS,* 1:260–61).

The semantic pole that opposes transgression, fear, and separation of lovers is that of steadfastness, joy, and unification of lovers. These meanings also we find signified by the falling on bended knees—by no coincidence, primarily in returned-unrecognized-lover ballads. Thus in a Nova Scotia version of "Pretty Fair Maid" (Laws N42), "When he showed her the token she had gave him / Down on her bending knees did fall" (*TSNS,* pp. 136–37). A version of another returned-unrecognized-lover ballad, "Waterloo" (II) (Laws N31), illustrates the ambiguity—and subsequent textual variation—

that can result when signifiers of the sort we are examining here become incorporated into a ballad's text. In this instance, rather than falling to her knees in joy, the girl does so in despair after her unrecognized lover has administered his test, informing her, falsely, that her lover died in battle. At this point, surprisingly, the ballad ends, thus qualifying as a tale of lovers' separation rather than unification (*BSSN*, p. 179).

The next Act-signifier in "The Bold Fisherman" is the bid to rise up from kneeling made by the fisherman to the girl:

"Rise up, rise up, my pretty fair maid.
Don't mention that to me,
For not one word that you have spoke
Has the least offended me" (*JFSS* 5 [1915]: 132).

This command to rise appears so infrequently in the folksong repertoire that one is tempted to doubt whether it has much of a signifying function; perhaps it is closer to the status of a sign—a necessary, empirical consequent of kneeling and pardoning. Nevertheless, it does appear and in a distinct slot, and its occasional uses certainly do not deviate from the by now established pattern. Thus, we find it in some Newfoundland versions of two returned-unrecognized-lover ballads, "The Mantle So Green" (Laws N38; *BSSN*, pp. 175–76) and "Janie of the Moor" (Laws N34; *BSSN*, pp. 180–81), where its significance is much the same as in "The Bold Fisherman." As for the separation pole, in "The Lowlands of Holland" the press-gang leader bids the husband rise from his wedding-bed for the journey to a war in Europe, the majority of the song then consisting of the wife's lament for her absent husband (*CSCEFS*, 1:108–13). In murdered-sweetheart ballads, where so far we have seen that the separation examples of our signifiers cluster, we do not of course find the "rise up" call following the cry for mercy. We do, however, see an interesting inversion in at least one murdered-sweetheart ballad, "The Cruel Ship's Carpenter" (A) (Laws P36A): the false lover bids his pregnant love to rise up from home or bed to the spot where he will, unbeknownst to her, carry out his criminal plan (*SNO*, 2:404–5).

The final Act is that of repairing to the father's house for the marriage ceremony:

Then we'll go to (your) father's hall and married we will be
And you shall have your fisherman to row you on the sea (JFSS
5 [1915]: 132).

Such an act appears in other ballads like "The Bold Fisherman" of successful courtship (e.g., Laws O15; *CSCEFS,* 1:464–65); but we also find a similar invitation by the male to an imminent wedding in murdered-sweetheart ballads like "The Cruel Ship's Carpenter" (A) (*CSCEFS,* 1:237–38), "The Wexford Girl" (*CSCEFS,* 1:235–36), and "Maria Marten" (*CSCEFS,* 1:308–9). The two may thus be in semantic opposition, though positionally exchanged; murdered-sweetheart ballads may *begin* with the man luring the maid *away* from the safety of home with a *false* promise of marriage, while ballads of successful courtship may *end* with the man leading the maid *toward* home with a *true* promise of marriage.

This analysis of the Act signifiers in a specimen text of "The Bold Fisherman" reveals clearly the two-valued pattern of meanings that those signifiers carry in the semantic inventory of British traditional folksong: the "comic" vision of unification and an ordered partnership on the one hand, and the "tragic" vision of fragmentation and unhappiness on the other. The second class of signifiers, Scene, presents few problems of analysis, and in fact turns out to strongly suggest a similar two-valued set. As in the vast majority of narrative folksongs, there is only one setting in the drama of "The Bold Fisherman": the riverside. Riverbanks are frequently the milieux for the reuniting of those long-parted sweethearts who feature in returned-unrecognized-lover ballads, as in Laws N29, "A Seaman and His Love" (*DBFS,* p. 3). In such stories, the river-bank—as well as the seashore (e.g., Laws N33; *CSCEFS,* 1:559–60)—would seem to be as much a rational as a poetic image since, after all, the man has invariably just returned from abroad; but river-banks are also extremely common venues for romantic liaisons be-tween landbound lovers, as in "Two Lovers Discoursing" (Laws O22; *EC,* p. 107), "The First of May" (*CSCEFS,* 1:491), and "The Banks of Inverary" (*CSCEFS,* 1:316–17). These are all songs of successful courtship or, as Laws calls them "Ballads of Faithful Lovers," in which the narrative is usually a quite simple and straightforward meeting, proposal by the male, initial refusal by the female, perseverance of the suit on his part, and her eventual ac-ceptance of him as a marriage partner.

But riversides also cluster at the opposing pole as scenes for solitary maidens despairingly to lament broken romances or to cast aspersions upon lovers who have sometimes false-heartedly absconded (*CSCEFS,* 1:495–99), sometimes been forcibly removed by third par-ties (Laws M8; *JFSS* 1 [1904]: 256–57). In such surroundings, in fact, false lovers may do their initial dirty work as well as leave their heartbroken (and sometimes pregnant) victims to lament (Laws P18;

CSCEFS, 1:659–60). In "Floating down the Tide," the false lover, while walking by the riverside, spies the body of the maid whom he had seduced and deserted (*CSCEFS*, 1:300–303); and as already mentioned in the discussion of the "rolling down the tide" signifier, true maidens may also find their dead lovers, the victims of third parties, in such locations. Finally, as before, there is the ubiquitous "Wexford Girl," in which the false seducer lures his victim to the riverside, slays her, and throws her body into the water.

The third category of dramatic action is Agent. Again, in "The Bold Fisherman," as in most folk ballads, there are only a very few agents: the maid and the fisherman/lord himself. In British folksong, a maiden's most notable feature is her state of high personal risk, especially in love relationships, which are far and away the most popular topic of British folksong, lyric and narrative. In most such songs the female's actions, emotions, and circumstances dominate the text's attention. In only a very small proportion of these songs do unmarried maidens have as their lot an indeterminate position on the scale running from despair to delight; in keeping with the high-risk status of their maidenhood in romantic involvements, girls are fated almost inevitably either to the ecstasy of a marital union or to the agony of being parted from their true lovers, parted often by third parties like disapproving parents and siblings, and even more often by the perfidy of the male lovers themselves. On rare occasion the girl may be the false one and initiate the separation of an honest union, but she almost always suffers for it—which is more than can be said for the false male lover (an indication that the folksong world view considers the female to be the dramatic, affective, and moral center of love relationships).[17]

The other agent in "The Bold Fisherman" is less generalized than is the female; he is not just a young man but a fisherman, and often "some lord." As a fisherman, this figure poses difficulties for us, since fishermen are just about nonexistent in the British folksong repertoire. There is only one unambiguous example: the predominantly Irish "Riley's Farewell" (Laws M8), which tells of parental disapproval of and interference in a daughter's romance with a fisherman. Riley leaves Ireland for America, eventually returning to take his faithful love away with him, but during the voyage their ship is wrecked and both drown (*JFSS* 1 [1904]: 256–57). Another faithful lover is the fisherman of "The Angler," an Anglo-Irish broadside of limited traditional currency that tells of a straightforward successful courtship and marriage.[18] If, however, as I think likely, in most English villagers' minds fishermen were synonymous with sailors, under the inclusive category of those who

make their living far off on the sea, then the repertoire presents us
with a plethora of examples, since sailors are a most common class
of lover in British folksongs.[19] They may just as easily be poor (and
suitably ragged and tarry) as be the possessors of great wealth,
gained doubtlessly from mysterious if unspecified exploits in foreign
lands. One never knows with a sailor, and many a ballad maiden
and many a ballad maiden's parent have made the wrong judgment,
to their subsequent discomfiture (e.g., Laws K36; *CSCEFS*, 2:316–
19). Sailors may be the most faithful of lovers, even in the face of
unfaithful partners (Laws P6; *CSCEFS*, 2:618–19), or they may be
that extreme of falseness, the sweetheart-murderer (Laws P36A;
CSCEFS, 1:237–38).

But the most fundamental polarization of meanings carried by
this Agent signifier stems from a Janus-like characteristic that is a
consequence of sailors' mobility. First, many returned-unrecognized-
lovers are sailors by profession, brought home after their lengthy
absence to final union in married bliss with their faithful sweethearts, whose patience has at last been rewarded:

So now this couple they've got married,
In wedlock's bands they are united,
They are married and joined together
So there's an end to the sailor bold (Laws N35; *CSCEFS*, 1:
552–53).

And second, that selfsame mobility which allows sailors to return to
a reborn union—or, for that matter, even to arrive on the scene as
potential partners in the first place—also permits them to easily
escape an unwanted permanent union. Indeed, it is often this ease
of escape that may propel them to the very initiating of what are in
their eyes casual liaisons (cf. Laws K43; *MB*, p. 42). As one of the
profession puts it in "The Rambling Sailor,"

With my false heart and flattering tongue
I'll court them all and marry none,
I'll court them all both old and young,
And still be a rambling sailor (*JFSS* 3 [1907]: 108).

Sometimes the separation and heartbreak that love affairs with
sailors bring to young girls are not the result of willful action by
either of the lovers but simply an ineluctable feature of the sailor's
profession; performance of the job itself means that he must leave,
and an enemy's cannon, or a gale, or even foreign rivals for the sea-

man's affections lurk ever at hand, threatening to make the separation a permanent one (e.g., *CSCEFS*, 1:547–49, 526–27, 522–25). In their debate, the lovers of "The Shepherdess and the Sailor" (Laws O8) imply several such significations integral to the sailor role:

> Young sailor, then said she, how can you fancy me?
> I never can give consent
> For when you're on the seas I could never be at ease,
> But you leave me to sigh and lament.
>
> Young shepherdess, said he, if you can fancy me;
> I have plenty of money in store,
> And the sea I will forsake and a promise to you I'll make,
> And be true to you ever more.

The ballad ends, "Take a sailor for your life and he'll make you his wife / And the sailor your fortune he will make" (*CSCEFS*, 1:388–89). To a significant extent, therefore, the fisherman/sailor image possesses the quality of a denotative sign. But strangely enough, it is precisely these literal qualities of ambiguity inherent in the life of a real sailor that contribute to his role as a symbolic signifier on the one hand (as we shall shortly see), while also allowing him to function as a denotative sign on the other (as chapter 2 will show).

We must also examine the gentry status of the male lover in "The Bold Fisherman," for in four of the English traditional texts the lady declares, upon spying the rich ornaments beneath his gown, that surely he is "some lord." Noblemen lovers can be very dangerous for girl commoners, as the maids in "Lord Thomas and Fair Annet" and "The Silvery Tide" can attest; however, they can also be as honest and persevering wooers as any ploughboy, as the young baronet of "A Cornish Young Man" (or "The Labouring Man's Daughter") proves (*FBI*, p. 308). But in almost all ballads in which a maid successfully weds an aristocrat, as well as in those numerous pieces whose male protagonists are "squires" (and thus not necessarily nobility), the lower-class lover has first to prove herself worthy of the match (by a show of cleverness or bravery, for example), which is not the case in "The Bold Fisherman."

Then what about the subcategory of aristocracy most immediately relevant to our ballad, that of noblemen incognito? This motif is also very weak in English tradition.[20] Successful matches between disguised nobles and maiden commoners are far more popular in ballads distinctly Scottish in both character and traditional currency.[21] Only English versions of "The Knight and the Shepherd's

Daughter" (Child 110), in which a knight without so much as a by-your-leave has his will of a girl laboring in the fields, might qualify. But even that, in our sample's version, is ambiguous.[22] It appears, therefore, that the fisherman's disguise gives the song a far more comfortable home in the returned-unrecognized-lover story-type than it does in the poor-girl-weds-rich-boy one.

The high status of the supposed fisherman is also indicated by his gold chains, and the data reveal that these chains also have significations that extend far beyond simply denoting social status. The fisherman's ornaments belong to our fourth and final category of signifiers, Agency, and in "The Bold Fisherman" they are the only objects with a degree of autonomy high enough to gain them recognition as independent agencies rather than as simply tools subsumed to an Act; it is her sighting of these chains that permits the girl to realize the stranger's true identity. In British traditional folksong, gold chains are used principally as love tokens, the primary referent, I have suggested, obtaining in "The Bold Fisherman." Love tokens signify that two lovers are affectively conjoined, even though they may be physically parted. So signifies "The Chain of Gold" the young lover hangs around his beloved's neck just before her father has the two forcibly separated, the wooer overseas, the girl to house arrest (*CSCEFS*, 1:335–37). And so does the token "Brave Wolfe" (Laws A1) gives his fiancée before sailing for Québec to fatally engage General Montcalm's army.[23] Gold chains exchanged between lovers, however, can also take on a negative signifying function if the chain wearer turns false, for they magnify that perfidy. A fine example is Laws P12, "Nancy" (II), in which the girl accepts the chain of gold, but will not accept the more denotative and contractual token, the wedding ring. Adding insult to injury, she wears the chain around her neck, prominent to his view every morning; at the same time, she orders him be gone, saying she can get better lads than such a "tarry sailor" as he (see *FD*, p. 76).[24] This is an unusually subtle example, for she has evidently interpreted a love token to be a commercial object, either to acquire wealth or to attract more acceptable suitors. (She gets the tables quite properly turned on her several years later when he meets her down and out on a London street; he gives her a debased transformation of his earlier gift, an *altruistic* handout of a *silver* coin.)

Thus in folksong's love relationships, gold chains signify the dualism of a couple's oneness in some instances and of one partner's extra-falseness, and thus the couple's extreme separateness, in others. Moreover, in the three occurrences known to me of the gold chain image in contexts other than those of love relationships, we also see opposing significations. In "The Old May Song," putting on a gold chain during a calendrical ceremony raises the existential status of the master of the house, for it signifies his live and functioning high position (*EFS*, pp. 6–7). But in the other two ballads, similarly placed gold chains lower the existential status of two nobles, bringing death by hanging to both "Geordie" (*CSCEFS*, 1:174–80) and the lady outlaw of "The Three Butchers" (Laws L4; *CSCEFS*, 1:274–75).

So far, this analysis of "The Bold Fisherman" has revealed three things: first, that the ballad's sequential structure of narrative events matches a common traditional ballad story-type, that of the returned-unrecognized-lover; second, that most of its imagery, and much of the surface language carrying that imagery, is shared with a larger category, songs of love relationships in general; and third, that the imagery and language embrace a range of meanings that is highly patterned—predominantly by two diametrically opposed concepts and correspondingly opposed values. A first reaction to this last discovery might be that it shows only that the course of love never did run smooth or that, in any case, the pattern of polar opposition is not entirely unexpected, since the preference of folkloric expressions for ideal states of good and bad is as old a characterization as Axel Olrik's "Law of Contrast" and as new as Claude Lévi-Strauss's "binary oppositions."[25] But both Olrik's "contrasts" and Lévi-Strauss's "binary oppositions" are structures composed of *two* or more distinct images; one character who is a hero might be counterbalanced by another who is a villain, or Oedipus marrying his mother will signify one meaning ("overrating of blood relations") in opposition to the meaning of a second signifier, Oedipus killing his father ("underrating of blood relations").[26] Analysis of "The Bold Fisherman," on the other hand, has shown that *the same image* can consistently project such antithetical meanings.

This property of "The Bold Fisherman's" signifiers brings to mind the characteristics of a very powerful kind of signifier, a symbol, a construct that the anthropologist Victor Turner has employed in analyzing ritual. Turner has found it useful to delineate three major properties of what he calls the "dominant symbol": *condensation,* which denotes the representation of a range of what are normally separabilia in a single image; *unification* of these phenomena so that they are represented as being conjoined in some way rather than disparate; and *polarization,* which is the particular kind of contrasting, two-valued quality that the cluster of referents signified by the symbol exhibits.[27] These three interrelated properties, it is apparent from our analysis, are contained in the signifiers of "The Bold Fisherman." Does this suggest, therefore, that we should consider those common folksong motifs—a riverside setting, a fisherman/sailor, a gold chain, a leading by the lily-white hand, a falling on bended knees—as symbolic? To do so would be in sharp contrast to our usual view both of those images and of their recurring textual vehicles, the view that they are "cliches" or "commonplaces." We usually ascribe their frequent appearance in a culture's traditional folklore to lack of artistic sophistication on the folk's part, need for ready-to-hand materials to replace forgotten ones, constraints that processing information orally imposes on the sheer amount and complexity of information that one *can* store and retrieve, and so on. However, if these commonplaces also have symbolic qualities, then a further explanation can be added to the somewhat mechanistic ones we customarily offer: since symbols are among the most value-laden, culturally important, expressively marked, and conceptually abstract representations of a culture's knowledge and ethic, they possess a high degree of longevity, of semantic load, of mnemonic strength, perhaps even of "ritualistic" significance.

But maidens, fishermen/sailors, objects of gold, all of the images we have been examining, have objective existence in the real world; if as signifiers they are to a large degree symbolic in the world of folksong, then we must ask, why these particular images? Poetic language, and especially folk poetic language with its strong pragmatic quality, is not a closed system; there should be some pattern to the relationship between the status of the symbol-vehicle in everyday perception (when the image functions denotatively) and its status in poetic perception (when the image functions connotatively). Is there a pattern to "real" rivers, kneelings, lily-white hands, and so forth? There indeed seems to be, and our earlier discussion of the sailor/fisherman signifier points the way: the phenomena all either mark the boundaries between two well-defined domains in routine meaning or possess ambivalent properties that allow them membership in at least two similarly well-defined but distinct domains.

In the Introduction, I spoke of the common love-adventure incipit, "As I roved out one May morning," as being more than simply a cliche: May, in the pragmatic world, is the interstitial period between spring and summer, two temporal categories that are firmly delineated ones in the seasonal calendar, while "roving out" indicates the interstitial space between the known and fixed home environs and the similarly unambiguous locus of a journey's destination. Consider, then, a river, the setting of both the events and the lover's mobility in "The Bold Fisherman." In the everyday experiences of the English countryman, a river was a common boundary marker between properties or parishes.[28] As a boundary marker, it "belonged" to neither of the contiguous domains it separated. Moreover, rivers run to the sea, and are thus of dual status: on the one hand a part of one's homeland, on the other, not of one's own country. In fact, only the skilled expert can clearly distinguish one's river from not-one's sea, as a villager implies:

> The Thames rises in the meadas close to Cricklet, an' runs away, an' gets bigger an' bigger, an' jines the sea at Greenwich, an' don' mix wi' the salt water for miles out, an' the skipper ull tell 'e when you gets into salt water.[29]

And like many such interstitial phenomena, rivers are transitions between well-defined classes of "facts" and thus in their ambiguity constitute a link between those clearer categories. Consider, once again, the Thames:

> . . . the first twenty-five miles of the river's course . . . embraces portions of three counties—Wiltshire, Berkshire, and Gloucestershire. This represents a distinct locality, with a common speech and folklore. The river Thames brought about this, for it had through the ages a unifying effect on those dwelling within the sphere of its influence.[30]

This unifying effect of the river in real, historical experience is similar to one of the functions of its symbolic representation in the conceptual experience of song poetry.

Similarly, we can point to the act of disrobing as a transitory state between the everyday one of fully clothed "culture" and the equally well-defined one of naked "nature"—most commonly associated with the two key phases in human life of birth and death (that is, when the body is unclothed and cleansed in a laying-out ritual). Not coincidentally, villages had two feminine role-slots that were perhaps the most specialized of women's tasks outside the home: the midwife role and the layer-out role.[31] The bended-knees position is similar: a "sacred" state between the common quotidian positions of the upright and the prone.[32] Even gold chains may have been, as gold, of intrinsic ambiguity to the working-class countryman. Toward the end of the last century, "Gold in plenty flowed through the country in a stream, but a stream to which only the fortunate had access. One poor half-sovereign was doled out on Saturday night to the lowest-paid workers; men who had a trade might get a whole sovereign and a few pieces of silver."[33] The ambiguity in the unskilled worker's perception of gold may have stemmed from these conflicting facts; on the one hand gold was plentiful, on the other he himself possessed it fleetingly but once a week (a half-sovereign was the lowest-valued coin minted in gold in the 1890s). Moreover, he had to part with that gold immediately to acquire the necessities of life, while gold was also "conspicuously consumed" by the wealthy for ornamentation.

One might also suggest that that stereotype of femininity, the lily-white hand, would be anomalous as well. In one way, it represented an epitome of femaleness, in real life seen possessed only by ladies of the gentry who relied on servants to perform household tasks. In contrast, rural working-class women performed constant manual labor in their own homes, as servants in the homes of others, often in the fields as agricultural laborers themselves, and would have possessed hands anything but lily-white. The paradox is that these female Significant Others in real experience did not exhibit a primary trait of "true" femaleness. We may also conjecture that in handholding, what is organically a part of Self becomes a part of Other while still remaining of oneself, and that like the river as an empirical unifier of distinct districts, handholding connects separabilia at their borders.

We need not rely on such conjecture in the case of the agents in "The Bold Fisherman," the man of the sea and the unmarried maiden, both of whom have a high denotative aspect in the song. The real-world status of seamen closely matches their duality as signifiers. A sailor is of society in that he is someone's husband or son, has shore leave and a home town to which he periodically returns. But he is also not of society in that he is away so often, partaking of that foreign otherness with which he has personal contact and which the more commonly landbound countryman knows only through imagination. Indeed, eighteenth- and nineteenth-century studies of the social structure of England appear to have placed sailors in an ambiguous category. For example, P. Colquhoun's classifications (his numerical data were taken from the first official government census, 1801) placed "The Army and Navy" in a category entirely divorced from landbound society, all other classes being ranked in seven categories ranging from everyone above the degree of baronet to "Paupers and their families, Vagrants, Gipsies, Rogues, Vagabonds, and idle and disorderly persons, supported by criminal delinquency."[34] A separate category for the army and navy indicates that while their members were considered a part of "the population of the United Kingdom of Great Britain and Ireland," they were yet at the same time quite different from all others tied to everyday terra firma.

As for unmarried but eligible young women, their status was very much a liminal one between that of the well-defined female child (who, whether residing at home while doing outdoors work or in service and living in her employer's house, was under the authority of her parents, to whom all her wages were handed over) and that of wife-and-mother. Flora Thompson's reminiscences suggest the ambiguity of this transitional stage, the phase of a girl first "at risk": Laura "had come to what the hamlet called 'an ok'ard age, neither 'ooman nor child, when they oughter be shut up in a box for a year or two.'"[35] It was during this period that Laura and her counterparts in the hamlet were liable to experience their first emotional attachments to the opposite sex.[36]

The ambiguity and, more particularly, ambivalence inherent in the empirical as well as poetic status of these images suggests a hypothesis about a subject that has long fascinated folksong scholars: that the ambiguity of such signifiers may cause them to be pivotal points of story variation in the texts of narrative folksongs. We have already had a hint of this in the stanza from "The Wexford Girl" in which the narrator seems to waver between making love to and killing his pregnant sweetheart after he has lured her to a deserted spot (see *FBI*, p. 713; *GG*, pp. 40–41), as well as in an unusual version of the returned-unrecognized-lover ballad, "Waterloo" (II) (*BSSN*, p. 179), which ends tragically. But let us also consider briefly a text of the internationally popular "The Twa Sisters" (Child 10), a quite unique version sung by Kilby Snow from the Blue Ridge Mountains of Virginia. While the many traditional British and American versions of this ballad display wide variation, the basic story line in the vast majority is fairly consistent; a suitor prefers the younger of two eligible sisters, and the older drowns her sibling out of jealousy.[37] Kilby Snow's unique rendition changes the basic story significantly from one of sibling rivalry and sororicide to one of the murdered-sweetheart type (though the murderer's motive is not made clear). The significance for our purpose of this unusual syncretic version is that in its dominant forms "The Twa Sisters" includes many of the images we have traced throughout the British repertoire in our analysis of "The Bold Fisherman"—the taking by the hand (which appears in several places throughout the ballad as antecedent to either killing or rescuing), the riverside setting, and the floating down the stream. In some versions we also find the undressing of the girl by a miller who fishes her body from the water.[38] In a few cases, we even find a gold chain.[39] And, of course, in Kilby Snow's murdered-sweetheart version, the two lovers are fishing when the murder takes place.[40] In short, could it have been these elements in particular that triggered associations leading to variation? Certainly, other studies have indicated that Southern Mountain balladry may have assimilated cultural premises about the nature of love relationships quite similar to the ones I will shortly posit for English village society, so the suggestion is not too far-fetched.[41]

Or take another example, "Little Sir Hugh" (Child 155). While "The Twa Sisters" has had almost no traditional currency in England, at least over the last hundred years, the opposite is true of the Sir Hugh ballad. Evidently originating in England, and with a loose similarity to events that purportedly took place in the city of Lincoln in 1255, the ballad's older versions tell of a Jewess luring a Christian boy into her home in order to slay him. His mother, searching for her missing son, is directed to a well in which the murderess has cast the body. From the well the dead child miraculously speaks to the mother, giving instructions for his burial. As is the case with "The Bold Fisherman's" suggested original Gnostic references, "Little Sir Hugh's" ritual murder and Jewish/Christian hostilities would not have been particularly meaningful to eighteenth- and nineteenth-century village society. Consequently, we find in many versions of the more modern tradition of "Little Sir Hugh" not only wide variation from the earlier story-type but also indications of amorous content and associated love-murder. D. K. Wilgus, using an analytic unit of ballad action called a "narrative theme," has shown that "Little Sir Hugh" fits comfortably into a matrix that includes several other love-and-death ballads like "Clerk Colvill" (Child 42), "Lady Alice" (Child 85) and its close genetic kin "George Collins," and "Young Hunting" (Child 68).[42] Significant in this cluster from our point of view is that they all, in the majority of their versions, feature not only intersex murder and one agent's venturing onto tabooed ground, but also bodies of water (the well in "Little Sir Hugh," rivers in the others) and often a taking by the lily-white hand—even in "Little Sir Hugh."[43] And in a most unusual text of the Sir Hugh ballad from Somerset, the boy meets his own mother on his initial entry into the Jew's house; he falls to his knees and asks her pardon, but she kills her own son and throws his body into the well (*CSCEFS*, 1:155–56). Once again, we have an intimate association between a certain set of imagery and a certain set of circumstances that, though covert, have to do with love relationships.

41

In interesting contrast, take the oft-collected "Lamkin" (Child 93); on the surface, one would expect the ballad to be drawn into this same semantic field, since it deals with a man's forced entry into a woman's house to kill both her and her children and often contains a certain sexual overtone (the woman offers her daughter who is "in flower" in place of her own life). But "Lamkin" never takes on further or more explicit romantic content, nor does it ever feature the kinds of signifiers we have been studying—no taking by the hand, no falling on bended knees, no body of water.[44] Whether it is the topic that triggers the subsequent incorporation of the "cliched" signifiers or whether it is existing textual "cliches" that trigger associations resulting in story variation is not possible to determine; but it is most challenging, both for interpretive analysis and for theories of textual variation, that the topics of love and death on the one hand and a small corpus of "cliches" on the other are so strongly linked that ballads like "Little Sir Hugh" and "The Twa Sisters" are changed in tradition to the point that a love relationship becomes their paramount concern.

We must now ask the following question: what major premise could underlie the poetic conception of love relationships so that a coherent world view is sustained, a premise that resolves the apparent contradiction between the two coexisting poles of, on the one hand, fidelity, hope, joy, unification, and love—of Life, in short —and, on the other, of infidelity, despair, fear, alienation, and exploitation—of Death? The repertoire of English traditional songs about love relationships indicates that the most likely answer is an intimate connection between transgression and redemption, a principle that accounts for more of the data than any other I can think of. It appears that, in the folksong universe of meaning, practically any love relationship is *ipso facto* a transgression and to succeed must be neutralized by a redemptive act before the ideal state of grace, union in marriage of two lovers, can be achieved.

A brief examination of the most common story-types in English folksongs that treat the topic of love relationships will reveal how this ethical principle of transgression and redemption is variously manifested. For instance, in the very simplest of story-types— straightforward successful-courtship—we find that the maid invariably refuses the advances the would-be lover puts forth on his first approach, and that he has to readdress his suit once or twice, incrementally (often by forswearing or making penance for past behaviors), before being accepted (e.g., *EC*, p. 107 [Laws O22]; *CL*, p. 3). Both the maid's initial refusals and the man's perseverance constitute the expiation that puts both into the state of grace permitting their eventual union.[45] As for the returned-unrecognized-lover story-type, both partners suffer through years of separation as well as through the test of fidelity to which the man must put the maid on his return (*CSCEFS,* 1:550–68).

Ballads whose stories are of the *un*successful-courtship type, in which a maid's refusal to accept a suit honestly tendered is allowed to stand (e.g., *JFSS* 2 [1905]: 91–92; *FD,* p. 76 [Laws P12]), of the lover's-infidelity type (e.g., *MB,* pp. 61–62 [Laws P31]), and of the more extreme seduction-and-abandonment type (see *CSCEFS,* 1: 651–84) may, individually, take on the surface a more one-sided view of either of the two partners, but the results are ultimately similar: the wronged party achieves his or her redemption in being victimized by the false lover, while the victimizer is punished—at the very least—by losing the chance to achieve happiness in true love. In the murdered-sweetheart story-type the girls are condemned, of course, not to a "living death" but to a real one, which seems in keeping with their more extreme transgressions of not only entering a love affair in the first place but of becoming pregnant to boot; their redemptive suffering is, presumably, proportionate to their crime (*CSCEFS,* 1:237–38 [Laws P36A], 295–96 [Laws P35], 292–93 [Laws P38]).

Story-types that feature unusually active maidens who are successful in capturing their mates demand that the girls undergo ordeals of redemption involving extensive bravery, cleverness, or trickery (e.g., *CSCEFS,* 2:61–62 [Laws O10], 91–92 [Laws N20])—or even the physical hardships that are the particular specialty of the warrior-maiden story-type (*CSCEFS,* 2:73–75 [Laws N6], 77–78 [Laws N14]). And in those many story–types that we may class under the general rubric of family-opposition-to-lovers (see *CSCEFS,* 1:328–72), *both* partners may be exposed to physical ordeals, often indeed having to wait till death to obtain the rewards of union, as the rose-briar motif indicates (e.g., *CSCEFS,* 1:69–71 [Child 73]).

If this thesis is correct—that the English country singer's folk-song world view of love relationships was premised on a transgression/redemption code—then we should expect to find instances in which someone went out of his way to render this implicit premise explicit. In other words, we need examples of what, for students of traditional English song, must often act in lieu of discursive native exegesis: examples of significant variation being wrought on established text-types so that what was apparently taken for granted, or subliminally apprehended (or even unconscious for that matter) is brought into clear view by an obviously intentional refashioning— a similar kind of evidence to that which we used to support the

thesis of the symbolic nature of some common folksong "cliches."
Certainly, we can rely on our own reading of many song texts already well established in tradition to illustrate a close love/death
association; the popular "Death and the Lady," for instance, in
which personified Death summons the lady to her final rest, is cast
in both language and imagery remarkably close to ballads of successful courtship and to lyric songs of false true-lovers.[46] But the
argument would be more powerful if we could find examples closer
to *native* exegesis: relatively new texts built from existing ones and
presumably motivated by a desire to make clear in surface meaning
what we suspect is present throughout in tacit meaning.

I can find two examples that are especially striking. The first
is a truly remarkable item, collected by Kenneth Peacock from Newfoundland tradition, its native title evidently "Flowery Garden"
(*SNO,* 2:588–89).

As I walked out in a flowery garden
A fair pretty maid oh I chanced to spy,
Stepping up to her thinking I knew her
I said, "Pretty maid, will you fancy I?"

"Perhaps you might be a man of honor,
A man of honor you seem to be."
"I'll marry thee, love, make you my true love,
I will get servants to wait on thee."

"Seven years I have loved a sailor,
Seven more he's been gone from me,
And seven more will I wait upon him
Till he returns from across the sea."

"If seven years you have loved a sailor
Perhaps he's married, dead, or drowned."
"And if he's married I'll love him better,
And if he's dead he's in glory crowned."

He drew his hand out of his pocket,
His fingers held a ring so small,
Saying, "Here's the ring, love, we broke between us."
Soon as she saw it down did she fall.

He threw his arms around her middle,
He gave her kisses, one, two, and three,
Saying, "I am yours, love, a single sailor,
Just returned from sea for to marry thee."

A short while after this fair young lady
Went to a dance one night so late,
This jealous young man he soon followed after
To prepare himself for a nobler fate.

He saw her dancing all with some other,
And jealousy came into his mind,
He then got ready a dose of poison,
He mixed it up with a glass of wine.

He gave it unto his own true lover.
She drank it down with a cheerful mind
Not thinking that her own dear loved one
Put a dose of death in her blood-red wine.

Soon as she drank it, so soon she felt it.
"Oh carry me home, oh my dear," cried she,
"The dose of liquor you lately gave me
Makes me so ill, love, as I can be."

" 'Twas in your liquor I put strong poison,
Sure I have drunk the same as thee,
In each other's arms, love, we'll die together,
Young men beware, don't court jealousy."

The first six stanzas of this Newfoundland text are nothing more nor less than that most common of returned-unrecognized-lover ballads, "Pretty Fair Maid" (Laws N42; see *CSCEFS*, 1:552–55), one of the most popular post-seventeenth-century ballads of the broadside type in folk tradition; it has been collected from country singers scores of times, on both sides of the Atlantic. And, to repeat, its story-type is replicated with enormous frequency in other popular folk ballads. It belongs squarely in the "comic" or Life-affirming paradigm of love experiences. The second half of the Newfoundland text is, of course, the almost as popular "Oxford City" (Laws P30; see *CSCEFS*, 1:310–12), a variant of the murdered-sweetheart story-type, and one that highlights the tragic Death paradigm of love relationships. "Flowery Garden" thus starkly conjoins at the most concrete level the two poles of Life and Death that love relationships covertly signify, in the process unmasking the code of transgression and redemption that informs a love affair. That the lovers had already spent seven years apart, and that the girl had had to undergo the test of fidelity on her young sailor's return, was not good enough for the compiler of this interesting amalgamation; the

45

cycle of transgression and redemption had to be repeated again in a far more explicit and extreme form, the final reward for expiation being signified in a topical and human analogue of the ancient rose-briar motif, the two dying together in mutual repentance and in final, spiritual unity.

The second example of a fresh product fashioned from already-existing wholes is not as startling as "Flowery Garden," since the two texts drawn upon both come from the Death semantic pole— in one case actual death being the girl's lot, in the other pregnancy and abandonment. The title of this song text is, significantly, "The Lily-White Hand"; briefly, its story is as follows. Walking "down by the riverside," the narrator meets a maid who comes "clinging to [his] side." He asks her to marry but she claims to be too young, only sixteen. Her youth attracts him all the more, however, and he takes her by "the lily-white hand" to lead her indoors, where they make love. Afterwards, he dresses to leave, but she berates him for breaking his promise to marry her. He asserts that he would never marry a girl so easily seduced and urges her to return home. But she cannot face the shame that would now befall her parents, and declares that she will drown herself instead. He again takes her by "the lily-white hand," leads her to the river, and pushes her in, marveling at how she floats "along with the tide." He seems to repent, but only weakly; he decides he will leave the country to escape discovery but also to find some other girl. The final stanza is a common lyric lament, warning young girls not to build their nests on the tops of trees, for the flowers will wither and the leaves die, as will a young man's love quickly fade (*GG*, pp. 38–39).[47]

"The Lily-White Hand" draws bits and pieces from several traditional text-types (we shall meet some of them in the following chapter), but the two that supply most of its text and narrative are "Pretty Little Miss" (Laws P18), which tells of an older man's seduction of a younger girl under a false promise of marriage, of his subsequent departure, and of his advice that she return home (see *CSCEFS*, 1:656–58; *WS*, p. 6; *FBI*, pp. 351, 373–74), and "Floating down the Tide," which tells of a seduced girl (her later pregnancy is sometimes explicit) who commits suicide by drowning herself because her lover will not marry her (see *CSCEFS*, 1:300–303; *FMJ* 1 [1969]: 309–10, 326–27). The stories of both "Pretty Little Miss" and "Floating down the Tide" are replicated with great frequency in the English popular folksong repertoire.[48] "The Lily-White Hand" has integrated their two stories and texts to *overdetermine*, in Freud's term, the transgression/redemption principle, as well as to sharpen the respective degrees of each (though here, as is quite common in English folksong, the girl bears the brunt of the explicit punishment). In addition, "Lily-White Hand" exhibits a small but significant change in the manner of the girl's death: the false lover pushes her into the river, thus converting the "Floating down the Tide" segment from a suicide narrative to the very common murdered-sweetheart story-type.

It is not necessary for us to dwell on the "cliched" imagery and language that these two syncretic texts, "Flowery Garden" and "Lily-White Hand," share with "The Bold Fisherman"; but I may reiterate that in these two striking versions we find "native speakers" of British folksong—that is, people who have assimilated the covert rules for generating culturally meaningful texts—going to unusual lengths to articulate individualistic products, though still firmly within the traditional mold.[49] That they have created texts that are clearly generated by the code an "etic" (or non-native) analysis has independently uncovered is strong support for my argument.

Ultimately, we can conclude that if this interpretation of the love relationships world view is correct, any of several possible concatenations of events could have become the British traditional folksong "The Bold Fisherman." The male protagonist could just as easily have seduced the lady and left her to grieve as he once more returned to sea as have revealed himself to be her long-absent, but now-returned-to-marry-her lover; just as easily have taken her by the lily-white hand or removed a gown to ravish her or to slay her and throw her body into the river, as have wooed her and taken her home to marry; just as easily have refused her plea for pardon and forthwith murdered her as have bidden her rise and be his bride. Almost any combination of these elements could have been generated by the ethic underlying English traditional songs of love relationships. And any such combination, I submit, would have been perfectly acceptable to eighteenth- and nineteenth-century English country singers and their audiences, with no perception of contradiction or inappropriateness on their part toward such a text —as acceptable, certainly, as the text-type that did solidify in the ballad's tradition.

And if I may be permitted my perhaps boldest speculation, let me direct attention to the usual second stanza of "The Bold Fisherman," in which the stranger moors his boat to shore. There is no clear preference in the available texts for a mooring object; the boat is tied "by the stern," to "the strand," to "a stand," and to the "stem." In one version, it is tied to a "spear," and in two others to a "stake," as in the following example from Dorset:

'Twas then he rowed his boat to shore and tied it to a stake,
And walked up to this fair lady her lily-white hand to take
(*JFSS* 7 [1923]: 37).

It is this last, the stake, that is most suggestive, for in the oft-cited
"The Wexford Girl" we find the same agency used as the murder
weapon ("But I plucked a stake from out the fence and I struck that
fair girl down" [*GG*, pp. 40–41]), as it is by the brothers in "The
Constant Farmer's Son" (Laws M33) to murder their sister's lover
before throwing his body into the stream.[50] We may hypothesize
about the semantic equivalence of "spear" as well, an unusual mooring object to say the least; the point, however, is that a stake, which
aids the bringing together of true lovers in "The Bold Fisherman,"
contradictorily assists their separation in the murder ballads. And
once again, in empirical experience, whether by itself or as part
of a fence or hedge, a stake was and is—like a river—a common
boundary marker.[51] We may therefore conclude that the love relationship ethic could have generated yet another appropriate alternative in "The Bold Fisherman": the man could just as easily have
plucked the stake from the ground and murdered the kneeling girl
as he could have granted her pardon and bidden her rise and marry.

We may now explore the relationship of the poetic province of
meaning that deals with love experiences to the English villager's
everyday, pragmatic world view. Why should love affairs in popular
songs be so highly marked as a focus of concern that the notion of
ipso facto transgression seems quite apt? If we turn our attention to
accounts of village life it becomes clear that relationships between
the sexes was an area of real-life experience fraught, in certain
important respects, with actively imposed rules and constraints. For
instance, although agricultural laborers (usually the largest single
category of village dwellers before the 1850s) lived on meager wages
in two- or three-room cottages, with the result that children of both
sexes shared a bedroom, a young person's knowledge of the opposite
sex was slim:

A lot of people shared bedrooms in those days—I mean four or
five to a room because of the big families. We never saw anything wrong. People think we did but we didn't. My sister and
me and my brother shared a room until we were married but
we knew nothing. I'm sure of this. Today they hear too much
about sex too early.[52]

The Anglican priest in the same village could testify to the restrictions that kept this young girl in ignorance, despite the living conditions at home: "They had a sort of code but all the natural human relations were covered by cruel and ugly taboos which obsessed some of them."[53] In Oxfordshire's hamlet society of Lark Rise, a mother's pregnancy would be carefully avoided in conversation between adults and children: "Even girls of fifteen were supposed to be deaf and blind at such times and if they accidentally let drop a remark which showed they were aware of the situation they were thought disagreeably 'knowing.' "[54] When Laura visited her cousins at Candleford, a market town where industrial occupations (that is, of the domestic and small artisan sort) were dominant, she was amazed at her peers' entirely different attitude:

> . . . one of them asked her: "Do you like boys?" . . . Laura thought at first they meant sweethearts and grew very hot and shy; but, no, she soon found they just simply meant boys to play with. She found afterwards that the boys they knew talked to them freely and let them join in their games, which surprised her, for the boys at home despised girls and were ashamed to be seen talking to one. The hamlet mothers encouraged this feeling. They taught their boys to look down upon girls as inferior beings; while a girl who showed any disposition to make friends of, or play games with, the boys was "a tomboy" at best, or at worst "a fast, forward young hussy."[55]

Despite these extreme constraints on adolescent knowledge about sexually relevant matters, prenuptial sex was by all accounts not uncommon.[56] George Bourne, who in opposition to the native villagers quoted above thought that there were in fact *few* restraints on sexual knowledge and behavior among the rural working class, asserts that "illegitimacy has been very common in the village."[57] And Flora Thompson herself notes that when attendance was taken at the village school, "the eldest children of several families answered to another surname than that borne by their brothers and sisters and by which they themselves were commonly known"— though when Laura was growing up in the 1880s there were no illegitimate babies born in Lark Rise.[58] But Thompson goes on to suggest a reason for this disparity between the surnames of siblings, and it is this suggestion that provides the best clue to explaining the world view that supported the folksong code of transgression and redemption in love relationships: the older children with the unfamiliar names, she says, were probably the children of couples who had married after the birth of their first child. This certainly resolves the apparent paradox of severe taboos against close male/female intimacy coexisting with premarital sexual activity; for it had long been the case in English rural culture that *intention to marry* constituted sanction for a love relationship, including sexual intercourse.[59] Thus the taboos and constraints against male/female liaisons were not enforced if marriage between the partners was the probable result of the relationship. *Marriage* appears to be the key, rather than love relationships per se.

There is considerable support for this thesis—that marriage and its sanctity was a greater focus of concern than the sanctity of unwed youth's and maiden's chastity. For instance, constraints on sexual activity out of wedlock came from parents' injunctions or neighbors' gossip, both essentially informal actions; there was evidently no highly formalized, ritualistic, community-conducted, highly public act of social control. On the other hand, there are wide reports that village communities included in their repertoire of formalized, public activities a ceremony meant to influence directly the sanctity of marriage—the custom most commonly known as "rough musicking." Almost all reports of this practice indicate that it was used to shame and change a husband or wife who had transgressed the norms of marital behavior; adultery, wife-beating, and pregnancy out of wedlock are the violations most frequently mentioned. In general, rough musicking involved the gathering of an organized band of villagers (invariably male) for several consecutive nights outside the offender's house to make as cacophonous a racket as possible by banging metal objects, singing contumelious verses, shouting insults and accusations. As one writer says, "public opinion is roused, and Jack must be taught that the whole community disapproves of his cruelty."[60] Threatening the continuity and stable functioning of the marriage unit, in other words, was an act the villagers considered threatening to the whole community and requiring corrective action by that community.

There is further evidence that marital rather than sexual purity was considered *the* condition to be protected. Even though George Bourne, for instance, noted that sexual mores were loose in his village, he was nevertheless quick to point out that "once a man and a woman are married, they settle down into a sober pair of comrades, and instead of looseness which might be looked for there is on the whole a remarkable fidelity between the married couples."[61] In the agricultural society of Cumberland's Gosforth, in this century, though premarital sex and illegitimacy were evidently more common than in other parts of England and viewed more broadmindedly by the general populace, "adultery seems to have been rare . . . and divorce and broken marriages are almost unknown."[62] An insider's account from Oxfordshire also reveals the relative attitudes toward premarital sex accompanied by marriage vis-à-vis sex without:

> If, as sometimes happened, a girl had to be married in haste, she was thought none the worse of on that account. She had secured her man. All was well. " 'Tis but Nature," was the general verdict.
>
> But though they were lenient with such slips, especially when not in their own families, anything in the way of what they called "loose living" was detested by them.[63]

The author goes on to describe two examples of "loose living": an adulterous relationship between a married woman and her lodger (the two were treated to rough music), and the moving into the hamlet of an unmarried woman with four illegitimate children.[64]

Thus does a picture emerge of the aspect of pragmatic world view that most rationally and coherently matches the folksong world view of love relationships. Love relationships are seen as transgressions in the expressive vision of song poetry because of the importance placed on the marital unit as a successful end to such affairs. The ordeals that lovers undergo in song courtships truly socialize them to the importance placed on the marriage they with such difficulty manage to negotiate. Failure to attain the desired end, whether because of falseness of one partner or interference by such agents of control as parents, means that the two have failed the test of the "survival of the species"; but in their failure the lover, or lovers, gain redemption for not setting up a fragile partnership that, when it failed, would endanger the community.

As a final note, we should take cognizance of the fact that while pragmatic world view is the immediate environment of folksong world view, normative beliefs and practices themselves constitute a figure on a larger ground—the objectively real conditions in which the majority of English country folk lived in the latter eighteenth and nineteenth centuries, especially in the south and midlands, conditions outside their control and perhaps even apprehension. I would suggest that the empirical conditions that most influenced the real-life concern with the proper functioning of the marital unit were in all probability economic ones. For with the decline in the lot of the rural working class in particular over the last half of the eighteenth century, marked by the loss of open fields, allotments, commons, and squatter's rights; with the change in the relationship between classes from one of mutual rights and responsibilities to one governed by market logic and wage labor; and with the change in intraclass relationship from one of collectivity and mutual assistance to one of more or less independent units of nuclear families, so did the rural worker's standard of living worsen to a level somewhat below—by rational standards—a tolerable subsistence level.[65] Rural economies thus demanded that the nuclear family be the unit of survival, and the proper functioning of this unit was essential for that survival, marginal as it may have been. Indeed, members who consumed more than they produced were drainers of the whole community's "limited good"—the total of very finite resources available in the ecosystem.[66] Such "overconsumers" would include not only the men who "consumed" women in love affairs that came to unsuccessful conclusions but the women as well—in fact, given the conditions of the time, *especially* women; for many daughters of the rural working class made their living in domestic service and would almost certainly have been turned out for the impropriety of indulging in a love affair. Most parents depended on children's incomes for a meager addition to their own finances and on their children's employers to provide the girls with board and lodging. Parents also needed the minuscule space at home for the younger offspring still maturing. Problems would be multiplied, of course, if a daughter bore an illegitimate child as a result of her unsuccessful love affair; and unwed mothers and their offspring often became nonproducing drainers of the community's resources by turning to the workhouse and other such forms of parish-supported relief for shelter. In short, a nuclear family of no more than two generations could just tolerably support its own members—and not all of them at that, given the large families that were common among the rural working class. For the second generation to become a viable part of society, it *had* to start its own successful nuclear families.[67] In the light of all these possibilities, it is not surprising that the girl is invariably the object of narrative, emotional, and ethical focus in English folksongs of love relationships.

While it is also not surprising that such a subject, with its potential of danger to the rural working-class population, should have been liable to expression by certain signifiers charged with symbolic implications, we must recognize that in ballads like "The Bold Fisherman" and others within the same semantic field the symbolic quotient constitutes in the main a tacit substratum. Most have a more overt infrastructure (and even more so, superstructure) that is in fair degree referential, with a logic of cause and effect that bears a strong denotative relationship to tolerably real cultural facts—the danger of partnerships with sailors being the most obvious example. In chapter 2 we will make the acquaintance of a distinct subtype of song about love relationships, a lyric rather than narrative one, which is predominantly coded by a much fuller symbolic language and world view, and in which the fate of young girls who engage in love affairs is far more consistently and tragically predetermined.

2

THE
SEMIOTICS
OF
SEXUAL
LIAISONS

Within the repertoire of traditional folksongs like "The Bold Fisherman" that fieldworkers in England have been so fortunate to collect from country singers over the past hundred years or so, easily the most popular topic is that of love relationships. Whether a song may have originated as long ago as the fifteenth century (the date of the earliest known version—but not necessarily of the composition—of "Riddles Wisely Expounded" [Child 1], for instance) or as recently as the nineteenth, the enduring relevance of love affairs allows songs which treat of them to transcend the narrow specifics of a particular time and place and achieve truly traditional status. There are differences, of course, in the degrees of general relevance that various sorts of romantic encounters may possess; for instance, while Anglo-Irish, Canadian, and American folksong collections of both native and imported pieces contain few songs on this favored topic of love with fairly explicit references to a sexual encounter between the two central *dramatis personae,* in England, and Scotland as well, what folksong scholars used to call "the way of a man with a maid" (but which we shall soon see was also, if to a lesser extent, "the way of a maid with a man") was evidently considered by country people to be a quite appropriate subject for song poetry.[1] Indeed, even in some versions of "The Bold Fisherman," which in its narrative outline as well as its language is usually a ballad of quite decorous courtship, the sexual possibilities of the meeting between fisherman and maid are more than a little hinted at. But there are many other well-known English traditional songs in which a sexual relationship between two lovers is an overt, integral, and consistent feature. And since this book's main purpose is to show that a poetic repertoire popular in a folk tradition during any given era will constitute a coherent system of meaning, a fair test of its success would be to reveal coherency in the sizable corpus of English songs that tell of "country matters."

The task of this chapter, therefore, will be to discuss such a system. From a sample of 152 distinct English folksongs on love relationships that specify a sexual affair between the lovers, I will show that coded into the texts is a set of world views that, while unified, display enough variation to be sensitive to different historical circumstances, contexts of action, classes of village audiences, and even occasions for singing. Despite this diversity, however, the different views are quite compatible with each other and with the larger category to which songs of sexual liaisons belong—songs of love relationships, with their all-embracing, abstract principle of transgression and redemption.

As we saw in chapter 1, the larger category, love relationships, can be played out in a wide array of narrative models: the returned-unrecognized-lover type, for instance, or the warrior-maiden. But these two, among others, almost never contain mention of a sexual intimacy between their protagonists. On the other hand, murdered-sweetheart ballads frequently do, since it is the girl's pregnancy that more often than not provides the false lover with a motive for doing away with his now-burdensome mistress. Successful-courtship and unsuccessful-courtship story-types may be of either kind, sexual or romantic. Consequently, since categories of this sort, delineated as they are by narrative model or story-type, can contain songs with sexual allusions as well as songs without, they do not provide a viable system of classification here. A sex act is a content, and only in very special circumstances is it a song's narrative topic. However, the population of songs that have such sexual content clearly suggests its own subdivision according to the surface language that carries the sexual referent.[2] I will, therefore, identify the subgenres according to their rhetoric of sex and call them the *symbolic,* the *euphemistic,* and the *metaphorical.*[3]

55

The first category, the symbolic, contains folksongs that, while relatively few in proportion to the whole corpus of songs of sexual liaisons, seem to have been the most widely admired—at least by outsiders—of English traditional songs. In fact it was the gardener John England's singing of one of these songs that first aroused the interest of his country's greatest collector, Cecil Sharp, in field-collecting native folksong.[4] Symbolic songs of sexual content are invariably lyric rather than narrative, are told by a first-person narrator, and deal with one lover's lament over a love affair spoiled by the partner's falseness or enforced absence. I use the designation symbolic for this class of songs because its dominant language-imagery signifies abstractions rather than "things," interrelates phenomena that are not empirically linked, and exhibits a distinct pattern of signification in which both positive and negative values are carried by the same image.[5]

The most signifying imagery in symbolic songs is drawn from nature's flora, fauna, and topography. James Reeves, who edited two anthologies of selections from the unpublished manuscripts of four prominent pre-World War I English collectors (Cecil Sharp, Reverend Sabine Baring-Gould, Henry E. D. Hammond, and George B. Gardiner), made the best-known attempt to draw attention to the widespread nature symbolism in English folksong and its sexual significance.[6] Hypothesizing a once widespread and well-known *lingua franca* of sexual symbolism, Reeves suggested some typical meanings for common folksong imagery: " 'Thyme' is virginity, the 'rose' is wanton passion, the 'violet' modesty, the 'pink' courtesy, the 'lily' purity, 'rue' and 'willow' stand for repentance and a broken heart."[7] But if such is the case, then we run afoul of a familiar problem, for what is one to make of lines like the following, performed for Sharp in 1907 by Robert Parish?

> I wish my love was a red, red rose,
> And in some garden grew
> With lilies I would garnish her,
> Sweet William, thyme and rue (*CSCEFS*, 1:497).[8]

It is not readily apparent why a lover would wish his beloved to be wantonly passionate so that he could embellish her with purity, virginity, and a broken heart. The usual way to account for such apparent discrepancies in sense is to suggest that by the time these songs were collected in the early twentieth century the formerly well-known *lingua franca* was in disarray and the older coherency of meanings lost. Or one might suggest that the same language can be intended sometimes literally, sometimes symbolically, sometimes purely for form's sake (thus the young man in the above lines is perhaps simply being "poetic" for poetry's sake and not necessarily "logical"). There is no doubt merit to both of these postulates, and Reeves in fact uses them both. However, as we saw in the last chapter, there is a surprising coherency of meaning in the folksong repertoire, even among versions collected in this century; and if we can by means of a certain analytic method discover consistency in meaning that accounts for more of the total repertoire than does Reeves's fixed dictionary-of-meanings approach and forgotten-meanings hypothesis, then the coherence criterion of validity is better met.

Reeves may have erred I think, in failing to draw a sharper distinction between symbol and metaphor. In his essay on the *lingua franca* he deals extensively with traditional sexual imagery that is clearly metaphorical and that we can unambiguously identify as "referring" to sexual phenomena; in "The Buxom Lass," for instance, the young farmworker attempts to "mow" the lady's "meadow" with his "scythe" (*WS*, p. 23). But metaphors differ from symbols in that, first, they are contingent upon the structure or behavior of their referents and thus are more particularistic and determined than symbols; second, metaphors are not associated primarily with abstract concepts but with tangible, or at least reified "things" (the metaphorical vehicle is at the same logical level of abstraction as its tenor or referent—as with music and food, say, or lions and kings); and third, metaphors do not exhibit the polarity in their range of signification that symbols do (metaphors bring to consciousness the similarities between significations, but not the antitheses). To distinguish between the two constructs symbol and metaphor is especially important here because there is in fact also a metaphorical type of song about sexual relationships, one that, as we shall see, is distinctly different in content, form, meaning, and use from the symbolic type. But this is not to say that symbol and metaphor are mutually exclusive constructs. As we discovered in analyzing "The Bold Fisherman," a symbol is not formed arbitrarily; there is a logical basis for the relationship between symbol and symbolized. Since a metaphorical relationship (structural, functional, or textural similarity) is one such logical basis, then one will find in some symbols a metaphorical substratum. But when that substratum becomes overlaid with a cluster of significations that reach beyond single reified referents to embrace polarized sets of concepts, then we are in the realm of symbolization and have transcended the more straightforward metaphor.

English traditional songs that follow the symbolic model are structured on a fundamental opposition between a conception of all that is vital and energetic on the one hand and all that lacks such life principles on the other. Two useful labels for these polar paradigms are "heterogeneity," implying multiple differentiation among active elements of the ecosystem, and "homogeneity," implying a sameness among nature's components to the extent that all meld into a static, uniform tableau. There are seven major semantic domains in the code-repertoire of this province of meaning, sexual liaisons, each domain encompassing a pair of more specific signifiers of heterogeneity versus homogeneity. Such are the variables; the value of each signifier may be both positive and negative, with the difference that signifiers in the heterogeneous paradigm have a primary value of positive, a secondary value of negative, while signifiers of homogeneity have a primary value of negative and a secondary value of positive. These variables, their values, and the very finite and simple ways in which they are combined constitute the structure of the code which generates a text of a symbolic song of sexual liaison. A chart will enable us easily to grasp this structure, a chart that represents the major resources that the full code allows. Since the semantic domains are homologous with each other, any one text will draw upon only a few domains.

Heterogeneity (primary value: + secondary value: −)	Homogeneity (primary value: − secondary value: +)
activity	lack of activity
intensity	lack of intensity
perpendicular	horizontal
multiple	single
free	bound
humans dominating nature	nature dominating humans
strongly fertile ground	weakly fertile ground

FIGURE 1.
The structure of the code that generates symbolic songs of sexual liaisons.

A sample text will allow the reader who is not familiar with this common type of English folksong to get a feel for the quite predictable language, imagery, form, and somewhat associational stringing together of ideas that characterize the lyric mode of symbolic songs:

THERE WAS THREE WORMS ON YONDER HILL

There was three worms on yonder hill,
They neither could not hear nor see;
I wish I'd been but one of them
When first I gained my liberty.
(Repeat last two lines.)

Then a brisk young lad came a-courting me,
He stole away my liberty;
He stole it away with a free goodwill,
He've a-got it now, and he'll keep it still.

Oh, for once I wore my apron-strings low
My love followed me through frost and snow,
But now they're almost up to my chin
My love pass by and say nothing.

Now there is an ale-house in this town,
Where my false love go and sit himself down
And takes strange girls all on his knee—
And don't you think that's a grief to me?

So gold will waste and beauty pass
And she will come like me at last.
That mortal man when he served me so
When I was down where the daisies grow.

Now there is a flower, I heard them say,
Would ease my heart both night and day.
I wish to God that flower I could find
That would ease my heart and my troubling mind.

Then out in the mead this poor girl run
To call those flowers fast as they sprung;
'Twas some she pickéd, some she pulled,
Till at length she gained her apron full.

On those sweet flowers she made her bed,
A stony pillow for her head;
Then down she lay and never spoke,
And now her tender heart is broke.

Now she is dead and her corpse is cold
I met her false-love, and him I told:
"A bad misfortune I come to tell."
"I'm glad," said he, "she have done so well."

Oh, so now she is dead and her corpse is cold
I met her false lover, and him I told:
"Come and walk after your heart's delight;
She will walk with you both day and night!"

So dig her a grave long, wide and deep,
And strow it all over with flowers sweet;
Lay on her breast a turtle-dove,
That folks may see that she died for love (*JFSS* 5 [1915]:
188–89).

I will not analyze specifically this text of "There Was Three Worms on Yonder Hill" (all versions of which I shall henceforth identify as Laws P25, "Love Has Brought Me to Despair") but instead will draw upon the whole sample of symbolic songs to exemplify each of the code's seven semantic domains and their fourteen signifiers, so that the reader will have no difficulty matching the relevant imagery in "Love Has Brought Me to Despair" with its cognate signifiers from the sample. *Activity* signifiers take premier place because they are among the most numerous in any one symbolic song, often dominating opening stanzas. For instance:

I sowed the seeds of love,
'Twas early in the Spring.
In April, in May and in June likewise,
When small birds they do sing (*CSCEFS*, 1:577).

The activity does not have to be peculiar to one of the lovers— "Up lanes and through meadows, how oft we'd wend our way, / Oh! my bonnie Irish lad and I would frequently stray" (Laws P26; *JFSS* 1 [1899]: 7)—nor confined to human movement, for, as is prominently the case in symbolic songs, the rest of nature acts in close accord with man and woman. For instance, "The lark in the morn she rises from her nest / And mounts in the air with the dew upon her breast" (*EC*, p. 172) illustrates animal activity parallel with that of the human actors, while at times there may be a veritable concert:

O hark, O hark, how the nightingale is singing,
The lark she is taking her flight in the air,
The turtle dove in every green bower is building,
The sun is just glimmering. Arise thou, my dear (*CSCEFS*,
1:404).[9]

60

These all signify the *positive* qualities of activity, the vitality of movement that is not just readiness for a sexual liaison nor just its necessary environs, but indeed, on the principle of metonymy rather than metaphor, the very act of sexual intercourse itself. But activity can also have a *negative* value—for instance, the activity of a lover inclined to mobility and thus into liaisons with others: "Why will you go a-roving / And slight your dear Polly?" (*CSCEFS*, 1:495), asks "The Irish Girl"; while another victim of an overly active lover reports that

> There is an ale-house in the town
> Where my love goes and sits him down,
> And pulls a strange girl all on his knee—
> And isn't that a grief to me? (*JFSS* 5 [1915]: 181).

Occasionally, it is the true-hearted male who is exploited by the roving of a false female, as in "The Grey Hawk," where the narrator once had a "sweet pretty bird" all his own; but the bird has now "flown away," where to no one knows (*EC*, p. 140).

In the cases above, different images carry opposing values of the same essential idea, activity; but we also find instances in which a single textual unit signifies both positive and negative values, as a symbol which has jelled into a linguistic "cliche" does. Thus, in order to recapture a departed lover, the deserted maiden must herself take to the road. Just as the heroine of "The Bonny Young Irish Boy" (Laws P26) must actively follow her absconded lover to London (*JFSS* 1 [1899]: 17), as the maiden of "A Shoemaker Courted Me" must go recapture her love who has gone harvesting (*CSCEFS*, 1: 613–14), so must the lass of "The Americans Have Stolen My True Love Away" journey across the Atlantic:

> The Americans have stolen my true love away,
> And I in old England no longer can stay.
> I will cross the briny ocean all on my soft breast
> To find out the true love who I do love best (*CSCEFS*, 1:
> 631–32).[10]

As this stanza indicates, it does not seem to matter much whether the lover has voluntarily departed for greener pastures or has been called to, say, war. (Nor, indeed do the maidens ever find their lovers, whatever the reason for the parting.)

What about the other of the pair, *lack of activity*? Just as the primary value of activity is positive, so the primary value of its opposite is negative, but the tension between its primary negative value and secondary positive value that makes it a symbolic signifier is evident here as well. Its dominant image is the death of the forsaken lover, the end of so many symbolic songs: "She laid herself down but she never more spoke / Because poor girl, her heart was broke," ends "Love Has Brought Me to Despair" (*CSCEFS*, 1:599), while the girl of " 'Twas Through the Groves" undergoes a surrogate death by lying alone all night on the "banks of lilies" (*EC*, p. 165). The secondary aspect of the lack of activity signification, its positive quality, is that it brings a measure of peace and relief from the unhappiness of the love affair: now "my love's dead and gone to rest" (*CSCEFS*, 1:171).

The second pair of oppositions is *intensity/lack of intensity*, a rich semantic domain in symbolic songs, replete as it is with sensory images of heat, luminosity, amplification of sound, and profusion of colors as well as with their contrasts—cold, the nonluminous, cut-off sound, and little color. Heat is signified by the daytime, as well as by the season when most of the love affairs flourish: "Early in the springtime of the year / As the sun did begin to shine" (*JFSS* 3 [1907]: 77). Contrasting is the coldness of the grave, so often the maid's final destiny: "Now she is dead and her corpse is cold" (*EC*, p. 97). Heat, however, like a lover's activeness, can also have a negative quality in that other girls may be its beneficiary:

> My love's gone across those fields, with his cheeks like roses,
> My love's gone across those fields, gath'ring primroses.
> I'm afraid the scorching sun will shine and spoil his beauty,
> And if I was with my love, I would do my duty (*JFSS* 4 [1913]:
> 279).

The case is similar for cold in its positive, if secondary, aspect; it sometimes signifies the ardent lover's indifference to the harshness of the weather while in pursuit of his lass: "O when my apron strings were low / My love followed me through frost and snow" (*CSCEFS*, 1:597).

Another type of intensity, luminosity, may be the positive quality of natural objects ("By a clear crystal fountain I saw my true love" [*EC*, p. 173]), of human actors ("So the first time I saw my love she quite surprised me / By the blooming of her cheek and the sparkling of her eye" [*EC*, p. 80]), or even of an emotion ("So love it is pleasing, love it is teasing / And love is a treasure when first it's new" [*EC*, p. 179]). But luminous phenomena like crystal fountains, sparkling eyes, and treasures have their negative sides as well: gold wastes and beauty passes, just as the luminous dew of the morning fades (*EC*, pp. 96–97, 179). Contrasting with luminosity is its lack, signified by the common case of those maidens who wish vainly that they had never had sparkling eyes but been blind and unable to see the false lover to begin with (*CSCEFS*, 1:604; *EC*, p. 96); another common image is that of girls whose cheeks once bloomed red as roses but which are now as pale as lilies (*JFSS* 4 [1913]: 279; *FD*, p. 90; *WS*, p. 32). But in its secondary value, such paleness may also be the positive shade of the pipes of ivory one's initially ardent lover plays upon (*FD*, p. 87), or indeed that of his breast on which the girl euphorically lays her head (*EC*, p. 163).

A further variable of the intensity/lack of intensity pair is amplified sound versus cut-off sound. Amplified sound is one of the most representative of images in symbolic songs; usually, the sound is a musical one, whether emanating from birds ("In April, in May and in June likewise, / When small birds they do sing" [*CSCEFS*, 1:577]) or from the lovers themselves ("There's no one in this country can whistle like Nancy my dear" [*EC*, p. 173] and "I placed my back against the old garden gate / And I heard my true love sing" [*JFSS* 2 (1906): 152]). In opposition to amplified sound is sound cut off, and once more the deathbed represents this in the human realm: "She laid herself down but she never more spoke / Because, poor girl, her heart was broke" (*CSCEFS*, 1:597). For the natural world the behavior of the cuckoo may provide an analogy:

> The cuckoo is a fine bird,
> She sings as she fly,
> And the more she sing Cuckoo
> The summer draw nigh.
>
> She singeth in April,
> She singeth in May,
> She singeth in June, my love,
> In July she fly away (*CSCEFS*, 1:623).

As for the multicolored aspect of intensity, we find this to be positively valued while the love affair is on the rise, as in the Irish-influenced descriptions of a loved one's appearance:

> His lips were red as cherries, and his hair was lovely brown,
> And the curls upon his forehead they so carelessly hung down,

His cheeks were red as roses and his eyes were black as sloes,
Complete in every feature, and as sweet as any rose (*JFSS 1*
[1899]: 17; *CSCEFS*, 1:495).

In its flowers nature parallels human multicoloredness and the
headiness of waxing love: "Oh yes! I'll arise and pluck lilies, pinks
and roses" (*JFSS* 5 [1915]: 176). The negative pole opposing multicoloredness is not necessarily lack of color but *few* colors, usually
one, occasionally two. In addition, and perhaps more importantly,
the few-color image differs from the profuse, almost indiscriminate
arrangement of the multicolored imagery in that the few colors are
"bound," that is, arrayed in an artificial and predictable configuration. Thus marble stones are formally placed at head and feet, with
the whiteness of turtle doves and lilies at the breast (*JFSS* 2 [1906]:
159). Occasionally, the single bright color of one red rose may be set
at the grave's center, green grass carefully layered below or above
the body (*GG*, p. 61). It is this very simply ordered, static arrangement of color that contrasts with the diverse profusion of color
accompanying an affair at its sexual prime.

The third major opposition in symbolic songs is the pair *per-
pendicular/horizontal*. Perpendicular denotes "height" as well as
"depth"; it is signified in relation to its immediate context, not in a
fixed metric. So, for instance, the positively valued euphoria of a
love affair and its concomitant sexual activity may be signified both
by the upward imagery of springing flowers and sturdily growing
trees, especially oaks (*CSCEFS*, 1:625, 171), as well as by the down-
ward imagery of being "Deep in Love" or of gathering love's flowers
down in meadows or valleys (*FBI*, p. 349; *CSCEFS*, 1:171). Even an
object of little absolute height, like a full-grown thorn, is an appropriate image when seen as a figure against the ground of an imma-
ture rosebush (*FBI*, p. 349). The negative quality of height is also
apparent as a secondary value: the false lover may abscond to the
arms of other girls who frequent houses "on yonder hill," for instance, or may lose interest when, pregnant, a maid is forced to
wear her apron "high" (*CSCEFS*, 1:597–604). The polar opposite
of perpendicular, the horizontal, is represented chiefly by the be-
trayed maiden's lying down to die or grieve, while nature partici-
pates sympathetically with withering leaves, fallen trees, or crushed
grass (*CSCEFS*, 1:171–72, 625, 577–78).

The fourth semantic domain consists of the pair *multiple*
versus *single*. The positive multiple in nature is often represented
by profusion of flowers (roses, lilies, pinks, violets) and birds (black-
bird, linnet, thrush), while multiplicity in the human domain may

be suggested by the legion of suitors from which the maiden makes her choice:

> First I lov'd Thomas
> And then I lov'd John,
> And then I lov'd William
> He's a clever young man (*JFSS* 5 [1915]: 174).

The negative value of the single pole is signified principally by the solitary narrator, parted from his or her beloved, or by a single species of bird (turtle dove) or plant (lily, rose, or grass) that marks the lamenter's grave. As for the fifth domain, the *free/bound* opposition, here the human imagery dominates the natural, although the notion of "free" color and "bound" color in the natural realm is an aspect of the many colors/few colors opposition already discussed. The positive aspect of free is that personal freedom (whether from parents, homegrounds, or prepuberty) is necessary if one is to enter a love affair in the first place, as the maiden of "Love Has Brought Me to Despair" reveals when she tells of "When first I gained my liberty" (*EC*, p. 96). But freedom has its negative side as well; it enables restless partners to ramble, to pay court to others, or to 'list in the navy. Freedom's opposite, the negative bound, applies to the abandoned girl constrained both by her own fidelity and by her inability to achieve emotional detachment from a lost lover; an illustrative plea is "Cupid, won't you set me free?" (*FD*, p. 77), a typical complaint, that of the tormented lover who, like a "thief," is "fettered and bound in some chains" (*WS*, p. 84).[11] Bound can also have a positive value, though of course secondary to and weaker than its primary negative value. Binding yourself is one possible, though not necessarily successful, way to avoid an unhappy experience in love, as the girl in "Seeds of Love" illustrates metaphorically: "O I locked my garden gate / And I choosed for to keep the key" (*FBI*, p. 367; cf. *EC*, p. 165).

The sixth opposition is between *humans dominating nature* and *nature dominating humans*. The former is most frequently represented by the maiden's picking of flowers, as in "The Seeds of Love"; thus humans attempt to corral nature for their own ends, not only by reaping the flowery harvest but also by sowing love's seeds in the first place. This image often occupies an entire stanza, indicating its importance as a signifier:

> Down in the meadows the other day,
> Gathering flowers both fine and gay,

Gathering flowers both red and blue,
I little thought what love can do (*CSCEFS*, 1:171).

The two poles of this opposition are often presented in juxtaposition, emphasizing their contrasting values. For instance, the girl of "Waly Waly" attempts to dominate nature by thrusting her hand into a bush to pluck a flower; instead she is immediately herself dominated by the bush's thorns, which prick her "finger to the bone" (*CSCEFS*, 1:171). The girl who plucks at the rose may gain unwittingly a willow tree that "twists and twines," dominating its environment (*CSCEFS*, 1:578–79). Similarly omnipotent is rue, which overruns the maid's garden that had once sported a heterogeneous profusion of flowers (*CSCEFS*, 1:577–78). Images of nature also dominate humans in the death scenes, where "rocks and hills shall hide me and bring me to my grave" (*EC*, p. 81), "the harmless lambs shall around me play" (*EC*, p. 165), the "leaves that blow from tree to tree / Shall be the coverlets over me" (*CSCEFS*, 1:603), and, the most final natural dominion of all, where "the grave it will moulder you / And bring you to the dust" (*CSCEFS*, 1:624).

The seventh and last of the symbolic model's major semantic domains is structured on the opposition between *strongly fertile ground* and *weakly fertile ground*. The former is signified by the location of so many of the waxing love affairs—flowering gardens, fields ready for harvesting, meadows, groves, and banks—while the weakly fertile ground may range from a grass-covered field, through mountains, hills, and rocks, to the nonfertile indoors of a death scene (but indoor settings are extremely rare in symbolic songs).[12]

The two paradigms of "heterogeneity" and "homogeneity" structure at the highest level the world view of all symbolic songs of sexual liaisons; in a minority of the songs, these two major oppositions may be synthesized dialectically into a third paradigm that we may call "dynamic equilibrium," in which phenomena are different-but-similar. This synthesis allows at least one possible escape from the extremely fatalistic view of sexual liaisons that symbolic songs espouse—the view that only separation and death, though they do provide some measure of peace, result from an affair. This median paradigm of "dynamic equilibrium" is a stronger, far more favored mediator than the but weakly positive quality of death, for it provides a live and happy ending; it signifies a controlled order of stability somewhere between the disorder of "heterogeneity" and the stasis of "homogeneity," and synthesizes the two poles by uniting the primary value of heterogeneous imagery (positive) with the secondary value of homogeneity (also positive).

When it does appear, the different-but-similar idea is expressed by a very narrow range of imagery and in only one or two stanzas of text. Any of the seven semantic domains may be represented in the image of synthesis. The first of the oppositional pairs, *activity* versus *lack of activity,* is synthesized in an image of *rest*; the second pair, *intensity* versus *lack of intensity,* in one of a muted harmony of snugness, comfort, a musical lullaby, and the creative intertwining of human and natural colors, an image to which we may give the general designation, *tranquility. Perpendicular* versus *horizontal* is mediated by an image of the *lateral, multiple* versus *single* by *couple,* and *free* versus *bound* by *interdependence.* The sixth opposition, *humans dominating nature* versus *nature dominating humans,* is mediated by imagery of *coparticipation* between man and nature in which neither exploits or overpowers the other; instead, humans employ nature's objects for human ends but retain those object's natural properties of vitality and nurturance. The final pair, *strongly fertile ground* versus *weakly fertile ground,* is synthesized into a ground of *controlled fertility,* where the articulated natural phenomena maintain their qualities as living things but at the same time shelter and rejuvenate the reunited couple.

The imagery that carries almost all the above information is usually manifested in a stanza like the following:

> If I had wings like an eagle I'd fly,
> I'd fly to the arms of my dear darling boy,
> And on his soft bosom I'd build up my nest,
> I'd lay my head down on his soft snowy breast (*CSCEFS,* 1:635).

Here we see the maid assuming positively valued activity in order to achieve the positive value of lack of activity so that circumstances may be adjusted to a union of these two polar states, *rest*; similarly does the lover of "The Irish Girl," in a signifier that exhibits an additional mediator, the *tranquility* of sweet and muted sound:

> I wish I was a butterfly,
> I would fly to my love's breast;
> I wish I was a linnet,
> I would sing my love to rest (*CSCEFS,* 1:497).

These examples also illustrate the *coparticipation* synthesis of humans dominating nature and nature dominating humans, for the actors wish to emulate the natural actions of birds; but over and above emulation, humans can also artfully fashion natural objects so that actual coparticipation is achieved. For example, in the following image flowers retain their natural functions while being put to human ends:

> With straw I'll make a garland, and dress it very fine,
> I'll mix the same with roses, lily, pink, and thyme,
> I will preserve it for my love when he returns from sea;
> I love my love, because I know my love loves me! (*JFSS* 2 [1905]: 93).

The last line of this stanza illustrates a further synthesis, the *interdependence* that unifies the antitheses free and bound. And as with the garland, the image of the bower or nest with the two lovers entwined in each others' arms signifies in addition the notion of *couple* (synthesizing multiple and single) and of their mutual *laterality* (synthesizing perpendicular and horizontal):

> If I was a blackbird I'd whistle and sing
> And follow the vessel my true love sailed in.
> And on the top rigging I'd there build my nest
> And lay there all night on his lily white breast (*CSCEFS*, 1:494).

In the texts of symbolic songs, however, the "dynamic equilibrium" paradigm is always presented as a hypothetical, potential, if-only state of affairs, never manifested as an achieved state. A far more common circumstance is the death denouement.

From this structural analysis of symbolic songs emerges a surprising consistency of meaning, even among those versions collected in the twentieth century, once we hit upon the right level of the signified, upon the relevant signifiers, and upon their relationships of analogy, homology, and to a lesser extent, dialectic. Or to put it another way, the analysis permits us to see through the apparent randomness that single images sometimes exhibit. For instance, at one level we may rightly claim that "green laurel" stands for young love, for fickleness, or for faithfulness (see *FBI*, p. 343). But if we were to examine the appearances of "green laurel" within the contexts of whole songs and whole models (such as the symbolic), discover its relevant semantic domain and plot its applicable paradigm (e.g., is it part of a multicolored profusion? Is it bound? Is it being dominated by humans? Is it doing the exploiting?), then the seeming arbitrariness of its referentiality may disappear. Or take the word "thyme," which, approached as a denotative and univocal sign by some commentators, has been assigned the meaning "virginity" (see *EC*, p. 31). When folksingers insisted on declaring that they had lost their "time," it was natural for the analyst to suspect morphemic confusion and to assert that the "real" meaning of the virginity sign had been forgotten. Yet "time" is quite consistent with the significations we have posited in our analysis, since to have "time" is, among other things, to have youth, freedom, and active vitality, while to have your time stolen from you is, also among other things, to be bound and rendered inactive: "Once I had time enough," complains a young man, to "flourish night and day"; but then along came a beautiful girl, who "stole all my time away" (*GG*, p. 5). And the girl who makes the assertion (rare for symbolic songs) of self-regenerative ability, "For the grass that is now trodden under foot / In time it will rise again" (*CSCEFS*, 1:588), is not signifying that nature is being dominated by humans, but rather that a state of affairs in which horizontality and being bound (which is what the trodden grass means here) obtain is going to be changed back to a state of affairs in which the perpendicular and the free will once more reign.

The second model that English traditional singers widely accepted as appropriate for expressing their world view of sexual liaisons we may designate the euphemistic, since the rhetoric of these songs is close to that of conversational and reasonably decorous speech. Euphemistic songs, in fact, recreate slices of experience that are far more mimetic of the real world than are the contents of symbolic songs; consequently, they are easier to decode, since their signifiers possess a strong denotative quality and since their referents are more concrete than abstract. To be sure, euphemistic songs use cliches freely, but their cliches—and not just the sexual ones—are those of everyday language, with tolerably everyday referents.[13]

The realism portrayed is primarily of the cultural, not the natural world. The actors frequently have social roles and statuses identified, unlike the extremely generalized "young man" and "young maid" of the symbolic songs. Euphemistic songs are also commonly narrated in the third rather than the first person, another indication of their objectivism. Their events usually take place in specific locations, named villages and towns, and often indoors, a distinctly cultural locus. The model's relatively empirical quality shows as well in its preference for the narrative technique; as in real life, events are interrelated by cause and effect, by before and after, by means and ends, rather than by the subjective associations that link image sequences in the symbolic model's lyric technique. Euphemistic songs also stress culture rather than nature as their chief concern by allowing their actors to make plans, choose from alternatives, put strategies into effect, and adapt to gain desired goals. For example:

THE SHANNON SIDE, OR CAPTAIN THUNDERBOLT

All in the month of April one morning in the Spring,
The violets and the primroses which made the copses ring,
The flow'r, the flower of the field, the fields were decked with
    pride;
And then I saw a fair maid down by the Shannon side.

I said: My lovely fair maid, where are you going this morn?
Where are you going, my honey, where are you going this way?
I'm going a-picking of sweet cowslips, this fair maid she replied,
And I'm going to seek my father's sheep down by the Shannon
    side.

The ground being moist whereon we stood and our feet from
    us did slide
And we both fell down together down by the Shannon side.

Three times I kissed the rosy cheeks as she lay on the grass
And coming to herself again: You've ruined me, alas.
But since you've had your will of me make me your lawful bride
And do not leave me here to mourn down by the Shannon side.

We kissed, shook hands and parted and homewards I did steer;
I did not go that way again for more than half a year.
And walking over those flowery plains my love I chanced to spy
Where she was scarcely able to walk the Shannon side.

I seemed to take no notice of her, but still kept on my way.
This fair maid turned her head aside and begging me to stay,
Saying: A thousand pounds in bright gold my father has
    provide,
Sixty acres of good land down by the Shannon side.

Said I: My love fair maid, I loves your offer well,
But I'm engaged already, the truth to you I'll tell.
It's to another fair maid all for to be my bride,
She is a wealthy grazier's daughter in yonder town resides.

O since you will not marry me, come tell to me your name,
That when my sweet baby's born it may be called the same.
My name is Captain Thunderbolt, the seas I'll never deny.
I've fifty jolly sailors ploughing the ocean wide (*CSCEFS*, 1:
    653-54).

The relatively concrete and realistic nature of their content and style suggests that euphemistic songs constitute a more varied collection than do the more abstract and quite redundant symbolic songs, and such is indeed the case. Yet their structure is rule-determined, and their code easier to discover than is the symbolic model's because of the relative paucity and denotativeness of the signifying variables; their texts' greater diversity results not from the components of the code but from the greater number of ways in which those components can be interrelated to generate different messages.

Most euphemistic songs contain only a single reference to the sexual encounter, another aspect of their realism; while always the central and motivating element in the total series of events depicted, the sex act is quantitatively just one of a larger set of interrelated occurrences. But it is the *raison d'être* of each song, and consequently a dictum about sexual liaison constitutes each song's message, or particularistic meaning. In our sample of ninety-two euphemistic text-types there are a total of thirteen messages, all of which can be derived from a single fundamental proposition contained in the euphemistic model as a monad.[14] This major premise as well as the thirteen more specific conclusions that derive from it I shall call "precepts," since they are, in keeping with the model's realism, fairly practical and often quite didactic bits of advice.

Of the thirteen, in all cases but one I take the precept to be directed toward the actor who undergoes the ordeal in the song's story. Theoretically, of course, the inverse precept could be applied to the other actors who do *not* undergo an ordeal, but the songs do not suggest that this is intended; the dramatic focus and the moral center of the song's theme seems to be the sufferer. In the one song type where there is no ordeal (precept 13) the relevant maxim is framed as applying to both of the main actors and worded not as a constraint—"you should not do such-and-such"—but as a sanction —"you may do such-and-such." However, while all but one of the thirteen precepts are cast as constraints, several of them have an "escape clause"—that is, the sanctioning of a variable that, if brought into play, will cancel the negative effects of ignoring the precept in the first place and convert a real or potential "tragic" experience into a "comic" one. For my analytical purposes, whether an experience is a "tragic" or "comic" one for the relevant actor depends on whether, at story's end, she (usually) or he is in the role of victim vis-à-vis a partner who is the victimizer (in which case the experience is a "tragic" one) or whether the two parties end on an equal footing (in which case the experience is a "comic" one). The victim's "tragic" fate can range from simple embarrassment to death, her "comic" fate, from tricking someone who has attempted to trick her to marrying a wealthy man.

In euphemistic songs, the signifiers ("the differences that make a difference") consist of five types of oppositional pairs, in the semantic domains of territory, experience, social status, personality, and motive. The best terms for the overarching paradigmatic oppositions would be "masculine properties" and "feminine properties," for at least three reasons: first, the signifiers are individual traits that map onto conventional perceptions of male and female in the traditional world view; second, these *cultural* properties contrast neatly with the *somatic* properties of masculine and feminine that our third model, the metaphorical, employs; and third, the actors in the songs who display the relevant traits are, in the great majority of cases, of the corresponding sex. A chart of the code structure is apposite at this point (see figure 2).

The fundamental precept of the euphemistic model's code (or, to say the same thing, the model's major premise in the province of meaning "sexual liaisons") is as follows: if you exhibit feminine properties and you engage in a sexual liaison with someone who exhibits masculine properties, then you will have a tragic experience; you might have a comic experience, however, if you can exhibit at least one masculine property yourself. (Note the words "might" and "at least." At least one masculine property is necessary to avoid a tragic experience, but it may not be sufficient.) This precept is *the* meaning of the euphemistic genre, and underlies all ninety-two songs in our sample. No one text draws upon all the

	Masculine properties	Feminine properties
territory:	acontextual	with a defined context (in or out of)
experience:	more experienced, older	less experienced, younger
social status:	higher	lower
personality:	innovative, aggressive, dominant, independent	conventional, passive, subordinate, dependent
motive:	liaison initiated over opposition of authority figure	initiate liaison for intrinsic reasons

FIGURE 2.
Structure of the code that generates euphemistic songs of sexual liaisons.

components of the code; in some instances, just a single signifier suffices, with the result that more concrete and particularistic precepts than the fundamental one appear throughout the population, thirteen being the smallest number of these precepts that can account for all ninety-two songs.

Since our sample is relatively large, and since the types of situations in which the lovers find themselves within the mimetic world that euphemistic songs portray are meaningfully different, we may subdivide the sample into three groupings on the basis of the actors' role relationships. First is the *prostitute/customer* type. Nine songs in our sample fall into this category, and two precepts apply, the first directed toward the victimized customer. Precept 1: If you engage in a sexual liaison with a prostitute that you *initiate for intrinsic reasons,* then you will have a tragic experience. This is the message of only two songs, "The Oyster Girl" and "Sweet Kitty." An indication of this rule's relative weakness is that in some versions of both these ballads a further signifier is added to strengthen the victimized status of the customer so that the message is a more forceful one: thus in a version of "The Oyster Girl" from Somerset (*CSCEFS,* 2:115–16), the customer is specified to be a Frenchman sojourning in England, while in a text of "Sweet Kitty" he is said to be Scottish *CSCEFS,* 2:107–8). Thus both texts strengthen the message of the song by assigning the customer the additional feminine trait, *out of defined context,* thereby bringing our second precept into play as well.

Precept 2: If you engage in a sexual liaison with a prostitute while *out of your defined context,* then you will have a tragic experience. Five ballads exemplify this precept: "Bonny Kate," "Gold Watch," "Portsmouth City," "Riding Down to Portsmouth," and "Tailor's Breeches." In each of these cases, the male customer is out of his well-defined natural context—visiting the big city, for instance; each man also makes the additional mistake of *initiating the liaison for intrinsic reasons.* His tragedy can range from catching venereal disease to being robbed, shamed publicly, and in general made to realize that he had better return to his natural context and stay there:

RIDING DOWN TO PORTSMOUTH

As a sailor was riding along
In height of his glory,
As a sailor was riding along
Telling a story,

He met with a pretty maid by the way
And those very very words to her did say:
Pretty maid, will you go along with me?
For I'm going down to Portsmouth.

Kind sir, if I go along with thee
I must be carried.
Kind sir, if I go along with thee
I must be married.
So she went along with him straightway
And she laid all in his arms till the day
And she leaved him all the reckoning to pay.

Now in the morning when he awoke
He found his love a-missing,
Now in the morning when he awoke
He paid dear for kissing.
O she robbed him of his gold watch and purse
And she took to him was ten times worse.
Don't you think she lay under a curse
In riding down to Portsmouth?

Now landlord, what have I got to pay
That I may reward you?
Now landlord, what have I got to pay
That I may reward you?
For my horse I will leave it in pawn
Until from the seas I do return.
Such gallus, gallus girls I will shun
In riding down to Portsmouth (*CSCEFS*, 2:117–18).

The customer does have a chance of neutralizing the negative effect of his out-of-context property by a sanction attached to precept 2, however; the victim might make the experience a comic one by being *innovative*. In the two instances that the customer comes out ahead by taking advantage of this sanction and asserting "masculine" traits, he turns the tables on the prostitute who attempts to cheat him—by robbing *her* in "The Rigs of London Town," by beating *and* robbing her in "The Frolic."

That the relationship between contrasting signs is the element of signification is clearly illustrated if we compare some of these prostitute/customer songs with the *man/maid* group to be discussed later in this chapter. In both "The Frolic" and "Riding Down to Portsmouth," the customer is a sailor on shore leave, as is the male

74

lover in several man/maid songs. When sailors consort with prostitutes, however, the sailor takes on the "feminine" value of someone *with a defined context*; consequently, on shore and in the city, the sailor is *out* of his natural context. But in his relationship with a marriageable country maiden in man/maid songs it is *she* who possesses the quality of defined context and *he* the value of *acontextuality*. (Acontextuality denotes a high degree of mobility that allows one, picaro-like, free movement within and through any milieu; in man/maid songs the acontextual role is very common, and most usually includes such itinerants as soldiers, sailors, and migratory agricultural workers.)

The second group of euphemistic songs deals with *husband/wife/lover* role relationships.[15] Our sample contains eleven songs of this class; from these eleven emerge three precepts, distributed equally among the parties of the triad. First, the message for wives. Precept 3: If your husband is engaging in liaisons with other women and/or neglecting his sexual responsibilities to you, and your response is of a *conventional* feminine kind, then you will have a tragic experience. This is a weak dictum when applicable to wives, evidently, for only one song, "You Bachelors You Know," illustrates it; the wife's conventional, role-determined behavior—shrilly badgering her husband to cease his carousing at the pub and to come home to his domestic duties—is but a spur to his further philandering. Similar to this dictum, but much stronger, is the next precept, directed toward husbands.

Precept 4: If you display feminine traits of *passivity* and *subordination* in sexual liaisons with your wife, you will have a tragic experience. The tragic experience is, perhaps needless to say, being made a cuckold. Thus in three songs, "My Good Old Man," "Rue the Day," and "Seven Months I've Been Married," the husband's passivity reveals itself in his sexual impotence, while in "Poor Couple" he is overly subordinate and conventional, blindly trusting that his wife observes the conventions of fidelity to the marriage bed as he himself does. In "Poor Couple," moreover, the wife possesses the masculine trait of *innovation* (she tricks her husband into leaving the scene while the lover escapes unnoticed); but this is a redundant trait, since the husband's gullibility is sufficient to assure him his role as the victim.

The final precept applicable to husband/wife/lover events is directed to the cuckolder. Precept 5: If you engage in a sexual liaison with a married woman while *out of your defined context*, then you will have a tragic experience. This is the fate of the lovers, both real and intended, in "Boatswain and the Chest," "Gamecock,"

"Grocer and Tailor," and "Mole-catcher," all of whom violate the dictum and get caught by the husband, with painful results. There is a single sanction available to the lover under the terms of this precept, however: he might make the experience a comic one by being *innovative*—that is, by analyzing the situation, deciding on a goal, formulating a plan for its achievement, and carrying out that plan with appropriate action. The lovers of "No Sir," "Rap-Tap-Tap," and "Sea Captain and the Squire" succeed in their seductions by employing this sanction. (None of the three husbands helps his own case, however; each exhibits the feminine trait of passivity, for he has done the conventional thing, leaving home to attend his work without making arrangements to prevent seducers calling on his wife, trustfully expecting the woman to respect propriety.) The young cuckolder in "Rap-Tap-Tap," in fact, possesses a further "masculine" property in addition to his innovativeness, a feature that suggests some influence from the metaphorical model:

RAP-TAP-TAP

So come all you farmers' servant-men
That are both stout and bold
And if you do as I have done
You never will catch any cold
For when my master goes abroad
For to view the fields so gay
I goes up to the door with my *rap-tap-tap*
O let it be night or day

'Twas every Thursday afternoon
My master to market did go
He asked me to mind his bus-i-ness
As servants always do
As soon as my master's back was turned
I went toddling out of the barn
I went up to the door with my *rap-tap-tap*
For sure I thought no harm

O no harm at all, my mistress said
And she asked me to go in
When I complained of the belly-ache
She gave to me some gin
I took it and I drank it down
But not a word did I say
For I thought I would come with my *rap-tap-tap*
So upstairs we went straightway

O there we lay in sport and play
For half an hour or more
My mistress she was so fond of the sport
I thought she'd never give o'er
O you've won my heart for ever, Jack
Your master's no man for me
For he can't come with his *rap-tap-tap*
Not half so well as thee

So when my master did come home
O he asked me what I had done
I told him I'd minded his bus-i-ness
Just as well as if he was at home
He gave to me some beer to drink
But not a word did he know
That I'd been there with my *rap-tap-tap*
If he had he'd a never done so (*FBI*, p. 468).

The third category of circumstances consists of man/maid relationships, in which both partners are potentially marriageable. Not surprisingly, most songs in the sample fall into this category. Accordingly, a larger number of precepts apply, though all are generated by the same code and basic premise as the others. Considering the number of songs (seventy-two), however, the precepts are surprisingly few. The first seems to be the only one of this category clearly directed in chief part to the man. Precept 6: If you engage in a sexual liaison with a maid who has the masculine ability to be *innovative,* then you will have a tragic experience. Eight ballads relay this precept: "Baffled Knight," "Broomfield Hill," "Crockery Ware," "Dabbling in the Dew," "Friar in the Well," "Horn Fair," "Maid with the Long Birches," and "Sweet Lovely Joan." In all of these songs the man's attempt to seduce the maid is foiled by an independent and innovative display on her part, whether in the form of a strategic act or of verbal dexterity:

THE BAFFLED KNIGHT

As I walked out one bright May morn
All in the month of May O
And there I met with a pretty girl
All by some new mown hay O.
The ri fol the diddle all the day.

I said: Pretty maid shall I lay you down
All on this new mown hay O?

77

There is a dew upon the ground
That'll spoil my silken gown O
That out of my father's purse
Cost many a pound and crown O.

He says: There's a wind blows from the west
That will blow the dew away O
And I will put on my riding coat
To lay on this new mown hay O.

If you will come to my father's hall
That is walled all around O
There you shall have your will of me
Upon some bed of down O.

When they came to her father's hall
That was walled all around O
She pulled at the bell and in she slipped
And locked this false man out O.

When you met with me it was all alone
You thought you had met with a fool, sir,
You may take your bible on your arm
And go a little longer to school, sir.

You may pull off your shoes and hose
And let your feet go bare O,
And if ever you meet with a pretty girl
You touch her if you dare O (*CSCEFS,* 1:142–43).

The following six precepts are all directed to the maid. Precept 7: If you engage in a sexual liaison with an *acontextual* man, then you will have a tragic experience. Acontextual men are those with extremely mobile and itinerant professions; in the sample, these are soldiers, sailors, thieves, tinkers, Irishmen, migrant harvest workers, and tramps. Judging from the number of songs that exhibit this precept in action, we could safely call this the most critical rule in the euphemistic song catechism. Soldiers are the guilty seduce-and-depart figures in "Cold Blow and Rainy Night," "Oh Yarmouth Is a Pretty Town," "The Sentry," "Shannon Side," and "Trooper and Maid," while sailors are the victimizers in "Bonnie Annie," "Home, Dearie, Home," "Indian Lass," "Just as the Tide Was a-Flowing," "Liverpool Landlady," "Sailor's Tragedy," and "Valentine's Day" (type I). A thief is the false lover in "Salisbury Plain," a tinker in "Jolly Beggar" (type I), an Irishman in "Hazelbury Girl" and "Banks

78

of Clyde," an itinerant harvest worker in "Barley Raking," and tramps in two songs whose titles specify the mobile and acontextual nature of the seducer, "Ramble-Away" and "Catch-Me-If-You-Can." The precept is not ironclad, however, and can be mitigated by any one of two masculine characteristics: the maid must be *innovative* ("Basket of Eggs"), or the liaison must be *initiated over the opposition of an authority figure* ("Gosport Beach," "Raking of Hay," and "Willie o' Winsbury"). In all such instances the denouement is a comic one and the acontextual lover is happily taken to husband, as in "Basket of Eggs":

THE BASKET OF EGGS

Three jolly sailors set out a-walking
With their pockets lined with gold,
As they were a-walking, so kindly a-talking
Two lovely maidens they did behold.

I said: Pretty maiden, shall I carry your basket?
The answer it was: Kind sir, if you please.
Sailors, O sailors, if you should outwalk me
Leave it at the inn called the "Chaise and Pair."

O landlord, O landlord, fetch me some bacon,
Eggs in the basket and we'll have a fry.
The landlord he went searching the basket
Thinking eggs there for to find.

O sailors, O sailors, you are mistaken
Instead of eggs it is a young babe.

One of them set out a-prattling,
The other he said: Wait awhile.
Here's fifty pounds I will lay down
If any one will own the child.

Then up spoke one called lovely Nancy
That I danced with last Easter Day.
I'll take the child and so kindly use it
If the money you will pay.

Are you the one called Lovely Nancy
That I danced with last Easter Day?
O yes kind sir, I pleased your fancy.
Now the fiddler you must pay.

Away we'll go to the yonder chapel
There the wedlock knot to tie.
Bells were a-ringing and sailors a-singing.
There he made her his lawful bride (*CSCEFS*, 2:111–12).

Precept 8. If you engage in a sexual liaison with a man *older and more experienced* than yourself, then you will have a tragic experience. The usual sign of disparity in age and worldliness between two lovers is the extreme youth and innocence of the girl—sixteen seems to be the conventional age. Five ballads feature this precept in operation: "Floating Down the Tide" (type 1), "Pretty Little Miss," "Seventeen Come Sunday," "Shoemaker's Kiss," and "Tripping over the Lea." The single allowance for neutralizing this dictum and changing the affair into a comic experience is a sanction that permits the liaison if it is *initiated over the opposition of an authority figure.* Only one ballad illustrates this, however, "Worcestershire Wedding."

Precept 9: If you engage in a sexual liaison with a man of *higher social status* than yourself, then you will have a tragic experience. This is a powerful precept; many girls who ignore it come to grief. But the attraction of a successful marriage above your own station also allows a significant number of girls to neutralize the dictum by taking advantage of its single escape clause with an ability to be *innovative.* Girls who run afoul of precept 9 may be found in versions of "The Astrologer," "The Bedmaking," "Betsy is a Beauty Fair," "Down by the Woods and Shady Green Trees," "Glastonbury Town," "Jolly Beggar" (type 2), "Mary Thompson," and "Pretty Little Miss."[16]

The girls who are able to adopt masculine traits and effect a comic experience may be found in "Basket of Eggs," "Brisk Young Butcher," "Knight and the Shepherd's Daughter" (whose heroine also displays the quality of social status higher than her seducer's), "Poor Nell and the Chimney Sweep," and "Pretty Betsy the Milkmaid." These lasses most often succeed by turning the tables on their seducers with a neat bit of trickery so that the final shame is his, or by evincing a plan of action of such unusual cleverness that it captures the man's heart and hand.

Precept 10: If you engage in a sexual liaison and exhibit feminine traits of *conventionality, passivity, nonassertiveness, or dependence,* then you will have a tragic experience. A large number of ballads display this dictum's effect, but the vast majority of these also include other reinforcing taboo violations to strengthen their message. Since the list is large, I will give only those that rely on this rule alone: "Floating Down the Tide" (type 2), "Molly and William," and "Through the Woods."[17] The last two are murdered-sweetheart ballads, while the first features a suicide following seduction (but is sometimes merged with the murdered-sweetheart story-type, as we demonstrated at length in chapter 1). The girls in these ballads show their conventional feminine dependency by pleading with the seducer to marry (indeed, even by becoming pregnant); like the wives to whom precept 3 is directed, they contrast sharply with those girls who convert their tragedy into comedy by replacing this Other-dependent behavior with assertive and innovative acts.

Precept 11: If you engage in a sexual liaison that you have *initiated for intrinsic reasons*, then you will have a tragic experience. Several maidens ignore this precept, but the taboo is evidently a weak one, since the majority of its violators also break precept 7 warning against acontextuals ("Indian Lass," "Jolly Beggar" [type 1], "Just as the Tide Was a-Flowing," "Ramble-Away," and "Trooper and Maid"). But initiating the liaison for its own sake is sufficient to bring about tragic consequences in three ballads: "Foggy Dew" (type 2), "Lark in the Morn," and "Valentine's Day" (type 2). However, more girls succeed in escaping the tragedy by means of a sanction—by possessing the masculine trait of *social status* at least equal to, or even higher than, her male partner's ("Foggy Dew" [type 1], "Forty Long Miles," "Jack the Jolly Tar," and "Oh As I Was a-Walking").

Precept 12: If you have a well-defined context and engage in a sexual liaison *within that defined context*, then you will have a tragic experience. Apparently, this is the weakest of all precepts, for just about all examples are also covered by other rules ("Blow the Candle Out," "Cold Blow and Rainy Night," "Glastonbury Town," "Home, Dearie, Home," "Indian Lass," "Jolly Beggar" [both types], "Seventeen Come Sunday," and "Trooper and Maid"), primarily precept 7. The only song in which precept 12 appears to be dominant is "Knife in the Window," and even that shows influence from the sanction attached to precept 5, from the interdiction of precept 4, and even from the metaphorical model that we shall examine shortly. A further indication of precept 12's weakness is that fully six songs allow escape from its consequences; four of these fall under the equal-or-higher-than *social status* sanction ("Forty Long Miles," "Jack the Jolly Tar," "Light of the Moon," and "Night Visit Song"), a further two under *innovativeness* ("Brisk Young Butcher" and "Valentine's Day" [type 3]), and one under *over opposition of authority figure* ("Open the Window").[18] Most of these songs are night-visit ballads, a story-type in which the maid's bedroom as the liaison's locus is an integral feature.

Finally, we have a precept that states the conditions under which a sexual liaison may successfully take place without victimization of one partner by another and without the suffering of any ordeal. The precept may be directed to either or both partners. Precept 13: If you engage in a sexual liaison in a *neutral context* with a partner of *equal age, experience, and social status,* then you might have a comic experience. Songs that illustrate this dictum are "Branded Lambs," "Brickster," "Dicky the Miller," "Gently Johnny my Jingalo," "Johnny and Molly," "Low Down in the Broom," "Nelly the Milkmaid," "Nutting Girl," "Oh As I Was a-Walking," "Roger and Nell," "An S-O-N-G," and "Spotted Cow." In these songs, both partners exhibit equal proportions of various masculine/feminine properties: they both have defined contexts but are both in a neutral setting (usually out in the fields) when they make love; differences in age and experience are not indicated, and thus one assumes that those qualities do not signify; and the partners are of equal social standing.[19] For example, here is a text of Laws O9, "Branded Lambs":

THE LONG AND WISHING EYE

As Johnny walk-ed out, one midsummer's morn
He soon became quite weary and sat down beneath a thorn
'Twas there he spied a pretty fair maid, as she was passing by
And young Johnny followed after with his long and wishing eye

Chorus: With his long and wishing eye, brave boys
　　　　　With his long and wishing eye
　　　　　And young Johnny followed after
　　　　　With his long and wishing eye

Good morning, gentle shepherd, have you seen my flock of
　　　lambs
Strayed away from their fold, strayed away from their dams
O have you seen the ewe-lamb, as she was passing by
Has she strayed in yonder meadow where the grass grows very
　　　high?

Chorus: Where the grass grows very high, brave boys
　　　　　Where the grass grows very high
　　　　　Has she strayed in yonder meadow
　　　　　Where the grass grows very high?

Oh yes, O yes, my pretty fair maid, I saw them passing by
They went down in yonder meadow and that is very high
Then turning round so careless-lie and smiling with a blush
And young Johnny followed after, and hid all in a bush

Chorus: And hid all in a bush, brave boys (etc.)

She searched the meadow over, no lambs could she find
Oft'times did she cross that young man in her mind
Then turning round, she shouted: What's the meaning of your
    plan?
Not knowing that young Johnny was standing close at hand

Chorus: Was standing close at hand, brave boys (etc.)

The passions of young Johnny's love began to overflow
He took her up all in his arms, his meaning for to show
They sat down in the long grass and there did sport and play
The lambs they were forgotten, they hopped and skipped away

Chorus: They hopped and skipped away, brave boys (etc.)

'Twas the following morning this couple met again
They joined their flocks together to wander o'er the plain
And now this couple's married, they're joined in wedlock's
    bands
And no more they'll go a'roving in searching for young lambs

Chorus: In searching for young lambs, brave boys (etc.) (*FBI*,
    pp. 310–11).

In at least four other songs in which precept 13 applies, there is the further variable that the lovers conduct their affair over the opposition of an authority figure, whether parent or employer ("Dicky the Miller," "Low Down in the Broom," "Nelly the Milkmaid," and "An S-O-N-G"). Note that this precept says *might;* these variables are necessary for a straightforward comic experience, but may not be sufficient. A significant contrast in personality type—an aggressive and independent male and a passive and dependent female, say—may override other factors of equality.

Of the eight precepts applicable to man/maid role relationships, precept 11, which warns girls against initiating the sex act, appears to be the most ambivalent. For one thing, more than half the songs that exemplify the breaking of the precept also contain violation of one or more other precepts. A more important indication of ambivalence, however, is relatively complex, and deserves some discussion. Three songs exhibit the breaking of precept 11's taboo only: "Foggy Dew" (type 2), "Lark in the Morn," and "Valentine's Day" (type 2). If we look at a number of versions of these three text-types that have been collected from British traditional singers, however, we find that the texts display an unusual amount of variation. Take "Valentine's Day," for example. In two versions (type 1), the male lover is an *acontextual* sailor. In another (type 2), it is the maiden who *initiates the sexual liaison for intrinsic reasons.* And in a third (type 3), she is permitted a sanction that eventually brings the seducer home to marry her: she is both *aggressive,* threatening him with prison, and to some extent *innovative,* admiring his boldness as both lover and adventurer, even though she is now pregnant and alone.[20]

"The Foggy Dew" also varies significantly in at least one version from its normal form. Usually, the two marry and enjoy a long and fruitful life together (type 1). In a distinctive text from East Anglia, however, the couple never do marry; moreover, she becomes ill about a year after their initial lovemaking and dies, blaming him for her sickness (type 2). While either of these two possibilities of love and death is quite consistent with the folksong world view of love relationships, it is unusual to find the same text-type existing in versions that differ so markedly. As for "Lark in the Morn," the variation is even greater. In the type illustrating precept 11, the girl becomes pregnant and, in response to her mother's queries as to who the guilty party might be, blames the ploughboy (*EC*, pp. 172–73; *MB*, p. 51). But in a Devonshire version, the text has taken on a stanza about cuckolds that implies that the girl is married to an impotent husband (*CSCEFS*, 2:182–83), and thus would be an illustration of precept 4 in the husband/wife/lover category. In yet another strain, the song appears to be a harmless eclogue, with no sexual content (*JFSS* 2 [1906]: 154; *SES*, p. 264). And finally, in a Scottish version (*FBI*, p. 317), we find explicit what is but barely hinted at in the eclogue type: a celebration of the sex act following the metaphorical model, the usual "Lark in the Morn" stanzas having been crossed with "Young Johnny Was a Ploughboy."[21]

The apparent ambivalence in the native value system toward precept 11 correlates with those characteristics that distinguish euphemistic from symbolic songs. In the symbolic model's world, sexual relationships inevitably lead to some form of separation, most often through the falseness of one partner, and to real or surrogate death. Almost half of the symbolic songs hypothesize a change in this course of events, to be sure, but the change is always an if-only one. The causes of a tragic experience are seen to be innate to the organic world—to the plant, animal, and human kingdoms. In the euphemistic songs, however, we do not see this "naturalization" of human affairs; the "causal" elements (the components of the code-structure) are "rationalized" as cultural realities. This is so even for the assumed personality traits of masculine and feminine: *independence and self-assertiveness* on the one hand, *dependence and passivity* on the other. Consequently, while the symbolic code generates only one meaning and only one hypothetical escape, the euphemistic code generates several more concrete meanings and several more concrete methods of attaining ends. In short, euphemistic songs portray a cultural world possessing a degree of contingency within it; meaning is dependent to a fair extent on circumstances grounded in the five phenomenal domains of territory, experience, social status, personality, and motive.

The ambivalence in the euphemistic model's precept 11—that a girl should not initiate a sex act for intrinsic reasons—provides a convenient transition to the third model, the metaphorical, for it is in this type of traditional song that woman comes into her own and not only is customarily and appropriately the aggressor but also dominates in a trait that she possesses by virtue of her physical properties of femaleness. English traditional songs may use metaphor to refer to the sex act in a variety of ways, since metaphor is, after all, a poetic figure of speech and a more conscious artifice than is a symbol, which is rooted in a belief system, or a euphemism, which is rooted in a behavioral system of general social propriety. Thus, metaphor to a certain extent distracts an audience's attention from the song's referential function (how its signs correlate with the real world) and toward the song's poetic function (the appreciation of the metaphor for its own sake—for its cleverness, its aptness, its aesthetic quality, or whatever).[22]

We will later see that this poetic function of metaphor matches the meaning of the metaphorical model, which, I will suggest, is that sexual intercourse may be enjoyed *for its own sake;* first, however, we should examine the range of uses of sexual metaphor in English traditional song.[23] In its manifest diversity, metaphorical usage can range from a single figurative phrase to depict the sex act (an act that, as in the euphemistic songs, is but one episode—though a central one—in a larger chain of causally related episodes not themselves sexual and not metaphorically expressed) to an extended metaphor in which the sex act constitutes the majority of

the song's content. The closer a song is to the left side of this hypothetical continuum (single metaphor as figure of speech), the more
fully the song is informed by other models of a sex world view, the
symbolic and the euphemistic; the closer a song's form to the
right-hand side of the continuum (extended metaphor), the more
the song belongs to the distinctive metaphorical model with its own
distinctive code-structure and meaning.

Let us look at examples from this continuum, starting our survey at the single metaphor end. In "The Maid of Australia" (*FBI*,
pp. 412–13), we have an example of about as minimal a use of metaphor as there can be. Traveling in the Australian countryside, the
narrator comes across a girl who, not seeing him, undresses to go
swimming in a nearby stream. She finally notices him, they exchange
some desultory conversation, and he helps her from the water at her
request, but slips on the bank. They both fall down, and he "enter[s]
the bush of Australia," almost certainly a metaphor for sexual intercourse. But the euphemistic model's code most informs the song, for
not only is there an extensive narrative going beyond the sex act
itself, and not only is the language chiefly euphemistic (they later
"frolic[ked] together in the highest of glee," and her pregnancy
causes her to curse "the hour that she lay on the ground"), but also
the message is entirely compatible with the euphemistic code's inventory of meanings; she is left pregnant and alone, having run
afoul of the precepts against sexual liaisons with *acontextuals,*
against sex *in her own defined context,* and against *initiating the
act for intrinsic reasons.* Similar is the fate of "The Handsome
Cabin Boy" (Laws N13), who breaks precept 7 while "eating the
captain's biscuits" (*CSCEFS,* 2:80–81; *MB,* p. 32).

"The Bonny Bunch of Rushes O" also combines a single metaphor ("break my bunch of rushes") with various euphemisms ("don't
me ill entreat," "You're going to delude me" [*EC,* p. 118]). After
what is evidently lovemaking (the text is a trifle obscure), she worries about the trouble she might "gain" and the resulting social disapproval. The song ends at this point (in the only other version in
our sample, he *promises* to return shortly and wed her [*MB,* p. 8]),
presumably with a tragic experience for the girl, who has broken
the interdiction against consorting with a man of *higher status* than
herself. Similar is a song—"Maids a-Rushing"—that uses another
single "rushing" metaphor (see also the fragment in *CSCEFS,* 2:600).
This song is also of the euphemistic code, and the girl's misfortune
stems from making love with either a *higher-status* male (*EC,* pp.
260–61) or an *acontextual* one (*CSCEFS,* 1:641–42; *EC,* pp. 261–63).

Moving further along the continuum of expanding use of meta-

phor, we have the example of "The Cobbler and the Butcher,"
where the sex act is described as follows:

O, says he: Me darling, have you got a job for me?
The butcher's wife, so cunning, says: I'll go up and see

Now she went to the bedroom door and gave the snob a call:
I have got an easy job if you have brought your awl
And if you do it workmanlike some cash to you I'll pay
O thank you, said the cobbler, and began to stitch away (*FBI*,
   p. 453).

This is a fuller metaphor than are the short phrases in the preceding
examples; in fact, the metaphor itself is very much like the extended
ones that figure in the fully formed metaphorical model in that it
draws its vehicle from a well-known occupation. But the euphemistic model still predominates in "The Cobbler and the Butcher";
not only is the narrative a lengthy and relatively complex one, and
not only does the butcher's wife later admit a policeman "along
with her to play," but also the song's message is clearly precept 5
of the euphemistic type: the lover *initiates the sexual liaison for intrinsic reasons* and *out of his defined context*. He is suitably punished by the husband at song's end (see also *CSCEFS*, 2:5–6; Cl,
p. 15).

Midway in our hypothetical continuum (so squarely midway,
in fact, that were there more examples—"Rap-Tap-Tap," given earlier, shows similarities—we would be forced to recognize it as a
distinct model in its own right) are two ballads which display a
symmetrical and exceptionally organic fusion of the euphemistic
and the metaphorical textual formats. The first half of each of these
two ballads treats the sexual liaison between a wife and her lover in
euphemisms (he "stumbled into bed" with his mistress and " 'kissed'
her twelve times that night" in "The Cluster of Nuts" [*WS*, p. 26],
while "ofttimes they would tumble" in "The Barley and the Rye"
[*JFSS* 8 (1931): 273–74]). The second halves, however, treat the same
sexual activity in extended metaphors, one of the lovers describing their frolic to the wife's husband figuratively so that the poor
cuckold has no suspicion of the real nature of the liaison and thus
permits it to continue. Within the context of its ballad, therefore,
the metaphorical description fulfills the function of the *innovative*
component of the euphemistic code, and the ultimate meaning of
each song is clear: even though you might be of *lower social status*
than your partner and might engage in a sexual liaison *out of your*

defined context, you can have a comic sexual experience with another man's wife by showing unusual *cleverness* (the sanctioned escape under precept 5 of the euphemistic model).

Finally, close to the right-hand end of the continuum, we have an example of fairly full metaphorical description in "I Sowed Some Seeds," in which imagery of the man's "sowing" of his "seed" in the girl's "grove" is carried throughout a substantial portion of the short song (*EC*, p. 160; *FMJ* 3 [1976]: 156–57; *WS*, p. 53; fragments in *CSCEFS*, 2:601–2). But the mimetic and didactic qualities of the euphemistic model still dominate, even though there is no clear use of euphemistic language to describe the sex act, only metaphorical language. The precept-message, nevertheless, is unequivocal: the girl undergoes a tragic experience because she does not heed the admonitions against *age differentiation,* against a sexual liaison *in her own defined context,* and even, perhaps, against an *acontextual* man (he is a "stranger" to London who lodges at her parents' inn).[24]

It is when we come to the right-hand pole of our hypothetical continuum, where extended metaphor, minuscule didactic content (if any), and almost exclusively sexual subject matter hold sway, that we find a predictable model and a large number of songs redundant with each other. There are two major types of this metaphorical model proper in the English traditional song repertoire, though the messages of the two do not differ significantly. The first type is in the common catalogue form, a form that can and does carry any content, sexual or otherwise. In catalogues, the key parts of a whole phenomenon are related not by cause-and-effect logic (as in the ballad, a narrative form), nor by analogic linkages of a sensory kind (as in lyric songs), but by summation; that is, each part is conjoined with every other part so that the parts added together make up the whole. So, for instance, a whole that is sexual activity is presented in a series of stanzas, each stanza depicting a vignette of that activity; thus in "The Keeper" (*CSCEFS*, 2: 232–33; *EC*, 289–90), the metaphorical huntsman chases an equally metaphorical series of "does" across the landscape, and "The Besom Maker" (*EC*, pp. 129–30; *FD*, p. 4) engages in sexual intercourse with a squire, a miller, a farmer, and a parson in a set of stanzaic vignettes. Other examples are "Pretty Wench" (*JFSS* 2 [1906]: 190–91) and "Mathew the Miller" (*EC*, p. 187; *WS*, p. 75). Similarly, several male lovers may repeat a parallel sexual experience with different women, as in "I Am a Coachman" (*EC*, p. 156) and "Four and Twenty Fiddlers" (*EC*, pp. 114–15). Or the stanzaic vignettes may catalogue in metaphor those parts of the human anatomy that are most relevant to sexual intercourse, as in "My Man John" (*CSCEFS,* 1:477–86; *WS,* pp. 71–72), "Balaam and Egg" (*CSCEFS,* 2:380; *MB,* p. 93), "The Furze Field" (*EC,* p. 117; *FMJ* 2 [1974]: 282; *MB,* p. 34), "Hares on the Mountain" (*CSCEFS,* 1:430–36; *EC,* p. 150; *FBI,* p. 395), "The Streams of Lovely Nancy" (*CSCEFS,* 2:533–36; *EC,* pp. 251–53; *JFSS* 1 [1901]:122; *JFSS* 4 [1913]: 310–12; *JFSS* 7 [1923]: 59–60), and the two Child ballads, "Riddles Wisely Expounded" (Child 1; *EC,* p. 161; *JFSS* 3 [1907]: 114–15) and "The Elfin Knight" (Child 2; *CSCEFS,* 1:1–3; *EC,* p. 243; *FBI,* p. 656; *JFSS* 1 [1901]: 83; *JFSS* 2 [1906]: 212; *JFSS* 3 [1909]: 274–75).[25] The chief characteristic of catalogue songs, whether enumerative, cumulative, or dialogic, is that each part can be deduced from a knowledge of the whole and the whole induced from knowledge of a part. Repetition is the paramount stylistic feature of both diction and imagery in catalogue songs, synecdoche their fundamental principle; the loss of a stanza or two does not result in any great loss of information, as would be the case in a lyric song and even more so in a narrative ballad, in both of which the whole is greater than the sum of the parts. Here is an example of the metaphorical model's catalogue type, narrated in this instance from a third-person point of view:

BLACKBIRDS AND THRUSHES

If maidens could sing like blackbirds and thrushes
If maidens could sing like blackbirds and thrushes
How many young men would hide in the bushes
Sing: Fal-de-ral, tal-de-ral, fal-ral-lal-day.

If maidens could run like hares on the commons
If maidens could run like hares on the commons
How many young men would take horse and ride hunting.

If maidens could swim like fish in the water
If maidens could swim like fish in the water
How many young men would undress and dive after.

If maidens could dance like rushes a-growin'
If maidens could dance like rushes a-growin'
How many young men would get scythes and go mowing.

If maidens could sleep like sheep on the mountains
If maidens could sleep like sheep on the mountains
How many young men would lie down beside them
    (*FBI,* p. 395).

To subject this catalogue type to structural analysis would reveal nothing, for the texts are little but structure; "deep" and "surface" structure, in other words, are the same. However, they do signify, though the key to their meaning is not just their overt structure but also, strangely enough, their point of view. I will delay discussion of this meaning, however, until I examine the more complex code-structure of the metaphorical model's other type, which does employ the ballad technique, but which, while structurally more complex than the catalogue, has very much the same meaning.

This narrative type shares with the catalogue not only the metaphorical rhetoric but also the almost sole concern with sexual activity itself—indeed, sometimes with just the sex act. The metaphors' vehicles (their tenors are, of course, whatever is integral to sexual intercourse) are drawn principally from the realm of occupations, as is the case with the catalogue type. These occupations may be the common ones of preindustrial village society's artisans ("Chilbridge Fair" [CL, p. 14; EC, p. 249], "The Miller and the Lass" [CSCEFS, 1:701–2; CL, p. 60], "The Jolly Tinker" [FBI, p. 405], "Bibberly Town" [CSCEFS, 1:703; CL, p. 103], "The Long Peggin' Awl" [FBI, p. 409], "The Buxom Lass" [WS, p. 23], and "The Wanton Seed" [EC, p. 276; WS, p. 115]—these last two from agricultural labor), or they may be primarily from town society ("The German Clockmaker" [FBI, p. 478] and "The Coachman's Whip" [FBI, p. 398]). An admixture of work and play lies behind various musical vehicles ("German Musicianer" [FBI, p. 458], "The Nightingale" [Laws P14; CSCEFS, 1:645–48; FMJ 2 (1973): 288; JFSS 8 (1930): 194–95; FBI, pp. 414–15; MB, p. 60], "The Devil's in the Girl" [CSCEFS, 1:704–5], and "Firelock Stile" [FBI, p. 399]) as well as hunting ones ("Three Maids a-Milking" [CSCEFS, 1:450–54; EC, p. 259; FBI, p. 422; JEFDSS 9 (1961): 75–76; JFSS 4 (1910): 93–94; MB, p. 2] and "The Bonny Black Hare" [CL, pp. 9–10]). Pure play provides the vehicles for "The Game of Cards" (CSCEFS, 2:247–50; EC, p. 43; MB, p. 35), and domestic bric-a-brac for "Young Johnny Was a Ploughboy" (EC, p. 281; WS, p. 118).

The *consequences* of sex for its participants, predetermined in the symbolic songs and contingent in euphemistic songs, are of little concern in the world view of metaphorical songs, for the relationship between the actors is not one of victimization. In one song, "Firelock Stile," the narrator does contract a venereal disease; the "moral" is hardly about sex, however, but about careless sex (there may also be the influence of the euphemistic model's precept 2, for he encounters the prostitute while *out of his defined context*). The other two examples in the sample that are rhetorically of the metaphorical category but that feature "tragic" conclusions are "Chilbridge Fair" and some versions of "Streams of Lovely Nancy." However, as was the case with those songs exemplifying precept 11 of the euphemistic model, both "Chilbridge Fair" and "Streams of Lovely Nancy" exhibit far more variation among their traditional versions than post-seventeenth-century folksongs usually do. "Chilbridge Fair," for instance, turns up twice in the sample; in one text, the girl ends up cursing the lover in a final stanza that is explicitly didactic (*EC*, p. 249), and I can only suppose that this version was influenced by precept 11 of the euphemistic songs' world view, since she does *initiate the liaison for intrinsic reasons*. However, the other version in the sample is an uncomplicated account in metaphor of sex between equal partners, and thus an unequivocal example of the metaphorical model in operation (*CL*, p. 14). As for "Streams of Lovely Nancy," this song is very popular in English country tradition, appearing in some nine full versions in our sample. It shows wide textual as well as narrative diversity, varying from, on the one hand, a paean to the sexual anatomy of a girl, in an unusual mixture of the symbolic model and the metaphorical model's catalogue form (e.g., *EC*, p. 251), to, on the other hand, an extended story in which additional narrative stanzas from "Oh Yarmouth is a Pretty Town" appear (e.g., *JFSS* 7 [1923]: 59). In this latter case, the influence of the euphemistic song of that title and its precept 7 against consorting with an *acontextual* male is explicit. Even when normatively tragic pregnancy occurs in the metaphorical model proper, however, that pregnancy is as much celebrated as the act that brings it about; if anyone gets upset it is the girl's parent, not the girl herself (e.g., "The Devil's in the Girl"). Indeed, in metaphorical songs, occupations of both men and women, leisure pastimes, sexual intercourse, pregnancy—all these human experiences are accorded the same hearty attitude and full participation.

Since the metaphorical model's narrative type is more complexly layered than is its catalogue type, structural analysis is required in order to reveal the underlying code that generates meaningful song texts. The contrasting paradigms in this code-structure are "maleness" and "femaleness," somewhat akin to the contrasting paradigms of the euphemistic code; the difference, however, is that the metaphorical model's semantic domains are principally somatic properties of male and female, whereas the euphemistic model's domains are cultural ones.

As figure 3 indicates, each partner exhibits superordinate position relative to the other's subordinate position in two areas: the maid is superordinate to her lover in *behavior* and *stamina,* the male

	Maleness	Femaleness
behavior:	subordinate	superordinate
physiology:	superordinate	subordinate
anatomy:	superordinate	subordinate
stamina:	subordinate	superordinate

FIGURE 3.
*Structure of the code that generates metaphorical ballads
of sexual liaisons.*

superordinate in *physiology* and *anatomy*. A song generated by this code contains a narrative that most often proceeds sequentially through its chosen semantic domains in the order from top to bottom indicated by figure 3; thus as the story unfolds, male and female each assume a fair proportion of superordinate and subordinate roles. The canceling out that results is integral to the model's meaning; for the mediator of these contrasting paradigms, which maneuver each other to a standoff, becomes *the sex act itself* as greater than, but at the same time not possible without, the differences between maleness and femaleness.

Since the metaphorical code's variables are more fully realized in any one of its representative ballads than is the case with the symbolic and euphemistic songs, we might exemplify metaphorical ballads by following the order of the semantic domains from top to bottom, the same sequence that provides the ballad narrative. First of all we find signifiers from the only truly cultural domain of the code, that of *behavior*. Female dominance in this sphere is asserted very early in a metaphorical ballad's story; as in the euphemistic songs that illustrate precept 11, she is the aggressive one and initiates sexual intercourse, either by a direct proposal or by challenging the male to give proof of his virility. In "The Miller and the Lass," for instance, the girl repairs to the mill where she forthwith exhorts the miller to "grind my corn so quick-e-ly" (*CL*, p. 60); in "The Wanton Seed," she spurs on the narrator with the assertion that "Oh yes, kind sir, you're the man that can do my deed / For to sow my meadow with the wanting seed" (*EC*, p. 276); and in "The Buxom Lass," the heroine hires the narrator to "cut down" her "field of grass" that grows "between two mountains at the foot of a running spring" (*WS*, p. 23). Similar assertiveness is displayed by the girls of "Jolly Tinker," "Three Maids a-Milking," "German Clockmaker," "Chilbridge Fair," "Long Peggin' Awl," "The Devil's in the Girl," "The Coachman's Whip," and "The German Musicianer."

At this point in the song, however, we usually find that the *physiology* variable comes into play. She is dependent upon him because her sex drive has created in her a "need," as the lass of "The Wanton Seed" puts it; he is now superordinate relative to her, for only he can fulfill that "need." This part of the transaction may be conducted with mutual felicity, as in "Three Maids a-Milking":

> I met with a man I knew well
> I met with a man I knew well
> And I kindly asked of him
> If he 'ad got any skills
> For to catch me a small bird or two
>
> O yes, I got some excellent skills
> O yes, I got some excellent skills
> Now come along with me
> Down to yonder shady tree
> I'll catch thee a small bird or two (*FBI*, p. 422).

Or a little persuasion may be required, as in "The Buxom Lass," where the young male worker requires the added inducement of five shillings "an acre and plenty of strong beer" since, as he puts it, "mowing is hard labour unless your scythe is good" (*WS*, p. 23). The sex act itself thereupon follows, presented in the metaphor that informs most of the song. As the couple's lovemaking is dwelt on in detail, he remains superordinate to her in the domain of *anatomy*. In filling her "need," he assumes a structurally dominant position, shooting at her "bonny black hare" with his gun ("The Bonny Black Hare"), sowing "high and . . . low" in her "field" ("The Buxom Lass"), grinding her corn ("The Miller and His Lass"), soldering her pan ("The Jolly Tinker"), and so forth. Male and female anatomical structure and conventional perceptions of that structure thus determine his superordinate and her subordinate positions; but this relationship lasts only for a while and is soon to be once more reversed, for when the initial bout of lovemaking is over the spent male wishes to cease, while she wants to continue:

> O come, said the soldier, 'tis time to giver o'er
> O no, says the fair maid, please play one tune more
> I do like your playing and the touching of the long string
> And to see the pretty flowers grow, hear the nightingale sing
>   (*FBI*, p. 415).

The sexual "need" of femaleness may have been temporarily satisfied but it is certainly not satiated, and maleness that has just shown its dominance in *anatomy* must now once more assume a subordinate role to female *stamina* and excuse itself, as does the spent young mower who proclaims upon leaving that even if he were to work the whole summer long he'd be unable to "cut down" the lass's "grass" to the extent that she would like (*WS*, p. 23).[26] Ultimately, however, the joys of sexual intercourse remain unchanged by shifting individual relationships of superiority and inferiority:

> So I took up my hat and I bid her: Good morning
> I said: You're the best that I know at this game
> She answered: Young man, if you'll come back tomorrow
> We'll play the game over and over again (*FBI*, p. 403).

The scenario above is an ideal one, to be sure, and a minority of the metaphorical ballads of sexual liaison present the fullest such portrayal. But even if a song uses only some of the code components in its text, it will still exhibit superordinate/subordinate exchanges. In some cases the ideal sequence of the full code might be rearranged; for instance, in "The Miller and His Lass" the man is unable to satisfy her "need" at the very beginning, and so her initial superordinate position, already established in *behavior* by her assertive wooing of his favors, is strengthened considerably:

> Come sit you down, my sweet pretty dear,
> I cannot grind your corn I fear.
>
> My stones is high and my water low,
> I cannot grind for the mill won't go (*CSCEFS*, 1:701).

But she is patient, and he is able eventually to perform to her satisfaction. And when he does he more than makes up for his initial lack of virility: "She swore she'd been ground by a score men [*sic*] / But never ground so well before" (*CSCEFS*, 1:702). Another example of deviation from the ideal scenario appears in "The Coachman's Whip." Here it is she who tires first; but she lends her partner to her maid until she herself has had time to recuperate and can reclaim him for her own pleasure. This reversal of the more usual female dominance over male in the *stamina* domain is here evidently a function of an additional superordinate property of hers that we more normally find in the euphemistic code's repertoire of signifiers —she is his *social* superior:

THE COACHMAN'S WHIP

I once took a job as a coachman
My money was paid in advance
I then took a trip down to London
From there I crossed over to France
There I met a charming young lady
Who 'dressed me and said with a smile
Young man, I'm in need of a coachman
To drive me in old-fashioned style

Chorus: O she was such a charming young lady
   And a lady of highest renown
   And I being a dashing young coachman
   I drove her ten times round the town

She then took me down in the cellar
She filled me with whisky so quick
I hadn't been there many moments
When she asked for a look at my whip
She held it, she viewed it a moment
And she then laid it down with a smile
Young man, by the look and the length of your slash
We could drive the best part of ten mile

She bid me get up to the chaise-box
So I climbed right up to the seat
Three swishes I gave with my cracker
And drove her straight down the High Street
I handled my whip with good judgement
Until I was up to her ways
But the very first turn that I gave on the wheel
I broke the main spring of her chaise

When my mistress grew tired or grew weary
She'd call me to stop for a rest
She'd shout for her serving-maid, Sally
The girl that I loved second-best
Sally, we've got a good coachman
He understands driving in style
While the spring on the chaise's repairing
I'll let him drive you for a while (*FBI*, p. 398).

We may now return to the catalogue type of the metaphorical model to see how the same meaning—the supreme rightness of sex as a leveler of male/female differences—is displayed, even though catalogue songs, because they are primarily concerned with the *anatomy* domain, apparently depict maleness as dominant throughout. But if we take the population of catalogue-styled texts, rather than consider each text individually, we see that the narrator's point of view is distributed equitably between men and women. While maleness might seem supreme in one text, therefore, in another text femaleness will be dominant throughout; consequently, the canceling-out of inequalities is achieved within the text population. For instance, a song like "The Keeper," which catalogues the huntsman's chasings and capturings of deer over plains, stiles, brooks, and so forth, will have its inverse in a song like "The Besom Maker," which enumerates a girl's sexual exploits (exploits that enrich her financially into the bargain) in "yonder vale" with a miller, "across the hills" with a squire, and on "the King's highway" with a parson. Or a maleness-dominant song like "Balaam and Egg," in which a trooper explains to an inn hostess's daughter just how his "horse" will drink at her "well," is counterbalanced by a song like "The Furze Field," in which the girl takes charge and maps out for the man just how to proceed when "hunting" in her "field" (superordination in the semantic domain of *knowledge,* not included in our code-structure because it does not occur too often).

One kind of catalogue song, the dialogic, does contain the equalizing process within individual texts as the narrative metaphorical ballads do.[27] In "The Elfin Knight" (Child 2), for instance, the man poses an initial set of impossible tasks (couched in sexual metaphors) to the girl; if she can perform them, he says, he will be her lover. But she reverses this skewed role-relationship in the second half of the song by posing to him a set of equally impossible and equally metaphorical tasks, saying that, on the contrary, she will allow him to be her lover if he can perform those. Other dialogue songs that share this kind of internal equalization are "Riddles Wisely Expounded" (Child 1) and "My Man John."

In short, if all manifestations of the metaphorical model's catalogue type are taken as a group, the underlying meaning of the model is little different from that of the ballad type: there are no losers in the "game" of sex. The play analogy is apposite, for in the metaphorical world view sex is undertaken for its own sake, one prominent feature of both play and poetic discourse. While in symbolic songs the qualities of sexual phenomena are given a naturalistic rationale, and in euphemistic songs a cultural rationale, the rationale in the metaphorical world view is primarily an existential one.

Each of our three models is a well-delineated and well-differentiated, though not contradictory, conceptualization of the nature and meaning of sexual adventures. It is indeed surprising to find that the models do not merge in single texts more often than they do, since they all treat the same subject matter and were all represented in the performance repertoires of individual singers. We did see that the metaphorical model's rhetorical technique is used occasionally in texts generated primarily by the euphemistic code, but that the metaphors are mostly isolated uses. There was also evidence that the euphemistic code's precept 11 warning maidens against initiating sex themselves, ambivalent in its application, may have indicated influence from the metaphorical model's value system. In addition, symbolic and metaphorical imagery occasionally draw upon the same phenomena for their vehicles, though with quite different referents. Moreover, euphemistic songs often begin with nature imagery of activity and its lack, or profusion of sound and color and their opposites; but such imagery in euphemistic pieces appears chiefly in the scenic frames of the song's introduction and is almost never sustained throughout as an encoder of meaning, unlike symbolic songs.

However, there is one notable instance of a song that is difficult to assign to any one model, and since this song was extremely popular not only in England but also in Scotland (where it may have originated), Anglo-Ireland, Canada, and the United States, we should be able to account for it within the code-systems we have established here. The ballad in question is the well-known "A-Growing" (Laws O35), which appears in our sample collections in seven reasonably full traditional versions, in several fragments, and in two broadsides (*CSCEFS,* 1:243–52; *EC,* pp. 265–69; *JFSS* 1 [1902]: 214–15; *JFSS* 2 [1905]: 44–47; *JFSS* 2 [1906]: 274–76; *JFSS* 5 [1915]: 190–91). Like "The Bold Fisherman," "A-Growing" seems to be older than most of the other ballads with sexual content and, again somewhat like "The Bold Fisherman," has been put forward by scholars as one of Child's remarkably few oversights, since "A-Growing" was available to him when he compiled the *English and Scottish Popular Ballads,* and yet he chose not to include it.[28]

Why did Child not include "A-Growing" in his canon of the British "popular ballad"? For one thing, the song's stanzaic form is of the extended type, seven stresses to the line and four lines to the stanza, commonly associated with the post-seventeenth-century street ballad, which owed much of its origin and vitality to the commercial city presses. In contrast, the majority of Child's canon conforms to the 4/3/4/3 or 4/4/4/4 metrical form; seven-stressed lines, when they occur in Child ballads, do so in two-line, not four-line, stanzas. Second, the story of "A-Growing"—an arranged marriage between an adolescent boy and a mature young woman that is soon terminated by the boy's death from no readily apparent cause—has no well-known traditional analogues. Third, the narrative element is relatively weak and the emotional element quite pronounced, thus militating against a firm "ballad" designation for the song. If we combine this strong lyric quality of "A-Growing" with a fourth possibility—that the song draws upon certain rhetorical conventions not generally shared by other "popular ballads" that Child did include in his anthology—then Child's decision to pass over "A-Growing" becomes clearer; much of the song's language is unmistakably of the lost-lover kind that permeates so many non-balladic symbolic songs of love relationships. And if we follow the implications of the song's rhetoric to possibility five—that the code that generates the meaning of "A-Growing" is not fundamental to the majority of the other domestic ballads in Child's canon—then we see that Child's decision to pass over this piece was quite consistent with his criteria for what constituted the "popular ballad."[29]

We are interested in "A-Growing" in this analysis because the song deals with a sexual relationship between a young boy and his older wife-to-be. Most often, their liaison is expressed in euphemisms:

> We went into the green wood
> To frolic and to play,
> O what did there befall
> I tell not unto thee . . . (*EC*, p. 267).

We find almost identical phrases in other euphemistic songs. However, when we attempt to match the song with the euphemistic code, some intriguing results emerge. First of all, we find in the *experience* domain that the girl is older than the boy, a direct inversion of all those euphemistic songs in our sample in which relative age signifies. Thus from the song's opening the girl exhibits the "masculine" quality of being older and more experienced, the boy the "feminine" quality of being younger and less experienced. Moreover, we find a similar inversion in the *motive* domain. In all other euphemistic songs that include this component of the code, the masculine variable of *liaison initiated over opposition of an authority figure* is one property the girl can assume in order to convert a tragic into a comic experience; but nowhere in the euphemistic song sample do we encounter the circumstances that begin "A-Growing"

—the liaison is initiated by the *father* over the opposition of the daughter:

O father, dear father,
I've feared you've done me harm,
You've married me to a boy
And I fear he is too young.
O daughter, dearest daughter,
And if you stay at home and wait along of me
A lady you shall be while he's growing (*CSCEFS*, 1:245).

Despite these inversions, however, the relationship of contrast between the two *dramatis personae* does not change throughout the course of events the song portrays, and the major premise of the euphemistic world view holds true: as long as a relationship of contrast obtains, the experience will be tragic for the actor who exhibits "feminine" traits only. Appropriately enough, not only does the boy die at the end of "A-Growing" but the girl's experience is also tragic, since she is left with a baby and no husband. She is also the target of the song's message as generated by the euphemistic world view, though that message is a direct inversion of precepts 8 and 11: don't engage in a sexual liaison with a man *younger* and *less experienced* than you or in a liaison *initiated by an authority figure over your opposition.*

But that is not all. There is just as much, if not more, symbolic rhetoric in some versions of this song, and it is revealing to apply the symbolic code to "A-Growing." Interestingly, we find that there are images of *activity* (on the part of both nature and humans) and of *lack of activity* (she must "lie alone" while he is off at school maturing; he is laid to rest in the grave after his death). There are *intensity* versus *lack of intensity* oppositions ("As it fell upon a day, / A bright and summer's day" versus "It is a cold winter's night / Here and I alone must weep" [*EC*, pp. 265–67]) as well as *perpendicular* versus *horizontal* ones ("The trees they do grow high" versus "He is dead and buried / And in the churchyard laid" [*CSCEFS*, 1:243–46]). There is even the ambiguity of antithetical values residing in the signifiers of *free* and its opposition *bound*; he is "freed" to go away for schooling while he matures, she attempts to counteract the potentially negative effects of this freedom by having him bound ("I'll bind a bunch of ribbons red / About his little waist" [*EC*, p. 265]), a positively valued binding that is mirrored by a negatively valued one when she, weeping, makes a holland shroud in which to bind his dead body. The song's overdetermined tragic ending (both lovers suffer) is also quite compatible with the symbolic meaning of sexual relationships: that the opposites of "heterogeneous" vitalism and a "homogeneous" void paradoxically are both innate qualities of love relationships, and a romantic liaison is consequently a very risky business. The protagonists' breaking of the cultural proprieties encoded in the euphemistic model matches the naturalistic determinism in the symbolic world view.

Thus the popularity of "A-Growing" might be explained. Not only is it quite compatible with the noncontradictory world views of two common traditional models, but it also stands out from the common run of songs about sexual liaisons by containing a perfectly symmetrical inversion of the usual male/female properties and child/parent role-relationships. It may very well be, in fact, that stanzas of symbolic rhetoric were added by "native speakers" later on in the song's traditional life in order to reduce possible confusion engendered by the unique inversion of roles and acts. An unusual Somerset version of "A-Growing," in which two stanzas from the fully symbolic "T Stands for Thomas" appear, provides support for this hypothesis.[30]

We have now accounted for our entire sample of English folksongs on the topic of sexual liaisons within the framework of our code-structures. Our remaining task is to relate each model's world view both to the country singer's pragmatic world view and to his or her everyday-life conditions, in the process indicating more explicitly how the three models themselves logically interrelate, so that a coherent universe of meaning is revealed.

Analysis of "The Bold Fisherman" in chapter 1 indicated that folksong's symbolic signifiers are not entirely arbitrary constructs; though poetic conceptions, they do display a certain correlation with practical perceptions of the same entities, which in the "real" world are themselves ambiguous. What kind of normative perceptions of ambiguity might signifiers of symbolic songs of sexual liaisons "reflect"—normative perceptions that are consistent with those posited in chapter one for the more inclusive province of meaning, love relationships? We might hypothesize that most such ambiguities stem from the fundamental one that human beings are an intimate part of nature and yet unresolvedly different from nature. From this could be derived such anomalies as the following: nature exhibits both the wild heterogeneity of disorder and the pure homogeneity of static order, but humans in order to live viably cannot countenance such extremes in their own lives, since in a heterogeneous state nothing is knowable and doable, while in homogeneity there is nothing to be known, no challenge, no growth, no allowance for change. Or again: nature's physical properties are regenerative seasonally but one of woman's most culturally valued physical properties is not—the maidenhead so often mentioned in folksong. Indeed, girls in many songs say as much with their "formula of impossibilities," as we call such tropes:

O I wish, I wish, but it's all in vain,
I wish I was a maid again.
O a maid again I never shall be
Till apples grow on an orange tree (*CSCEFS*, 1:604).

In other words, there is no analogy in nature for the distinctly human condition of irreversible loss of virginity. Or yet another paradox: nature's fauna and flora mate without spillover effects in an emotional domain, but humans cannot do so. This suggests a logical extension: in the human realm a love relationship is an inseparable whole of *both* physical and emotional commitment, but while the physical effects of loss of maidenhead can be predicted, the emotional effects cannot be, for those are contingent on circumstances (to some extent, symbolic songs compensate for this uncertainty with their extreme fatalism).

That these songs may have addressed conceptually such far-reaching questions is suggested not only by their nature imagery and code-structure but also by formal features they commonly exhibit in their texts. For instance, symbolic songs are invariably in the first person singular of the universal self. They are seldom situated in historical time or place, and just as seldom identify their participants in terms of specific social categories like chambermaid, tailor, or lord of high degree; overwhelmingly, the designation is simply "I" and "he," or "young man" and "young maiden." Moreover, these songs are the most "cliched" in English tradition, sharing a body of commonplaces so redundant and so often used that they have been called "floaters," which indicates both their capacity to be generalized and their quality as symbolic expressions.[31]

Ethnographic support comes from an account of a typical evening's singing at a country pub during the last century—though the facts are only partial, since the pub was a male preserve, the females staying home. The songs performed at the Wagon and Horses that evening included a wide range of genres, from a Child ballad to a music hall song; most songs were associated with specific singers, specific functions, or specific times and places of performance (such as outdoors or at the night's end). Interestingly, the two verses recorded of a song on the symbolic model constituted the only performance over the course of the evening not linked to a specific social persona or any other such constraint:

> Then there were snatches that any one might break out with at any time when no one else happened to be singing:

> I wish, I wish, 'twer all in vain,
> I wish I were a maid again!
> A maid again I ne'er shall be
> Till oranges grow on an apple tree

or:

> Now all you young chaps, take a warning by me,
> And do not build your nest at the top of any tree,
> For the green leaves they will wither and the flowers
>   they will decay,
> And the beauty of that fair maid will soon pass away.[32]

It is difficult to find ethnographic evidence for a pragmatic world view underlying the symbolic code, since symbolic songs are so abstract in their meanings. But an indication at least of the code's validity is that we can find a similar code, or major parts of it, in other rural expressive forms of social behavior. Take, for instance, that minor ritual I alluded to in chapter 1, "rough musicking," which villagers occasionally put on to chastise a husband or wife who had transgressed the bounds of proper married behavior. Here is a more complete account of the East Riding example partially quoted in the preceding chapter:

> The village is in an uproar. The very sparrows, by their lively movements and twittering, and the rooks, in the rookery bordering one side of the village green, by their wheeling flight and incessant cawing and clamouring, seem to partake of the general excitement. A throng of men and boys, aye, and women too, some with sticks and some with old tins and pans, are as eager as bees at swarming time; and are talking long and loud, with faces red with excitement and intensity of purpose.

An effigy of the offending husband is

> carried by two men through the village, accompanied by a motley crowd, with instruments more famed for sound than music.

A drum is a decided acquisition, and he who has a horn is envied by those who have nothing more melodious than a tin whistle, an old kettle, or their own hoarse voice.[33]

This description is strikingly similar to the heterogeneous paradigm of symbolic songs in its images of *multiplicity, activity,* and *amplified sound.*[34]

There is more, however; rough musicking as a signifier had symbolic aspects as well, since a very similar rite occurred in what was on the surface an apparently quite different context—on a couple's wedding night:

> When the newly married couple retires to bed a gang of young men gather round outside the cottage, with tin pans and anything that will make a noise and start banging the pans and hallooing; the wretched bridegroom has to rise and come downstairs and give them all a drink before they will go away.[35]

As with the empirical status of the symbolic vehicles in "The Bold Fisherman," the immediate application of both kinds of rough musicking is to potentially dangerous *junctures* between well-defined, well-known, and safer categories of reality. The transgressing partner of the marriage has created a liminal state of affairs; events are in disordered suspension, their future direction unpredictable, and rough musicking is an attempt by the community to reinstate normative order by saying to the offending party, either mend your ways or leave the village. Rough wedding music is appropriate to the critical period of the wedding night, when the brand new nuclear family finds out just how compatible its members are. At the higher, abstract level of the symbolic referent associating these two rites is the shared feature of sexual "licentiousness" and its potential danger to the small rural society.

As for the "homogeneity" paradigm of the code, apparently village communities did not have a formalized custom for expressing this idea (something analogous to, say, the social ostracism of "sending to Coventry" that was common in public schools); but it was certainly expressed in more informal, though still group-conducted, behaviors. In the north Oxfordshire village of Candleford Green, for instance, lived in solitude Mrs. Macey with her young son, vaguely letting it be known that her husband was somewhere abroad in service to a traveling gentleman. Though locally born and locally resident for half her life, the husbandless woman (Had she been deserted? Widowed? Never married? Only one other person knew the truth, that Mr. Macey was in jail) "had no friends in the village." And in Lark Rise hamlet several hours' journey away lived the clergyman's spinster daughter, who had the added disadvantage of being above the class of the majority of the local women, almost all workingmen's wives. "Considering her many kindnesses to the women, she might have been expected to be more popular than she was. None of them welcomed her visits. Some would lock their doors and pretend to be out; others would rattle their teacups when they saw her coming, hoping she would say, as she sometimes did, 'I hear you are at tea, so I won't come in.' "[36] The synthesis of these two poles, the hyperactivity of rough musicking on one hand and the passivity of silence and avoidance on the other, was doubtless the customary interactions of everyday neighborliness—gossiping, dropping in to "have a chat," and the inevitable borrowing and returning of sundry household items.

Consider another genre, one closer to practical culture than are song and ritual, clothing. Flora Thompson has this to say of her community in the 1880s:

> Then they had colour prejudices. A red frock! Only a fast hussy would wear red. Or green—sure to bring any wearer bad luck! There was a positive taboo on green in the hamlet; nobody would wear it until it had been home-dyed navy or brown. Yellow ranked with red as immodest. . . . On the whole, they preferred dark or neutral colours; but there was one exception; blue had nothing against it. Marine and sky blue were the favourite shades, both very bright and very crude.
>
> Much prettier were the colours of the servant girls' print morning dresses—lilac, or pink, or buff, sprigged with white—which were cut down for the little girls to wear on May Day and for churchgoing throughout the summer.[37]

Three "emic" or native categories of dress color are implicit in this quotation: one category contains red, green, and yellow; the second, navy, brown, marine, and sky blue; and the third, lilac, pink, and buff, with a small repetitive white motif distributed evenly over the pastel ground. Category 1 was not suitable for respectable women, while category 2 was; category 3 was appropriate for mature unmarried girls.[38]

There is a remarkable closeness between the code that appears to underlie this color system of everyday public dress and the code we see in the symbolic songs, especially in the *intensity/lack of intensity* semantic domain. The luminosity of the stark natural colors, red, green, and yellow, was associated with the heterogeneous paradigm in songs of love relationships and with a primary positive value, while in everyday living the set had a negative value. The pastel shades of lilac, pink, and buff parallel the homogeneous *lack of intensity*, here positive rather than negative and proper for "maidens at risk" when not in a context of courtship. To counteract the extreme plainness of the nonluminous pastel color, however, it was permissible to incorporate a touch of heterogeneity—"sprigged with white"—since, after all, they were *available* for courtship. Appropriate for married women was the median state between intensity and its lack, colors that had been subjected to a cultural process, dyeing, thus achieving a proper synthesis of nature and culture. The acceptability of marine and sky blue, which Flora Thompson explicitly identifies as "very bright," presents some difficulty to the logic of this classification, though "sky blue" does seem to be close to the nonintense pastels, marine to the synthetic "navy" and "brown." (It may be significant that folksongs never mention the sky or the color blue, only flowers, trees, birds, grass, sun, and their appropriate hues.) But the majority of the variables Thompson mentions certainly form a system compatible with that underlying symbolic songs.

The interpretation is clearly allowable that songs about sexual liaisons generated by the symbolic code affirm an ontological extension of the ethical transgression/redemption principle: that sex is a very risky business because it possesses a dangerous quality that is innate to the whole organic world. Since an adult love affair is such an integral part of nature, it partakes of nature's indivisible properties of both disordered, unpredictable, and uncontrolled heterogeneity on the one hand and ordered, absolutely predictable, "lifeless" homogeneity on the other. But neither state is viable for humans— that is, surrender to the instincts of the Id or the constraints of the Superego. In order to escape either of these unacceptable alternatives, a solution is presented, though its successful achievement in the song world is rare and more hypothetical than actual: one must work to use both the exotic and the monotonous in proper proportions in order to articulate the syncretic medium of a contented, stable, productive, socially complete, married couple. The appearance of this same code in other stylized traditional behaviors suggests how fundamental such a proposition must have been in the rural world view—a true infrastructure. And indeed, the symbolic model shows evidence of being a very old one in traditional English song. Truly, its message was relevant to every sexually mature person of every era and to the very fabric of the community.

In contrast with the symbolic songs, those structured on the euphemistic model use signifiers that are far more denotative to indicate a different aspect of world view, one of "becoming." The conception of "becoming" envisages life in more processual and evolutionary terms than the symbolic vision of "being," for in the euphemistic song world one both adapts to and influences one's environment. If you can do neither, then you will suffer, unless a very narrow range of conditions obtain in the first place (precept 13). But most often, an array of choices is available, choices more numerous and more realistically achievable than the if-only synthesis some symbolic songs imagine. The euphemistic world view seems more fitting to an industrial era, and, not surprisingly, most of its songs have the broadside stamp to them; many take place in urban environments, and most seem to date from between 1750 and 1850.

The Industrial Revolution brought about accelerated change within English society. Increased mobility between villages and between village and town, the displacement of settled folk caused by enclosures, the increasing movements of individuals both up and down the social ladder—all these became far more prominent features of life toward the end of the eighteenth century than they had been before. It is to be expected that a model like the euphemistic, which depended less on shared, unstated assumptions about the nature of the world than did the symbolic, would become more prominent. Relatively concrete, context-sensitive signifiers were more widely communicable carriers of more apposite information than the overly abstract and multivocal symbolic signifiers. Euphemistic songs contained their symbolic elements to be sure, as we saw in chapter 1; but these were used selectively, maintaining as a substratum a link with the still-present but fading world view of the preindustrial countryside. These signifiers do not constitute *the* language of a euphemistic song, as their cognates do in symbolic songs.

Precept 13 of the euphemistic repertoire of dicta takes the safest route and counsels that chances of a "comic" sexual experience are enhanced if conditions of age, social status, and territory are equally distributed among the two partners. Probably, up to the mid-nineteenth century at least, most village girls married village boys; but those girls may often have had a twinge of regret at choosing this conservative route when confronted with childhood peers who had succeeded in raising their status by assuming risk. In the late nineteenth-century villages, tradesmen were especially favored as husbands, for one thing because their social status was not that far above the status of laborers' daughters in service, and for another because such a marriage might give one an opportunity to rise even higher in the world, as marriage to farm laborers did not:

> Butchers and milkmen were favoured as husbands, perhaps because these were frequent callers at the houses where the girls were employed. A hamlet girl would marry a milkman or a butcher's roundsman in London, or some other distant part of the country, and, after a few years, the couple would acquire a business of their own and become quite prosperous. One married a butler and with him set up an apartment house on the East Coast; another married a shopkeeper and, with astonishing want of tact, brought a nursemaid to help look after her children when she visited her parents. . . . The girls who had married away remained faithful to the old custom of spending a summer fortnight with their parents, and the outward and visible signs of their prosperity must have been trying to those who had married farm labourers and returned to the old style of living.[39]

By this time, the 1880s, the custom of young country girls going into service had long been established.[40] In villages that had no local industry of either the factory or the cottage type, domestic service was the main occupation available to adolescent girls, since in the south of England field work was not now generally considered respectable and since enclosures had for at least a century disenfranchised many families from the small farms, open field allotments, or commons they had formerly worked together.[41] Domestic service was simply another example of the greater mobility and more diverse environments within reach of the nineteenth-century young woman, in contrast to her pre-nineteenth-century counterpart. Service enabled her to encounter a wider range of experiences than had formerly been possible, but it also required that she be able to call upon her own resources in unfamiliar situations. Thus a capacity for innovativeness, a readiness to go contrary to the safely old-fashioned authoritarianism that parents represented, an ability, in short, to counteract the liability of traditional "feminine" traits must have been indispensable qualities to the new woman of the industrial era. Thus were cultural realities "reflected" in the sign-aspects of the more modern (though after 1850, fast becoming themselves old-fashioned) euphemistic pieces.

That the signifiers of euphemistic songs had fairly direct correlates in real life cannot be doubted. For instance, the marginal nature of gypsies, who constituted major followers of the tinker profession—one category of *acontextuals* in euphemistic songs—was
taken for granted by native village folk from as far back as the
sixteenth century and is still, in fact, up to the present day.[42] Irishmen—not necessarily immigrants but the itinerant workers who
crossed the Irish sea every May to work the summer harvest on
English farms before returning home at season's end—were similarly
marginal; in fact, they were used as figures of fear to control country children's behavior: "Laura had been used to seeing the Irish
harvesters from a child. Then some of the neighbours at home had
tried to frighten her when naughty by saying, 'I'll give you to them
old Irishers; see if I don't, then!' "[43] Similarly were soldiers seen as
socially marginal, even though many of them were local lads who
had gone a-soldiering and returned: "Entering the army," says
Alfred Williams of one such village boy, "he served through the
South African War in the cavalry; but as is so often the case, he
contracted habits of dissoluteness, from which he could never free
himself afterwards."[44] The opinion of a local village shoemaker was
that a soldier's life simply added to an already unsettled personality: " 'The young chaps who go for soldiers are mostly wild and up
to all sorts of games. You can pretty near always tell who's going—
it's the uneasy kind that finds our life dull. . . . There's some of the
roughest tramp chaps too in the army that the recruiters bring in,
so wild, some of 'em, they don't know what to do with 'em after
they've got 'em.' "[45] One girl who in real life ran afoul of precept 7
warning against such acontextuals was Bertha, in service with
Laura's aunt at Candleford town; Bertha bore an illegitimate child
by a soldier, and only the kindness of her mistress kept both mother
and daughter from the workhouse.[46] As for males whose social standing was significantly higher than that of working girls, they were
just as much a potential source of danger and tragedy in the area
of sexual relationships as were acontextuals. In 1858 Joseph Ashby's
mother, Elizabeth, for instance, was seduced and made pregnant by
the master of the house where she was in service, necessitating her
return to her native village in shame.[47] The town experience of a
female operative in Staffordshire later in the century was not much
different, she being seventeen and her seducer being her employer,
"a gentleman of good position and high standing in the town."[48]

I have suggested that the most relevant audience for symbolic
songs must have been any and all sexually mature village dwellers.
The mimetic quality of euphemistic songs, on the other hand, their

third-person point of view, their internal closure (that is, events in the song's fictional world are resolved in the text, for good or ill), and their decorous language suggest that they were more in the nature of structured "performance" items than were symbolic songs and with a target audience of lesser sweep—people who had greater potential contact with a world outside the hermetic ones of their own village and its long-established social networks.[49] What about songs on the third model, the metaphorical? Treatment of sexual subject matter metaphorically is certainly as old as, if not older than, symbolic rhetoric; this antiquity alone suggests that metaphorical songs were not necessarily more appropriate to the relatively heterogeneous society of the nineteenth century than to a more homogeneous preindustrial one. Instead, a reasonable inference is that they were most appropriate to restricted social situations where the personae of the participants were either very well-defined and secure or else of entirely no consequence; two systems of role relationships, in short, in which the participants would not be rulebound, would be freed from allegiance to the deterministic premises that the symbolic model's "naturalized" world view implied, as well as from the constraints of the "socialized" world view in the euphemistic model. In both such situations, participants would be free to enter the realm of the imaginary, of play, of "poetry for its own sake," to enjoy vicariously a world subject to naught save the physical facts of sex itself, and to ignore temporarily the transgression and redemption ethic. The aspect of world view most addressed by metaphorical songs is not the basic "being" of the symbolic, nor the processual "becoming" of the euphemistic, but the existential "behaving," where simple action and reaction within a closed system of *now* are what chiefly signify.

Most typically, situations of this sort might involve an all-adult male or female peer group. As is often the case, available ethnographic literature helps us but little in this sphere. Perhaps we can infer something from allusions like that of Bob Copper to the Saturday noontime all-male sessions at his pub in Bedfordshire, where the men off work for the weekend and on their way home would share a quick pint and recount bawdy stories and memorates of firsthand encounters with woman.[50] Flora Thompson has a similar allusion to noontime raconteurs, though the occasions were not restricted to Saturdays; after the bread, cheese, and bacon had been eaten, and a few moments of rest were still to be enjoyed before work was resumed, the boys would wander off "with their catapults down the hedgerows," and the men "would while away the time in repeating what the women spoke of with shamed voices as 'men's tales,' " tales that were "kept strictly to the fields and never repeated elsewhere" and that "formed a kind of rustic *Decameron*."[51]

Both of these reports are of stories and not of songs, and we have little indication whether they were of metaphorical or idiomatic (that is, "filthy") rhetoric, though Thompson's own inference that they were probably "coarse" rather than "filthy" suggests the former. But this author does mention songs as also being a feature of these all-male lunch breaks, and characterizes their content as being little different from the tales: "Songs and snatches on the same lines were bawled at the plough-tail and under hedges and never heard elsewhere. Some of these ribald rhymes were so neatly turned that those who have studied the subject have attributed their authorship to some graceless son of the Rectory or Hall."[52] This certainly sounds more like metaphorical than idiomatic or even euphemistic song, but the evidence is simply too skimpy to say— and sometimes downright muddied, in fact, by Bob Copper's assurance that metaphorical songs like "Three Maids a-Milking" had *no* sexual connotations for his male singers, an assertion that one is tempted to dub a mite fantastical.[53]

With a little imagination, we might see in at least one account an indication that an all-married-women gathering—again, a social situation in which role identities are unambiguous and well-known —may have been also an appropriate occasion for metaphorical song performance. Mrs. Arless, age forty-five, had been brought into the hamlet as the young bride of a local man and was different from the more usual hamlet housewife and mother not only in her greater zest for life and in her inner vitality, but also in that, not surprisingly, she was rumored to have gypsy blood.

> Her idea of wise spending was to call in a few neighbors of like mind, seat them around a roaring fire, and despatch one of her toddlers to the inn with the beer can. They none of them got drunk, or even fuddled, for there was not very much each, even when the can went round to the inn a second or a third time. But it was just enough to hearten them up and make them forget their troubles, and the talk and laughter and scraps of song which floated on the air from "that there Mrs. Arless's house" were shocking to the more sedate matrons. Nobody crooked their finger round the handle of a teacup or "talked genteel" at Mrs. Arless's gathering, herself least of all. She was so charged with sex vitality that with her all subjects of conversation led to it—not in its filthy or furtive aspects but as the one great central fact of life.[54]

This passage reinforces several of our hypotheses about the probable social milieu most conducive to metaphorical song performance; the event takes place in woman's territory (just as underneath the hedgerows or in the pub at noontime was men's territory) and the participants are a homogeneous group ("a few neighbours of like mind"); time and space are "closed," the group is shut off from everyday restraints of decorum and propriety, the matrix is a "play" one, and the somatic is foregrounded ("so charged with sex vitality").

Ultimately, we have to rely on inferential leaps in using such data to advance hypotheses. The single unequivocal reference to an actual use of sexual metaphor that I can discover (though in a proverb, not a song) was in the context of our other hypothesized ideal situation: one in which, in part at least, social roles were not known, and were not particularly relevant to the actors. The event took place just after World War II, considerably later than the nineteenth-century period we have concentrated on, to be sure, but in the milieu of a Suffolk agricultural village at harvest time. The story is told by a local man who was then a sixteen-year-old farm laborer. During the summers, woman gangers would come up from town to earn money working the apple harvest. One of these took a fancy to the young lad, and approached him during work one day asking to "see his watch." Playfully, she took the watch from the pocket of his waistcoat lying nearby, wearing it throughout the day around her neck and periodically taunting him to "come and get it!" She returned the timepiece at day's end, but the following day corralled the boy in the field during lunch break and seduced him. Later:

> At tea-time the women went rushing home with their aprons full of apples—shrieking, you can be sure. They shruck a bit more when they saw me and a couple of them rang their bike bells. My old woman shouted, "Don't torment him! He's like his old watch—not so bad when he's wound up!" Laugh! You should have heard them!
> It was my first time.
> Christ, that was a summer and no mistake.[55]

In this use of sexual metaphor we have the major elements of our "ideal" contexts: the women are away from the everyday setting of their home town; the primary audience for the remark, the other gangers, are socially equivalent with the speaker; the social personae of boy and women vis-à-vis each other are of no consequence outside that context itself; and the occasion—for the woman, certainly—is out of normal time and place with their customary constraints, a ludic occasion.

The three models as ways of thinking and communicating about sexual matters thus can all be logically interrelated within the cultural system of an agricultural village community. The symbolic model represented an older, more traditional, and more fundamental world view, defining the ontological "being" of sexual liaisons. The euphemistic songs, particularly appropriate in the changing period of the Industrial Revolution's formative years, spoke more directly to the quickly evolving contemporary environment and to the phenomenon of process, of "becoming," even though they themselves were quickly to become passé. The metaphorical model, closest to fantasy, fit a more artificially restricted context of both meaning and performance where only a few variables were of causal efficacy, portraying a "behaving" world reduced to mechanics and to energy.

3

THE
LOCAL
SONG
IN
YORKSHIRE

Signifiers
of the
Everyday-Life
World

The first two chapters have dealt with songs of the ideally tradi-tional sort: they contain quite formulaic language, tirelessly repeat the same story-types and themes, are cast in a limited array of formal verse models, were popular over most regions of Great Britain and Ireland, show a certain amount of music and textual variation between their various traditional manifestations, main-tained to some extent an existence apart from print, lasted for a significant length of time as popular performance items, and were generalizable enough in their topics and meanings to outlive nar-rowly time-bound, place-bound, or occasion-bound relevance. When we think of "folksong" and what it denotes, it is these characteristics that come foremost to mind. But we also know, of course, that such characteristics can seldom be plotted on a binary scale of presence or absence, since they all come in varying degrees of more-or-less. Invariably lying toward the "less" end of the scale is a song-genre popular in most domestic and community performance repertoires, which we call the "local song."

The eminent Yorkshire collector, Frank Kidson, summed up the feelings of many people—including folksong collectors—when confronted with a local song pertinent only to a certain district. In his *Traditional Tunes,* he printed but two stanzas of a North Riding hunting song, allowing a comment to fill in for the rest of the text: "I have no wish to inflict upon the readers more than two verses of this effusion. Like all songs of its class, it runs to about twenty verses, and the prowess of every fox-hunting squire and yeoman of the district is chronicled; highly interesting to those who know the descendants of the persons mentioned, but rather monotonous to the general reader."[1] Monotonous to the general reader, perhaps, but evidently not to the folk of the relevant district itself. Herbert Halpert, from a North American vantage point, asserted that often local songs are in fact far more vital, functional, and meaningful in a community's network of song communication than are older, more traditional songs, even though a local song's lifespan as a performance item may be short.[2] Halpert's discovery of local songs' pragmatic has justified in recent folksong study an additional emphasis on these topical pieces. Most such studies, when they are interpretive, elucidate either referential meanings of several local songs or conceptual meanings of individual texts; in this chapter, however, I will try to contribute to this fast-growing body of scholarship by searching for conceptual meanings in a significant number of local songs from the same culture region to discover just how they support a unified world view. The results, I hope, will suggest that local songs need not be "monotonous to the general reader."

While it has sometimes been asserted that folksingers themselves do not make distinctions between "old songs" and "new songs," or between traditional and local songs, the apparent lack of such "emic" distinctions may very well be a function chiefly of our failure to discover them, as a recent study from Newfoundland that makes native classification its particular goal suggests.[3] For village folksinging in England we can infer one kind of native classification system from Flora Thompson's account of an evening at a small country pub, the Wagon and Horses.[4] Before we begin discussing our local song sample, let us examine Thompson's account in some detail, with the goal of interrelating as logically as we can the several subgenres of the community's popular song repertoire, a repertoire that included items widely traditional throughout most of Great Britain and Ireland as well as more topical pieces like the local songs.

The young bachelors usually began an evening's singing; their specialty consisted of "such songs of the day as had percolated so far. 'Over the Garden Wall,' with its many parodies, 'Tommy, Make Room for Your Uncle,' 'Two Lovely Black Eyes,' and other 'comic' or 'sentimental' songs of the moment." The songs of these "boy-chaps" (as unmarried youths were called) are easily recognized as fairly recent hits from the city stage—the music hall, in this case —circulated into the country by word of mouth or by penny song-books. Next, middle-aged male singers would take the spotlight, and their preference was for "long and usually mournful stories in verse, of thwarted lovers, children buried in snowdrifts, dead maidens, and motherless homes." These songs were evidently a mixture of sentimental parlor song and broadside balladry; their chief characteristic was that they posed problems and provided solutions, homiletic, didactic, or practical for those problems, all within their texts—problems and solutions with which the audience that night could for the most part identify. This was a feature of those eighteenth- and early nineteenth-century ballads, mostly from broadside presses, that we examined at length in chapters 1 and 2; it was also a feature of the more lyrical, modern, and genteel parlor songs that these middleaged hamlet singers also favored, "songs of a high moral tone, such as: 'Waste not, Want not, / Some maxim I would teach. . . .' "

Next that evening at the Wagon and Horses came songs that belonged to the company as a whole, regardless of age, individual talent, or experience. Suitable for either indoor or outdoor performance, loved neither for its message nor its contemporaneity, but for its general conviviality and the opportunity it provided for group participation, a song of this sort was most meaningful as an act of singing itself rather than as a product or as a lesson. Catalogue form with all its repetition was the stylistic mark of this kind of song, in the manner of the cumulative "Barleymow," the song that raised the rafters that night in Lark Rise.[5] Following these communal songs would come "personality" pieces—traditional songs, but each associated as a performance item with a specific hamlet singer, whether because of his unique way of singing it or perhaps because of some specific circumstance in his life that rendered the song's content particularly apposite to him, a relevance known full well to the company. Thus at The Wagon and Horses, the only bachelor of mature age present, Lukey, would sing "The Old Maid's Song," his performance given public "point by Luke's own unmarried state."[6] Next to be performed was a local song, whose rendition on this occasion was the privilege of its maker (as is often the case with local songs):

One comparatively recent settler, who had only lived at the hamlet about a quarter of a century, had composed a snatch for himself, to sing when he felt homesick. It ran:

Where be Dedington boo-oys, where be they now?
They be at Dedington at the 'Plough';
If they be-ent, they be at home,
And this is the 'Wagon and Horses.'

The evening would end with performances by the oldest singers present, who appropriately specialized in "summat . . . as stood the testing o' time." On this particular evening, old Master Price gave his rendition of "Lord Lovel" (Child 75), while Master Tuffrey closed out the evening with a version of "Lady Isabel and the Elf-Knight" (Child 4), the sound of which, filtering through the evening air and into the cottage kitchens, signaled the housebound hamlet women that " 'They'll soon be out now. Poor old Dave's just singing his 'Outlandish Knight.' " One final class of song, which could be sung any time during the evening between a "boy-chap's" latest hit and an octogenarian's Child ballad, was that of lyric lost-lover pieces like our symbolic songs, "snatches that any one might break out with at any time when no one else happened to be singing."

Flora Thompson's account indicates that, whether the participants themselves would have articulated it or not, there was indeed a native system of song classification within the natural context of performance, a system grounded in a felt if not intellectualized appropriateness between multiple variables such as singer's community persona, time of evening, place of performance, audience, song topic and message as well as form, style, and age. Two prime, though much more hidden, elements in this configuration, however, are communicative function on the one hand and relative closeness or distance of the song's phenomenal province of meaning to the company's experiential present on the other. Take, for instance, the catalogue-form-with-chorus songs like "The Barley Mow"; dealing as they so often do with ever-real and present social subjects like drinking, working, and playing, the prime "meaning" of such songs was the act of group singing itself, their prime communicative function a phatic one—the affirming in action of spatial, cultural, and affective union of its face-to-face participants. At the other end of this scale from close to distant were, not surprisingly, the songs of old Masters Price and Tuffrey, ballads that told in a style popular even during the Tudor reign of the doings of noblemen who wore fine jewelry, lived in stately castles, and rode the swiftest steeds. In the 1880s, the performance of this class of ballad could have had both a poetic function, the appreciation of the song for its own curio value, and an emotive function, as apparently was the case at the Wagon and Horses; the singer and his uniqueness (the fact that he was born in the previous century, for instance) constituted the song's chief appeal.

Also primarily emotive in function would be the personality numbers like Lukey's "Old Maid's Song." The difference, however, is that the Child ballads would have had little referential function, being antique pieces referring to a world past and gone, quite beyond the reach of the company's experiential present; but Lukey's song did have a referential function, for in large if figurative measure it referred to Lukey himself, a real member of the everyday community, as well as a conative function, for it would influence the audience's attitudes and behaviors toward Lukey in everyday life after the evening was but a memory.

The referential function would have been dominant in the middle-aged men's ballads and homilies; these songs' provinces of meaning were within potential reach and closer to hand, their messages to be stored in mind for retrieval if needed. They affectingly described a typical kind of event that just may happen to you, for instance, and proposed an ethic and course of action that you might one day soon have to adopt yourself should you be placed in circumstances involving "thwarted lovers, children buried in snowdrifts, dead maidens, and motherless children." Close to this phenomenal realm would have been the world depicted in the hits of the day, the specialty of the young bachelors, whose songs also treated a world of potential reach. The two differed, however, in that the orientation of the music hall songs was toward the relatively trivial and topical incidents that occupy the attention of youths, whatever strategies for living they espoused being directed at "modern" humor and even irreverence for their dominant culture's sacred cows. The fathers' songs, on the other hand, unashamedly embraced the norms of more universal, traditional, long-lasting, important adult experiences and an old-fashioned, now decidedly un-hip, ethos.

And somewhere between these two generations' differing views of the world-within-potential-reach on the one hand and the chorus songs' world-of-the-here-and-now on the other lay the world-within-actual-and-manipulable-reach, the world of paramount reality that the local song dealt with. The topics of such songs—like the ditty by the immigrant from Dedington—are real places, peoples, and events within the sphere of experience ready at hand, their dominant functions, at the level of the community, what the personality songs are at the level of the individual: referential in their treatment of a known (or at least knowable) world, and conative in that they call for the audience to take a responsive stance toward the real topic.

Clearly, a phenomenological perspective of this adumbrated sort reveals a logical classification that must have been implicit in Lark Rise cognition.[7] And it gives the local song, a genre often slighted by scholars, its own proper but meaningful and functioning place within the folk community's repertoire of song. In general, local songs both treat experiences from the manipulable (and manipulating) environment of their singers and audiences, and also have the fairly immediate and practical purpose of encouraging an appropriate response in thought or deed toward that real environment and its implications. Consequently, work and play within primary groups, calendar occasions by means of which a rural society orients its annual round, features of the landscape that directly affect one's activities, topical events within the community and of community-wide impact, and especially details about Significant Others whose social roles and actions closely complement one's own —these are all particularly favored as topics of both local songs and of the working-class poetry with which our next two chapters will deal. Should the topic be reasonably abstract, of more national import, or even of the historical past, then the emphasis invariably is on how in the present it concretely embodies *our* particularity.

One consequence of this emphasis on regional specificity is that local songs center their world view in the Self/Other relationship, whether at the interpersonal, geographical, or cultural level. It is how the boundaries between these two roles are conceived in the local song that gives us our most revealing insight into how the songs signify. Take, for instance, a piece like the following, from the agricultural North Riding of Yorkshire:[8]

HUNTING IN FLYINGDALES[9]

Come all you brave sportsmen I pray you give ear,
Come listen to me and your spirits I'll cheer
If a day of foxhunting you'd like to enjoy
It's with Flyingdale's Parish I'd have you to go.

Chorus: The hills and the valleys with a sweet echo
        Resound the sweet sound of a loud "Tally-ho!"

There's Readman the huntsman on his horse he does go
And he's not far behind when he hears "Tally Ho!"

He climbs the steep hills like a wild mountain goat
In his black velvet cap and his bright scarlet coat.

There's his son Will-the-Whip a very good man
He rides to the hounds as fast as he can.
And he always remembers to give a good shout
To let followers know bold Renny is about.

There is John from Laithes a good hunting sort
Likewise Will Beeforth an excellent sport
There is Francis and Lesley and Uncle Reg
They gallop along taking stone wall and hedge.

There's Knightley the grocer he hunts when he can
Likewise Matt Welburn a real sporting man
But to keep the hounds going money has to be found
Subscriptions are useful if you don't keep a hound.

There's Grainger and Mennel to the Meets they both go,
They like to be there and to shout "Tally Ho!"
After a hard day's hunting how hungry they feel
So they toddle off home where they are sure of a meal.

There is one brave sportsman we must not leave out
A sound foxhunter without a doubt
He sails the wide ocean by night and by day
His name is Will Mackie from Robin Hood's Bay.

There is Reveller, Volter, Pleasure also
There is Faithful and Handmaid they valour do show
There is Chorister and Cobweb they stick to the line
There is Cowslip and Sepia and Valentine.

Now I have finished my song so pass the bowl round
And drink to the health of hound-keepers and hounds
It's through a few local sportsmen the Hunt does survive
So it serves as a tonic to keep us alive.

This amiable piece is typical of local hunting songs. Its focus is the
core value of its bracketed world. Each actor—those members of the
hunt so goodheartedly catalogued—is defined by his special characteristics, but the characteristics of all so blend and merge with each
other across the boundaries distinguishing individuals that we are
presented with a monistic whole that is the sum of its parts; for
each part is but a microcosm of a unity of good-fellowship and
singular enjoyment. Even boundaries potentially more highly
marked—those separating members of the hunt from nonmembers

—are not regarded as differentiating bits of information but as integrating ones; others are invited to join, their capacity to smoothly merge with the hunt's prevailing bonhommie taken for granted. (This fifth stanza, by the way, also illustrates the pragmatic aspect so pervasive in local songs: the hunt obviously needs funds.)

Even the hounds of "Hunting in Flyingdales" are presented as almost indistinguishable from the huntsmen, and in fact only their names identify them as animals—Reveller, Volter, Pleasure, and so forth. This kind of analogous relationship between animal and man is a very common feature in sporting songs; in fact, it is customary to assign dialogue to animals, who converse not only with each other but with the human *dramatis personae* as well. Moreover, this anthropomorphizing is frequently extended to include the quarry itself, which, though it may be energetically chased and eventually killed, compliments its victors freely and receives high praise in turn from them. Such paeans are not necessarily hyperbolic; they simply select a choice quality from the topic and restate that quality in a catalogue of the topic's components (whether people, animals, agencies, or even parts of the landscape) that embody it.

A useful term for this kind of conceptualized relationship between distinguishable parts is *match*; the parts are analogous, even redundant, and fit together organically into an aggregate by *contiguity, similarity,* or *complementarity* rather than by *negotiation* or even *interaction*. Local songs frequently display this model of participant relationships, especially when the topics are leisure-time activities like sport, or a series of individuals who each encapsulate the essence of a narrowly defined group. For instance, another hunting song, "The Dallowgill Hunt," begins its celebratory paean thus:

All who delight to see and hear
The fox and hounds in full career,
Attention give unto my song
Of what was done—'t won't keep you long—
By men and hounds in Dallowgill,
Which Yorkshire scarce can parallel.[10]

Men and dogs working in unison unearth the equally "noble" fox, and as the long chase begins the song pauses to "expound / The name of every gallant hound." Even inhabitants of farms and hamlets in whose path the chase lies cheer the hunt on in its wild career. Not too strangely, the noble fox wins this particular contest by escaping, for this is not a world of good and evil, of winners and losers, but of mutual participation in common allegiance to the ethos of the hunt:

> O'er hills and dales, mountains and rocks,
> These noble hounds and gallant fox,
> Without a pause, without a stay,
> Ran more than fifty miles that day. . . .

The song ends with a praise to the patron of the hunt, the "honourable Aislbre," and a promise to soon engage the fox again.

While the Dallowgill hunt took place in the latter half of the eighteenth century, a similar song of a hunt almost a hundred years later is little different in style or conception. This time it was the "Holme Moss Hunt," whose quarry was a "gallant old hare."[11] The hare is caught and killed after proving quite equal to the abilities of hunters and dogs, and the song ends with praise to both hounds and sportsmen, men who are as adept at hunting as they are at drinking and singing. Another song of a hunt by the same pack a few years later is much the same, though on this occasion the several quarries prove far more elusive; but seven hares are finally brought to ground, and the hunt is praised as the equal of many famous ones from previous eras—in fact, "It ranks with any hunting this pack had ever seen / Since Robin Hood and Little John cheered them in Sherwood Forest green."[12]

Another hunting song tells the story of "The Wharfedale Otter."[13] The hunt here is not conducted by an organized pack; instead, the folk of Langstrothdale in the pastoral farming region of Yorkshire's West Riding notice that 1901's fishing is poor, and the reason soon comes to light: an enormous otter has been beating fishermen to their catch. The text catalogues attempts by a series of local residents to capture the predator, efforts that prove vain. By the following spring the otter is still free, and the admiring songmaker ends by comparing the animal to the Afrikaans hero of the Boer War: "But I think we might as well have tried to catch De Wet / As catch the Wharfedale Otter." Many local sporting songs similarly praise the skills of individual animals. One such song, by a blind fiddler named Thomas Mercer (or "Massey"—he traveled the East Riding's district of Holderness in the middle of the last century singing his own compositions at fairs and pubs in return for money and drink) is called "Nancy," in celebration of a Holderness-bred-and-trained racehorse that won the nationally renowned Chester Cup in 1851.[14] The mare Nancy represents to this songmaker the quintessence of his district's finest qualities, while to the author of "The Cliffs of Oad [Old] Whitby" it is the topography and historical monuments of the old fishing town and surrounding rural landscape that encapsulate the ideal of "our district."[15]

Yet another song that conforms to the match conception but that concentrates almost solely on people is the "Song of Upper Wharfedale," which begins:

> Though Langstrothdale chase cannot boast of being long,
> It's often been put into rhyme and song;
> But I'll not sing of the Dale itself,
> But about the good folks who in it do dwell.[16]

Its stanzas proceed to catalogue the salient hamlets and homesteads of the chase from west to east, concentrating its descriptive and panegyrical resources on the residents, each of whom is celebrated for one or two sterling qualities that mark his or her valued local persona, whether that quality be farming, singing, or even the keeping of a photograph collection.

All the above songs displaying the match model of relationships among the components of its depicted environment were from sparsely populated agricultural districts of the three ridings of Yorkshire. The one possible exception is "The Cliffs of Oad Whitby"; but even today Whitby has very much the tone of a fishing village, and in 1851 (which is closer in date to the song's composition) the town, although it had a fairly large population of just over ten thousand, was part of a district where primary-production economy, chiefly fishing and farming, was entirely dominant.[17] The final song in our sample that exhibits the match conception is indisputably urban, however: "Sheffield Is a Wonderful Town, O!"[18] But this appears to have been a professional stage number, and was disseminated internationally through publication in the *Universal Songster*.[19] No doubt Sheffield's worldwide reputation for cutlery manufacturing contributed to the song's wider interest; but I include it in the sample because it does contain highly concrete and specific references, indicating local composition, local popularity with residents of Sheffield themselves, and local perceptions of place.

The chief characteristics of the match model are that even though distinct boundaries of the empirical or the perceptual kind may be present in the song's world (as in the difference between the landed squire who acts as patron of the hunt and the ordinary hunt members who may be simple tradesmen), such boundaries do not "make a difference" to the song's conception; separabilia, whether animate or inanimate, human or animal, are coequal in value orientation and common purpose, so that consensus and wholism obtain. One assumes that the overt social function of such songs when performed in their native local contexts was one of reinforcement and affirmation.

But there are also many local songs that depict conflict within a rural setting rather than the pure consensus portrayed by the match songs. In these songs of conflict, boundaries become important as signifiers, and it is not sufficient for the active components of the song-universe to simply coexist or participate; instead, they have to interact in order to resolve a certain divergence of interests between them. Consequently, boundaries have to be negotiated, and the model of relationships that obtains is more complex than match. An example of probably the most minimal conflict and negotiation appearing in our sample is an untitled song on the sale of a cow. Most probably from the Nidderdale region of rural north Yorkshire, "Sid Metcalfe had a cow . . ." treats in five short stanzas the bargaining between seller and buyer, who quickly agree on a price for the cow but cannot agree on the amount of "luck money," which is a small portion of the purchase price returned from seller to buyer and a thoroughly traditional custom in rural cattle sales. The buyer, James Richardson, wants a pound in luck money; but the seller refuses to give more than half-a-crown, which is finally accepted and the sale completed:

> So the bargain was sealed, James set off to lead,
> With his half crown, up town, and into his field.
> With his mind well eased, and looking very pleased
> And making sure with the halter, the cow was well seized.[20]

We can designate such a model of boundary negotiation *negative feedback*; the system is a self-regulating one, able to draw upon its own internal resources to achieve equilibrium and unity among its active components whenever those components conflict.

A very common type of local song that follows the negative feedback model is the satirical song, a local type that has been well studied in North America but very little in Great Britain.[21] Songs of consensus that follow the match model talk only of what is culturally valued; satirical songs on the negative feedback model, however, highlight the differences from cultural norms that people display, those slight deviations that make for individualism and even eccentricity. But by appealing to qualities of consensus like good humor, or common residence in the same district—some normalizing property from the existing environment of the actors—the song will ultimately resolve the conflict deviations bring about. Occasionally, especially when the song is a narrative one, the deviations may be resolved in the text's story; the deviant suffers for his behavior, learns his lesson, and is reintegrated into the *communitas*.

Satirical songs, therefore, can cover a fairly large assortment of deviations as well as corrective mechanisms—ranging from a gentle joshing, so good-humored that the tone of the song provides the resolution, to fairly biting criticism of behaviors that require some active adjustment on the part of the offender. In our sample of Yorkshire songs, however, this latter sort is rare; far more common is the gentle, friendly joshing. For instance, "Li'l Jackie Beresford, the Lad from the Dales" takes as its subject a well-known local "character" from Wharfedale in the pastoral farming northwest Dales; it plays variations on the theme of Jackie Beresford as a true-to-life (though punning) "Jack of all trades." His various occupations, from driving a school bus to digging sewers, are made fun of in catalogue form. But the subject's normative status, which his adherence to fundamental cultural values supports, and his kinship ties to the locality, which go back several generations, provide the negotiation of boundaries that center him squarely within a system-in-equilibrium. To this end a closing stanza brings in the approved stability and continuity that Jackie Beresford's domestic-cum-marital identity provides:

> His charming wife Margaret when the weather was fine
> Went to fish in the Wharfe with a rope and some twine
> But what did she catch at the end of the line?
> Li'l Jackie Beresford, the lad from the dales.[22]

Similar is another good-humored joshing of the horsemanship displayed by members of the North Riding's Glaisdale Harriers in a song that catalogues the falls taken by hunt members during a chase. There seems to have been little in the hunt itself to celebrate on this particular occasion, since "the fox was fast and the hounds were slow." The songmaker thus took as his topic the humorous events of the day to tell of Jim's falling from his horse into the river, which elicited an "Oh heck!" from the victim, and of the District Nurse Kate's tumble onto a portion of her anatomy that the songmaker "dare not state." But these incidents and their potentially embarrassing effects are canceled out by the unifying jollity of the hunt itself, with the beer, the horn, the shouts of "tally-ho!" and the general camaraderie of shared embarrassments.[23]

Also from the rural North Riding is "The Mangy Fox," which tells of a young man's day-long tramp from house to house and village to village trying unsuccessfully to sell a fox that becomes an increasingly rank and uncomfortable bit of baggage as the day wears on. In a benign variation of the "biter bit" motif, the young man receives his "just deserts" and is redirected back to normalcy:

THE MANGY FOX[24]

Come all you sportsmen far and near and listen to my song,
The words are few, the verses short, it will not take me long;
'Tis about a lad, they called him Joss, at Esk valley he did dwell,
One day he set off down the road, a mangy fox to sell.

Chorus: To me ri-chol ur-ol-laddie, to me tu-rol-tally-ho,
To me ri-chol ur-ol-laddie, to me tu-rol-tally-ho.

Now Jossie unto Aisleby, he quickly did repair,
And as he passed along the road, how folks did look and stare.
He tripped about from house to house and gave syke [such]
fearful knocks,
But they only looked and laughed at him, for none would buy
his fox.

At Woodlands Hall it chanced that day, the Cleveland hounds
did meet
And Joss said as they passed him by they were a goodly sight;
A happy thought flashed o'er his brain, said he: "I'll bet my
socks
If I unto Squire Wharton gan [go] he's sure to buy my fox."

And unto Squire Wharton then poor Joss he quickly flew,
He politely said: "Good morning, sir, can I sell this fox to you?"
"In Cleveland's woods," the Squire said, "there's been foxes
up to now,
I think, my lad, a fool I'd be to buy a fox from thou."

Now next at Sleights at Station Hotel poor Jossie did appear,
And in he went so briskly and he says: "I'll take a beer,"
He viewed the company round and round for he was almost on
the rocks,
"Is there anybody here," says he, "who'd like to buy a fox?"

They all did slowly shake their heads, they were not inclined to
   buy,
But one of them stood poor Joss a gill, he looked so fearful dry;
One of them said to him: "Young man, you'd better take him
   yam [home],
Or else be shifting out of this, he stinks so fearful ram."

Now next at Goathland to John Hills poor Joss he made his
   way
Determined he would sell that fox before the close of day;
But Johnny unto Jossie said: "We've plenty of varmint here,
And if tha wants ten bob for him he's sadly o'er dear."

Now next to Beckhole Joss he went when he chanced all for
   to spy
A chap called Husband mending roads or reckoning to try,
Says he: "With carrying this damned fox my back is full of
   pains,
A sixpence I will give to thou if thou knock out his brains."

No sooner said than it was done, and Reynard he lay dead;
Joss stopped to take one lingering look at him and away from
   t'spot he fled;
Kind friends when next you meet with Joss, stand him another
   gill.
For the memories of that awful day they haunt his conscience
   still.

From the same district is "The Lord Nelson Inn," a local song
dating from 1801.[25] It pokes subtle fun at a deceased cobbler-inn-
keeper, whose wife is constrained to take over the task of host when
her husband dies. Unfortunately, she is accused of cheating custo-
mers in some unspecified manner; found innocent of the charge by
the local J.P., however, she refurbishes the inn and oversees a local
celebration raising a new pub sign, an effigy of Lord Nelson, the
then-current English culture hero and protector against a possible
French invasion. The song ends defying the French to approach
England's shore now that Nelson's image hangs protectively, exhort-
ing all listeners to

Now fill all your glasses let each honest soul
Drink success to old Peggy's Hotel at Beck Hole,
In a chorus we'll join till we make the woods ring,
With health to brave Nelson and God Save the King.

Three sporting ballads, in which the central actors are once again animals, also exhibit a negative feedback model. In the North Riding song, "Blue-Cap," the squire of Methills Hall vows to pit his dog singly against a local hare that no other dogs have been able to run to ground.[26] Despite the mockery and counter-bets of his neighbors the chase is begun, Blue-Cap finally prevails after a spirited run, and Squire Hewitt wins his wager. Opposing allegiances are then dissolved, as everyone retires to the hall for punch and roast beef and to relive the race in talk. A toast to the squire and to Blue-Cap is drunk by all. A thematic replica of "Blue-Cap" is the East Riding song "Camerton Races," though here the differences among the actors are more intense, for the opposition lays stones on the track in order to unseat the local favorite's rider, Young Wright.[27] The jockey's skill prevails, however, and the local champion wins, at which point all enmity and ill-spirit is forgotten:

There's health to the Umpires for what they have done;
They all must agree that brave Dutchy has won;
Each party resorted to Camerton Hall,
And a welcome was given to all that did call.

Similar is the song in praise of a North Riding racehorse from the village of Wigginsthorpe, "Otho," who beats a worthy adversary, Doctor Syntax, at Richmond and, according to the songmaker, is likely to do so again whenever they meet in future.[28] "Here's fair play in racing and Garforth forever" ends the song.

Two further songs are associated with areas more urban than the examples we have seen so far. One, "Blossom," tells of a match race between two greyhounds, run toward the end of the last century.[29] The district from which this song comes was at the fringe of the urban manufacturing region just west of Huddersfield in the Industrial West Riding. The other song, "Wibsey Fair," is from a more fully industrialized region, Hunslet (now a part of Leeds), and dates from the early nineteenth century.[30] It tells of the wide range of personnel who attend the cattle fair in this mining region. It welcomes all to the festival (which few others "in old England can . . . excel"), even the inevitable "sharpers," who are kept in line by the police. Since the prime purpose of the fair is to sell cattle, there is a strong rural element in the world depicted, even though the setting was highly industrial.

Two other songs on the negative feedback model are both set in the most urban of Yorkshire milieux; they date from the last century, were printed on broadsides, and—like "Wibsey Fair"—take as their topics special holidays. The first, from 1853, is titled "A New

Song on the Opening of St. George's Hall, Bradford, Yorkshire," and is set in one of the West Riding's three largest cities.[31] It begins as a typical celebration of a festive occasion, but quickly devolves into an ironic catalogue of what one should expect on the day in question: "Sporting Ladies" from some of the county's major cities and towns—York, Leeds, Halifax, and Huddersfield—will make young men regret they ever came to the event; working men of few means will ruin themselves paying their sweethearts' way to the spectacle; all laborers and tradesmen will strike and refuse to work on this day; and the lasses should be careful that they "do not fall" on the way home, or they'll rue the day they went to Bradford's celebration, presumably because they'll later be giving birth to fatherless children.

The second broadside, with remarkably similar content, is on a similar topic, the opening of a new town hall in 1858. This time, however, the city was Leeds and the occasion of more note because Queen Victoria herself was to preside over the ceremony. "A New Song on the QUEEN'S VISIT to LEEDS" visualizes the vast crowds that will come from most of the West Riding's major manufacturing towns and cities and urges local merchants to decorate their premises as grandly as possible.[32] As in "Wibsey Fair," however, conflict arises in this joyous setting when the pickpockets go to work among the festive crowds; but communal celebration holds sway, and once again the young lasses are urged to hold their petticoats fast or risk pregnancy—evidently a conventional ending.

All other examples of the negative feedback model come from country districts. Two "bothy" songs from the agricultural North Riding, "The Country Lad" and "The Old Yow," tell of farmworkers' experiences on the job.[33] But the experiences are fraught with the pitfalls of such an occupation—being overworked by the farmer, being fed farm-baked bread and cakes that "rattle in your guts like an old tin can," and being made the victim of pranks by more seasoned workmates. These do not have the bitter divisiveness that characterizes many Scottish farmworkers' song, however, and are more in keeping with the idea of nonsense songs that treat the ludicrous affectionately, or with the friendly joshing that characterized examples already given. The narrator of "The Country Lad," for instance, ends by implying that he'll have to adjust his ways to those of the farmer and thus resolve the conflict, since the alternatives are even more unpalatable:

Now I'll never have no fun when me daily work is done,
For me maister thinks that I've never done enough;

I would run away to sea and a sailor lad I'd be,
But I can never stand t'water when it's rough.

A similar kind of nonsense song pits a farmer against a recalcitrant
plough horse; he finally feeds the beast treacle in a spoon as a cure
for what seems to be a fatal illness.[34] The song has a none-too-clear
resolution, as is the case with many local songs, since they rely on
their target audience's intimate knowledge of the topic, a knowledge gained not only through firsthand experience but also through
gossip, yarns, and whatnot. But one assumes the unusual cure
worked.

Another East Riding song by the blind fiddler Thomas Mercer
is "Donkey Race," a most humorous ditty telling of a donkey race
that took place in a park near the village of Sproatley.[35] Some of
the entrants and their failings as racers are catalogued; the eventual
winner (to whom the songmaker assigns a pseudonym from a more
famous forebear, "Creeping Jane") is apparently just as flawed as
the losers, but victorious nonetheless.[36] We are fortunate in possessing an eyewitness account of the songmaker's performance of
"Donkey Race" in a natural setting, wherein the song's negative
feedback conception is matched with the release into communal
laughter its performance effected among the antic company at the
inn:

> Lusty acclamations and a drink from every man's jug re-
> warded the fiddler, and a vigourous cry was set up for "The
> Donkey Races," another of his songs, which, as Lazy Mat told
> me, "had been printed and sold by hundreds." The blind man,
> nothing loth, rattled off a lively prelude, and sang his song with
> telling effect. The race was supposed to be run by donkeys from
> all the towns and villages of the neighbourhood—from Patring-
> ton, Hedon, Hull, Driffield, Beverley, and others—each pos-
> sessed of a certain local peculiarity, the mention of which threw
> the company into ecstacies of merriment. And when the "Don-
> key from York" was introduced, with his "sire Gravelcart" and
> his "dam Work," two of the guests flumped from their chairs
> to laugh more at ease on the floor.[37]

From the West Riding Dales comes one of the most popular of
Yorkshire local songs, "The Yorkshire Horse-Dealers."[38] Its county-
wide popularity is probably a consequence of the stereotyped Yorkshire character traits its protagonists display—knowledge of horses,
shrewdness, and pertinacity, among others.[39] It tells of two farmers

trying to best each other in a horse trade. After the deal (a straight swap) has been made, one farmer claims victory in the transaction, for his horse is dead. The other tops this, however, by revealing that not only is his own horse also dead but already flayed; thus while neither gets a live horse, one farmer does get the skin and hooves still on the deceased but unflayed horse. The relationship thus returns to equilibrium; the two are old trading rivals and will surely match wits again.

The next three songs depict boundaries that are more sharply delineated, more divisive of highly variant interests, and thus more difficult to negotiate in bringing about consensus. For example, yet another sporting ballad, "Pride of the Pack," tells of a race run in Wensleydale between a local hunt-dog, Butcher, and Spanker from Teesdale on the Yorkshire/Durham border.[40] The home favorite is victorious, and the unsuccessful visitors good-naturedly dismissed:

> Hurrah! jolly fellows, to Teesdale go back,
> You've nought like the pride of the Wensleydale pack.

Differences in culture region and allegiances remain, but the expression "jolly fellows" tempers these differences somewhat, and so some kind of negotiated relationship remains. Much more biting and divisive, however, is "Beautiful Swaledale," which approaches the viciousness, if not the cleverness, of the Canadian lumberman bard, Larry Gorman, in his earlier years.[41] The song locates its topic in two Dales hamlets, Low Row and Feetham, and then proceeds with allusions to unusually deviant behaviors of unspecified local folk, accusing them of avarice, greed, and laziness. Perhaps the repetitive refrain may have performed the negotiating function, resolving the extreme differences under the unifying principle of common residence in

> Beautiful Swaledale, the land of rest,
> Beautiful Swaledale, I love thee the best.
> The land, it is set in a cultivate style.
> The extent of Swaledale is twenty long mile.

But this may be irony, in which case resolution is certainly not achieved and the conceptual structure of relationships in the song's world view would not be that of negative feedback. However, the fact that irony is almost nonexistent in folksong, whether traditional or local, and the prosaic literalness of the closing line in the refrain suggest that there is resolution intended. Another West

Riding Dales song, "Ruscoe," tells of a young swell's clumsy attempt to woo a young lady in an adjoining dale.[42] But the locals play a prank on him, and he returns home to Cravendale shamefaced, astride a horse sporting an artificial tail, since the local tricksters have cut off the real one. He thus "soon left behind him the famed Nidderdale."

We would require greater knowledge of native perceptions to know whether these three songs are grounded in a negative feedback conception with, presumably, a correspondingly regulatory function in their effectiveness. Certainly, the return to equilibrium among actors who disagree is not clearly depicted in the texts, although the relatively muted hostility displayed and the songs' rhetoric and tone would suggest that the correcting of deviations and minimizing of adversary relationships were chiefly intended. Whatever the case, these three come close to the third model of relationships across boundaries, a model I will call *positive feedback*. In this type of relationship, the differences that boundaries mark between active components are amplified rather than lessened, and one may suppose that the song's persuasive purpose was to heighten those differential identities, contribute to widening the gap, and reify the boundaries as literal signs of conflict.

Just as almost all the songs of the negative feedback conception come from rural environments, so the majority of songs about conflict conceived on the positive feedback model treat of urban milieux. The first three examples are rural folks' perceptions of urban environments. "The Wensleydale Lad," along with "Yorkshire Horse-Dealers" one of the most widely known of Yorkshire local songs, tells of a North Riding youth's visit to the big city to enjoy Leeds Fair.[43] In fact, however, he never does get around to fulfilling the ostensible purpose of his trip; instead, he visits a factory, which fills him with wonder at its quantity of machinery. He is especially awed that a single engine can run so many wheels, belts, and looms, and anthropomorphizes the engine (or perhaps supernaturalizes it) by exclaiming that "Owd Harry's a gay strong chap." He then attends an Anglican service at Leeds Old Church and, a Methodist or Wesleyan presumably, is quite confused by the strange behaviors—men without hats, priests dressed in outlandish outfits and carrying mysterious implements, a sermon that lauds the rich and damns the poor, a prayer to the king, a cacophony that purports to be hymn singing (he himself joins in with a rendition of "Darby and Joan"). He finally leaves in confusion, though in quite amiable temper, and departs the city for his country home. This is the most muted positive feedback relationship in our sample. Another visitor to Leeds (though here from a semi-industrial rather than completely agricultural milieu) appears in "Tewsdi at th' Afternoon," and is at greater odds with his environmental Others.[44] This narrator journeys one weekday to the big city, only to be quite mystified by the topsy-turvy world of crowds and shops. She (or he) parades the market until "ah wor nearly sick," subsequently visiting a pub that is little different from the shops and streets. The song's chief targets for attack are the women who, decked up in their best finery, crowd the stores and taverns "Wal ther' 'usbands they wor workin' 'ard," but who as soon as five o'clock comes hurry home, change clothes, get tea ready, and swear to their husbands who come in from work at six o'clock that "bi damned th'd nivver been ey-at" (never been out). Their haste is fortunate, for positive feedback is the dominant structure of relationships in this urban society:

> An' if yar Johnnie should beeat mi whom [beat me home]
> Well, oss [I shall] feel 'is heavy shooin [shoes]
> Cos 'e'd clatter them abey-at [about] mi ribs,
> This Tewsdi at th' afternooin.

The third example of a rural view of the urban personality is "The Sportsman of Leeds" by W. Foster of Langstrothdale, also the poet of the match songs, "The Song of Upper Wharfedale" and "The Wharfedale Otter."[45] In contrast to those two songs that deal with Mr. Foster's own rural district, however, "The Sportsman of Leeds" is a bitter attack against a city man who, unable to bag a rabbit in the normal way because of his poor marksmanship, finally cages one in a box and obliterates it at point-blank range with a shotgun.

Almost all our other examples of positive feedback relationships in local Yorkshire songs are apparently urban visions of urban settings. Almost all date from the nineteenth century. For instance, another Leeds broadside, "Meeting of the Leeds Town Clocks," dating from about 1860, is an extended conceit presented within the frame story of a drunken reverie.[46] It is evidently a satire on the City Council's inability to agree on the style of clock that should grace the facade of the new Town Hall—the same hall opened not too long before by Queen Victoria. Each clock (they are all well-known and already-established features of the city's landscape) debates its own merits as deserving of the new setting in the Town Hall's tower. The arguments heat up until bedlam reigns, and all the clocks begin striking together in a frenzy of competition—at which point the narrator is roused by a bobby's truncheon and hauled before the magistrate. This technique of extended metaphor, which we have not met with so far, appears several times in our local song sample, but always, as we shall shortly see, in conjunction with our fourth and final model of relationships.

The topic of a broadside on the "Leeds Election" is a quite natural context for the divisiveness that the positive feedback conceptualization entails.[47] The electorate is urged to unseat the Tory majority in Parliament and to vote for the local Liberal candidate, Barran. The following arguments are offered:

> The Tories they look to the rich, not the poor, sir;
> They don't care if Poverty knocks on your door, sir,
> You can go to the Workhouse by the dozen or score, sir,
> So long as they're all right themselves.
> They go to St. Steven's laughing and grinning,
> But the work that they do could be done by old women,
> So with Taxes and Rates we can scarce have a shilling,
> Then so much for the Tories, I say.

The song ends with a proposal for the Tory candidate, William Jackson: that when he has lost the election he repair to the East and "fight for the treacherour [sic] Turk."

Three further songs are set squarely in the context of factory work. "The Factory Bell" draws an explicit antithesis between rural and urban conditions as it posits match and positive feedback contrasts between the two:

> Oh happy man, O happy thou
> While toiling gaily at thy spade and plough,
> While thou amidst thy pleasures roll,
> All at thy labour uncontroll'd
> While at the mill in pressing crowds
> where high built chimneys puff black clouds
> And all around the slaves do dwell,
> Who are called to labour by a Bell.[48]

The boundaries within this urban milieu that most occupy the song's attention are those which unalterably divide the working-class foreman from the working-class operatives and, indeed, operatives from each other. In the case of the first, "Some wheedling foreman every hour / Makes big himself with stolen power," while in the second, "You're all beset by unknown spies / For envy long sits forging lies." Another song, "Poverty Knock," reputedly local to the Heavy Woolen District, a conurbation of small factory towns and villages in the central West Riding, exhibits a similar vision of the adversary relationships between supervisors and workers as well as between man and industrial apparatus.[49] The supervisors skimp on piecework remuneration, dock pay for the slightest tardiness in reporting for work, and show more interest in courting the young female workers than in keeping the weavers' looms tuned so that they may boost their production and thus their pay. Anthropomorphized machinery speak "Poverty, poverty knock," and autonomously shoot shuttles from their insides to knock an operative senseless and bleeding on the floor, while no one, not even a fellow worker, heeds the unfortunate's plight, since to do so would be to lessen one's own output and thus one's wage. A third "factory" song, "Terrible Accident and Loss of Life at Bradford, Dec. 28, 1882," dwells on the victimization of people not by other people, but by the technological artifacts of industry.[50] Fifty-four residents of Bradford were killed in this actual disaster. In reality, human greed and carelessness did indeed play a large part in the collapse of the mill chimney and the resulting deaths; but either the songmaker's ignorance of these facts, or his sensibility about the human grief caused by the tragedy, led him to focus on the chimney as the main actor in unbridgeable opposition with its victims: "The chimney falling was inflicting / The wounds that causes death."[51]

Two songs from the Spen Valley area of the textile district deal with management/labor strife, and date from the time of the Luddite disturbances in the early years of the nineteenth century, when the advent of machines threatened to make many workers and their skills redundant. An untitled song beginning "You Heroes of England . . ." draws its sharply delineated boundaries between the interests of the manufacturers and their lackey militiamen on the one hand and the workers whose livelihoods are threatened on the other.[52] Another Luddite piece, "The Cropper's Song," is a hortatory item proclaiming war between members of this particular craft and the militiamen.[53] This is a quite inflammatory set of verses and understandably so, since the Luddites were best known for their active role in machine breaking. As in so many other industrial songs, man-made objects are active personnel in the drama portrayed: the croppers' hatchets, pikes, and guns against the (unstated) bayonets of the "specials," and the rioters' sledgehammers against the Industrial Revolution's offspring, shear-frames. Again, artifacts are anthropomorphized; thus the sledgehammer is "Great Enoch."[54]

Three further songs from urban milieux exhibit positive feedback relationships between official representatives of the law and individuals who have broken that law. The first treats of an event in Leeds that took place in 1864–65. The cook of a local J.P. had seen fit to give away fat drippings from the kitchen, thinking the control of such detritus was her prerogative. Her opinion was not shared by her employer, however, who charged her with theft. She was tried, found guilty, and sentenced to a month in Leeds's Armley jail. "Since her committal to prison the indignation of many of the working classes, and especially of their wives and daughters, had been very plainly manifested in various ways, and this feeling had been stimulated by the publication from time to time of various doggerel rhymes and occasional anonymous placards."[55] Indeed, there was a small riot outside the prison the day of her release, and five protesters were arrested and charged, one going to jail for ten days himself. A song on the event, stressing the antithetical interests between employed and employing classes and unashamedly depicting the trial magistrates as concerned more with class solidarity than with justice, may serve as illustration of the positive feedback conception:

OH DON'T I LOVE MY DRIPPING![56]

Tune: "The Ratcatcher's Daughter"

In Leeds there lived not long ago,
A Justice of the Peace;
He was a doctor by his trade,
And wasn't he fond of grease!
He had a Cook—a jolly Cook,
Eliza was her name;
She took bad fat from off his meat,
And rendered down the same.

Chorus.—Dripping oh! dripping ho!
        Oh don't I love my dripping.

Says Eliza: "This 'ere fat's my own—
"A cookey's per-qui-site";
For she had never understood
That right must bow to might.
So when this Justice of the Peace
Who was Eliza's master,
Heard that she had took his grease,
There came a sad disaster.

Chorus.

Says he to Cook: "I've got you now,
"And don't begin your fibbing;

"You've took my fat from off my meat
"And boiled it down for dripping.
"As a Magistrate I know the law (?),
"I'll call in the police,
"And send you into durance vile
"For taking off my grease."

Chorus.

Poor Cookey she was dragged away
Into a private court,
But afore she could say "Jack Robinson"
She was completely floor'd.
Two brother beaks sat on the bench,
Trying to look quite wise;
Said they, "How dare you steal this fat?"
And then cast up their eyes.

Chorus.

"We must protect our brother's rights—
"He's a Justice of the Peace!
"And we know he's werry fond of stuff
"That's rendered down to grease;
"So for a month in Armley Gaol
"You will be kept quite tight,
"And dripping never take again
"As your own per-qui-site."

Chorus.

MORAL

Now all you cooks and servant gals
Wot's very fond of "tipping,"
Don't take your master's scraps of fat
And boil 'em down for dripping;
For if you do, bear this in mind,
The Magistrates won't fail
To try you in a private court,
And send you off to gaol.

Chorus.

The other two songs dealing with legal institutions both take jails as their topics. "Wakefield Jail" catalogues the indignities and hardships its prisoners are subjected to, paying particular complaint —as in "The Factory Bell"—to the role of clock-time in determining the performance of human activities.[57] The usual prisoners' complaints against forced labor, pitiful food, and behavior of the guards sustain most of the verses. "Beverley Gaol" is set in a semiurban milieu, Beverley being an ancient abbey and market town as well as the East Riding's county seat.[58] The town itself was and is in a predominantly agricultural region and has never had the high degree of industrialization that characterizes the central West Riding region. Like "The Wensleydale Lad," "Tewsdi at th' Afternoon," and "The Sportsman of Leeds," however, "Beverley Gaol" seems to be primarily an agricultural laborer's view of a "big city" phenomenon, for, the collector writes, it "is an old song which I learnt by hearing it sung by my grandfather's ploughmen at Swine, some half century ago. I suspect there are various recordings of it, that it had originally been composed by some rustic bard and added to and altered as it passed down from one generation to another, or from one village to another, orally. . . ." Features similar to those in "Wakefield Jail" alienate the narrator of this song, and he will forthwith remove himself from the environment of Beverley forever once he's served his sentence: "But if ivver Ah gets oot ageean, an' can bud raise a frind, / Oh! the divvel tak' toll-shop at Bevlah toon end." The toll booth is thus one prominent sign of extreme contrast between the town and the countryside just beyond its borders.

One unusual example of a positive feedback conception appears in a modern song collected in contemporary Bradford from Irish Catholic working-class men. Titled "Oh! My Bradford in the Sun!," it is a vicious satire on the large population of West Indian Negro immigrants to that city, portraying them with the usual racial stereotypes (pimping, living twenty to a room, eating animal food, themselves slum-landlording, and, in particular, living off the fat of the British welfare state and getting rich on it to boot).[59] Taking its subject's point of view, the song ends: "Bless white people, one and all, we think Bradford very nice place, / But no good no more for the white man's race."

Two final examples of songs modeled on positive feedback relationships differ from all other examples above in that they are set in rural environments. Both deal with poaching and are told from the poacher's point of view. "The Sledmere Poachers," from the East Riding, is a defiant avowal to continue the night-game despite the danger of the keeper's gun, which on one expedition badly wounds the poacher's dog.[60] Nevertheless,

... if we meet a keeper bold his body we will bray;
For we are all bright Sledmere lads, our names we will not tell,
But if we meet a keeper bold his head we'll make to swell.

Finally, a song in which the boundaries between actors are the most
extreme of all is "Bill Brown," an eighteenth-century ballad from
a rural portion of the southern tip of the county, now closely aligned
with industrial Sheffield. One of the poachers is killed by a keeper,
and the song vows vengeance in far more resolute and inflammatory
terms than does "The Sledmere Poachers":

With sword and gun now we will run,
Though the law it doth maintain them,
Yet poor Brown's blood lost in the wood
For vengeance cries amain then.[61]

So far in this discussion of local Yorkshire songs I have identified three ways of envisaging relationships between the active components in the song drama, whether the components be people,
animals, landscapes, or cultural artifacts: the match model depicts
an ordered consensus among components conceived in their tolerably real-life guise; the negative feedback model depicts conflict of
interests, but conflict that can be resolved within the community's
existing frames of reference consisting of real-life perceptions and
habits; and the positive feedback model portrays sharp conflict that,
in contrast with negative feedback, cannot be resolved with existing
perceptions and means—indeed, the indication is that the conflict
will only grow greater and the gulf between interactants widen, with
potentially explosive results. We also saw that each of these models
correlates very strongly with a certain type of environment; thus if
we construct a matrix with *rural* and *urban* environments on one
axis, *consensus* and *conflict* relationships on the other, we have four
possible cells, three of which we have already filled in our discussion.
Models of *consensus* in a *rural* environment are overwhelmingly of
the match type, while conceptions of *conflict* in *rural* settings are of
the negative feedback sort. *Conflict* in an *urban* milieu, on the other
hand, exhibits positive feedback relationships.

Three cells of our four-cell matrix are filled, therefore. The
final cell must be filled with the way *consensus* within an *urban*
environment is modeled. The term I shall give to this model is
transcendence, the urban counterpart of the rural match. In the
transcendence model, boundaries are not negotiated by calling upon

definitions of the situation that inhere in its existing and real-life identity structure, but by employing definitions that come from an entirely different system or frame of reference. The literary methods of achieving this transcendence through the medium of the text are the common ones of metaphor, allegory, hyperbole, and conceit.[62]

We have encountered the use of tropes like these in songs already discussed—for instance, in "The Factory Bell's" brief hope for a return to the Golden Age, "When man to man shall kindly say / We all forget we all forgive," the "Holme Moss Hunt's" reference to Robin Hood and Little John, and the "Lord Nelson Inn's" visualizing of the pub sign as an embodiment of the naval hero himself and thus as protector of the hamlet's and of all England's shores. But in all cases these are the briefest of vignettes, not encoders of meaning informing the song as a whole; they are to the transcendence group what euphemistic songs with occasional metaphor were to the metaphorical model in chapter 2. Only one song so far has been fully informed by a metaphorical technique, "Meeting of the Leeds Town Clocks," a merry piece depicting a mild case of conflict in its positive feedback conception. The six other songs in our sample that are coded figuratively are all from urban settings and all envisage consensus.

The simplest kind of transcendence is displayed in an amusing piece of fantasy titled "ON Leeds Becoming A SEA-PORT TOWN," issued on a broadside by Richard Barr, a Leeds printer in business during the middle of the nineteenth century.[63] Apparently, its purpose was to satirize the rage for constant change and improvement, which other commentators of the times saw as so unfortunately characteristic of the new Industrial Man.[64] The conception of Self/ Other relationships espoused in this text's world, however, is one of consensus, where all is joy and harmony and similarity among parts; in other words, the manifest function of the song notwithstanding, in order to depict such consensus in an urban setting, to make it acceptable to belief so that the intended message could be effective, the songmaker had to draw upon a frame of reference that could not be found within the existing definitions of the city itself. He conjures up a fantasy in which Leeds has been transformed into a seaport town; as the first ship docks the city erupts in merriment, all social classes freely intermingling:

> Then we shall meet with touts and prigs, sirs,
> Aldermen too in their gowns & wigs sirs,
> The heads of the town with all their forces,
> And the _____ new Mayor they'll draw with Horses.

There'll be free boatrides for all, and the shipping trade will bring in a cornucopia of exotic products not presently enjoyed. The narrator ends hurriedly; he must be off, for he does believe there's a ship coming right now. The satire and fancy stem, of course, from the fact that despite its canals Leeds is just about the most landlocked city imaginable.

Another song of a transcendence depiction was intimately associated with an actual celebration, complete with a pageant, that took place in 1809 to honor George III's Jubilee. The setting was the small mining town of Rothwell, east of Leeds, and its close neighbor, Lofthouse; the band was from yet another mining town, Castleford, a bit further east, past Wakefield. "They formed a procession, and several well-known people were dressed in fantastic costume. Edward Walton, maltster, of Rothwell, impersonated the king, and Nancy Tetley the queen. Men were yoked to a conveyance loaded with coal, and driven by 'Captain' Garrett, governor of the gaol."[65] A song describing the occasion was composed and printed:

A NEW SONG IN PRAISE OF THE REJOICINGS AT ROTHWELL

To the Tune of "Retford March."

Of all the places hereabouts, if I the truth must tell,
This loyal town of Rothwell now must bear the bell,
In honour of his majesty they roasted a fat beast,
And gave away most freely that all should have a taste.

    Chorus.
  Stand firm, be free, and you shall see,
  The glory of this town,
  That Rothwell name shall bear the fame
  All the country round.

There are three loyal Miners hereabouts doth live,
In honour of his majesty great gift they did give,
And now for this loyalty it causes us to sing,
They did it in respect and honour for our king.—Chorus.

A loyal maltster in this town behaved very well,
In acting of his majesty none could him excel;
And in the afternoon we appeared in Lofthouse town,
So now they plainly see we are bucks of high renown.—Chorus.

Our king he was attended by a jovial crew,
And to these loyal subjects great praises are due;

By Castleford's assistance they did most sweetly play,
And marched round the town at night, so concluded the day.
  —Chorus.

The coals that made the fire for to roast this ox
Was drawn by sixteen stallions, and they were jovial bucks,
A gentleman he drove them with a stick and a bladder,
And took great delight in keeping them together.—Chorus.

Near unto the churchyard a public-house is there,
At which he stopped his team and watered them with beer,
There was a great report we should be short of ale,
But if there had been more our barrels would not fail.—Chorus.

A guinea there was given by a noble gentleman
For a posset and a dance, disprove it if you can;
On Tuesday afternoon the women merry were
In drinking of this posset and plenty of good cheer.—Chorus.

So here's a health unto his majesty, likewise to Mr. Pitt,
Likewise to Doctor Willis, we've not forgot him yet;
Here's health unto these Miners, they are men of great renown,
Likewise to all true subjects of famous Rothwell town.—Chorus.

As befitting the "ritual" occasion, the "mythic" frame of reference
of Royalty and Court supply the ground for negotiating an abundance of what are in everyday life sharply delineated boundaries
into *communitas*—boundaries between the south (London and Buck-
ingham Palace) and the north; between the usual activities of upper
class, middle class, and working class (though one wonders whether
the men who were "yoked to a conveyance loaded with coal" and
driven by the middle-class "Captain" Garrett were miners); between
kings and commoners; between the serious and the comic; between
necessary and conspicuous consumption; between food and drink
paid for and the same freely given, among others. The license that
often characterizes such festive occasions is also present in the attitude taken toward women publicly drinking on Tuesday afternoon;
recall that in the song with a positive feedback conception, "Tewsdi
at th' Afternoon," women drinking in public was seen to be the
antithesis of desired norms, while on this Tuesday at Rothwell it
becomes an intimate part of the rightness of the occasion.

The use of the external system of meanings that is Royalty to
provide the transcendent frame of reference is most popular in our
sample's six songs of urban consensus. For instance, a Halifax broad-

side from 1844 celebrates the famed West Riding reformer, Richard Oastler, who for many years fought vigorously on behalf of legislation that would mitigate the harsh effects of existing Poor Laws and factory practices on the working class.[66] The song expands Oastler's popular cognomen as "King of the factory children" into an extended imagery in which his everyday actions are fittingly "regalized": he has been jailed but now freed from his "dungeon"; he will be crowned with "laurels," defend his factory "subjects," oppose the "Bastile Laws," and so on.[67] Interestingly, Oastler's original cognomen of "King" is reputed to have been assigned in derision by one of his critics, Edward Baines (editor of the *Leeds Mercury*), which is an example of the use of metaphor for antagonistic purposes. Oastler's humbler constituents, however, negated this ironic use by adopting the title for their own panegyrical ends.[68]

Another famous reformer of the Industrial West Riding, though of a quite different sort to Richard Oastler, was Titus Salt, who rose from humble beginnings to be an extremely innovative and enormously wealthy textile manufacturer. His role as reformer was manifested principally in his building a mill complex surrounded by a whole new town to house his workers. The town, not far from Bradford, was called Saltaire, and was for its era a "model town" of a civilized if somewhat austere comfort, quite superseding the cramped hovels that characterized so many living quarters in other working-class districts. There were gardens, parks, baths, a church, and so forth—but no public house. Salt was also a patron of the arts, and indeed in a small way patron of the author of a song about him that passed into oral tradition, "The Lord of Saltaire."[69] In these verses the imported frame of reference is the aristocracy rather than royalty in particular; the "Lord" of Saltaire is the "noble" architect of the "palace to labour" that will "equal the Caesars of old." The peer extends his nobility even unto his workmen, each of whom lives in his palace "In contentment, and comfort, and plenty, / Secure as a peer of the land!" This standard panegyric in honor of a patron, written in 1853, foresaw in part what was later to become a reality. Sir Titus Salt was knighted in 1869, an honor somewhat below that to which the song had earlier exalted him.

Yet another paean to textile economy is an early broadside from Halifax on the opening of "The Halifax Piece Hall" for the selling of cloth. This song draws from the royal, from the legendary, and even in a semi-inverted way from the Edenic myth for its transcendence imagery of unity. It was issued on broadside by a Halifax printer, E. Jacob:

A SONG[70]

Sung at the Opening of the Manufacturers' Hall, in Halifax,
    January 2nd., 1779

When Adam and his Consort Eve,
Lived in a Garden fair,
They dressed themselves in Green-Fig-Leaves,
For want of better wear:
But we, their Sons, are wiser grown,
Than Leaves of Figs to pull;
We clothe ourselves from Head to Foot,
With ever honour'd Wool.

    Chorus.
God save King George, and bless our Trade,
Let not our prayers be vain,
May all our Foes to Friends be turn'd
And Peace and Plenty reign.

O let us not forget the good
The worthy Bishop Blaze,
Who came from Jersey here to us,
As ancient Hist'ry says.
He taught us how to Comb our Wool,
The Source of all our Wealth,
Then let us still remember him,
While we have Life and Health.

    God save King George, &c.

Now our desires are crowned by "Hope"
We'll be no longer seen
Dispers'd around in every Street,
As heretofore we've been;
But to a Hall whose beauty vies
With Palaces of Old,
Our Handy-work shall now be brought
And straight be turned to Gold.

    God save King George, &c.

To him now let our Thanks be paid,
(At once he's good and great)
Who gave the ground whereon to build
Fair Manufacture's Seat;

O! may the Building stand as long
As shall his Fame be known,
And may our Industry be blest,
And Riches be the Crown.

  God save King George, &c.

Come ye, who oft' in Council met
To raise your future Fame,
And ye, from whom our noble Hall
Is honoured with a Name.
And ye, whose lab'ring Hands have rais'd
The Colonnade so gay,
All, All, with Joy of Heart, come share
The Glory of this Day.

  God save King George, &c.

Then let us all, with one Accord,
With open Heart agree,
The young, the old, the high, the low,
To spend this Day with Glee.
Join in the Chorus, lift your Voice,
Join with me, one and all,
Then shall ye drink in Sparkling Ale,
Success t' our noble Hall.

  God save King George, &c.

While the frames of reference imported for "The Halifax Piece Hall" may seem overly hyperbolic at times (consider the touch of alchemy-cum-classical mythology in stanza three), many of its images are still firmly grounded in a believable environment of which it speaks. It does not forget to salute both the great who donated the land and the small who carried the hods.

One final example of urban transcendence, the only one not from the Industrial West Riding, is set in York's debtor's prison and dates from about 1840.[71] In contrast with the views of urban jails we examined under the positive feedback model, those incarcerated here see themselves as escaping a divisive social environment into the safety, comfort, and communality of the debtors' retreat. The dominant borrowed image is that of the closed village and its attendant ambiance of pastorale. The inmates' meals are reminiscent of harvest home suppers, with their beef and pudding, while the warden plays the role of the benevolent squire. Their common activities are to "merrily laugh, chat, dance and sing." The decadent commodities of drink and tobacco are eschewed in favor of Edenic fruits and sweets. There may also be a touch of the Last Supper; there certainly is a hint of purification taken from the Biblical image of Christ's sojourn in the wilderness: "there forty days I lay, / Then whitewashed I went out. . . ." But as all local songs do, the text still retains pragmatic touch with reality; the jail was, after all, a debtor's prison and thus in one sense a true retreat from constant dunning in the outside world.

Were we asked to suggest "causes" for the clear patterns the analysis has so far revealed—the preponderance of match and negative feedback conceptions in rural songs, positive feedback and transcendence in urban—few of us would have difficulty offering some immediate hypotheses. For instance, it is probable that country songmakers had few models of extended poetic metaphor at hand, a technique basic to transcendence, while urban songmakers had greater acquaintance with official literary forms, like panegyric, that used such techniques. Or some of us may not be too reticent to suggest a difference in personality type between rural folk and town folk; "The inner meanings of things concerned them very little," wrote George Bourne, and told of his gardener, Bettesworth, who had served in the Crimean campaign:

> What was most strange was to hear these places, whose names to stay-at-home people like myself have come to have an epic sound, spoken of as scenes of merely trivial incidents. As it was only of what he observed himself that Bettesworth told, this could hardly have been otherwise. . . . To this harum-scarum English ploughboy, ignorant, rollicking, reckless, it was not the great events, on a large scale, that were prominent, but the queer things; the little haphazard details upon which he happened to stumble.[72]

Another contributing factor might be that since most of the urban songs came from financially motivated broadside presses, the models of positive feedback, with its sensational antagonisms, and transcendence, with its aura of literary sophistication, were more salable than the tamer conceptions favored by the amateur country poet, whose motives were primarily social ones. In addition, perhaps the rural songmaker, his identity known in the locality of his song's dissemination, could not afford to be overly hostile in telling about his own community, while the city songmaker, invariably anonymous, could. And rural songs were often performed in face-to-face contact as well, while urban songs were communicated chiefly through the medium of print.

Closely related is the matter of how knowledge-of-Other is manifested in the two types of milieu. In rural communities, with their relatively small and stable populations, knowledge-of-Other is greater than in urban systems. Consequently, in villages there would be greater tolerance for individual deviance, since the song-maker has knowledge of the Other's multifacetedness, that is, of additional qualities that compensate for particular deviances. In towns, on the other hand, where so much in the environment is outside one's primary network, knowledge of the Other is sketchy, and is thus measured against a rigid and solipsistic standard. Alfred Williams gives an example of these contrasting attitudes toward one kind of environmental Other, the weather:

> Do you know what the town folk say of dull, wet weather in winter? They say it is "rotten." . . . I do not know if any of you have ever seen "rotten" weather or no; for my part, I have not, and let me tell you this, you never hear a countryman say the weather is "rotten." If it is wet he says it is a "damp mornin'," if heavy it is "terrible dull," or it may even be "main uncid," but never "rotten"; it is not so monotonous to him.[73]

The kind of binary, yes/no categorizing that a positive feedback conception entails has a neurological basis as well. Consider what Flora Thompson has to say about the differences between her small hamlet of Lark Rise and the more complex market town of Candle-ford:

> What impressed Laura most about Candleford, on that first holiday there, was that, every day, there was something new to see or do or find out and new people to see and talk to and new places to visit, and this gave a colour and richness to life to which she was unaccustomed. At home, things went on day after day much in the same manner; the same people, all of whom she knew, did the same things at the same time from week-end to week-end.[74]

In contradistinction to rural systems, urban systems contain a great amount, rate of change, and diversity of information that each individual has to process. Rural information can be handled by exist-

ing cognitive maps (match) or by slight adjustments that still permit knowledge of the whole (negative feedback), while in urban
systems the whole can be grasped only by combining information
bits into more abstract patterns (transcendence) or by similarly re-
ducing it to positive feedback's either/or pattern of knowable
simplicity.[75]

Any or all of these factors may have contributed to the different poetic conceptions as to the nature of Self/Other relationships
in Yorkshire local songs. But they all are "causes" from the realm
of the *physics* of the two systems, whether those physics be of the
social, cultural, or physiological kind. None of them account for
the *meaning* of the different concepts, for the signifying aspect of
the poetic world view. Our principal concern is with meaning of
this sort, and we may start our search for signification by examining the possibility that the poetic representations in large part
meant literally and denotatively; that they "reflected" the reality
that rural life was indeed harmonious and exhibited little conflict,
while urban life was in reality extremely divisive.

At one level, this reflection hypothesis has much to recommend
it. The reports of the many Royal Commissions and other investi-
gative bodies that studied the factory system in both old and new
towns, as well as the domestic and social conditions that accompanied that system, portrayed some of the most appallingly brutal
and alienating circumstances imaginable, especially throughout the
first half of the nineteenth century.[76] True, much modern scholarship dealing with the social and economic history of the era has
argued with the support of quantifiable data that in fact the quality of life improved with the Industrial Revolution; but the weight
of contemporary accounts as well as of modern-day scholarship of
the "pessimistic" school, which questions the relevance of statistical
methodology as well as economic data to drawing conclusions about
the *meaning* of an industrial culture, argues strongly against the
"optimistic view," just as the local folk poetry from Yorkshire
does.[77]

Nevertheless, one might say, even if it is true that exploitative
and alienating conditions existed within industrial and urban environments in the north, was not the same thing true of the countryside after the enclosures? The "General Ludd" riots in the north
and midlands had their rural counterpart in the "Captain Swing"
riots of the agricultural south not long afterward.[78] And by all
reports life for most inhabitants of the agricultural working class
was just as bad as—in fact, often worse than—it was for the urban
working class.[79] Even social relations in villages were said, often by

natives themselves, to have been riddled with ongoing and irre-concilable conflicts.[80] Consequently, if depressed conditions and social antagonisms characterized the reality of both urban and rural life in the nineteenth century, why should the Yorkshire local songs' depictions of those two environments be so different?

Part of the answer may be that these stereotypes of a poverty-stricken and divisive country life are based overwhelmingly on data from the south of England, where enclosures that disenfranchised so many of the working class from access to land had been recently rampant; where weekly wages, the tied cottage, and piece rates had become common; where the cultural and social gulf between employer and employed had grown steadily wider after 1750. In the pre-enclosure village, in contrast, "labourers and cottagers and small farmers were neighbours. They knew each other and lived much the same kind of life. The small farmer was a farmer one day of the week and a labourer another; he married, according to Cobbett, the domestic servant of the gentry. . . . The new farmer lived in a different latitude. He married a young lady from the boarding school. He often occupied the old manor house. He was divided from the labourer by his tastes, his interests, his ambitions, his display and whole manner of life."[81] Consequently, "the rich and the poor were thus growing further and further apart, and there was nobody in the English village to interpret these two worlds to each other."[82]

In contrast to this southern experience, however, rural Yorkshire (especially the West Riding Dales from which so much of our song sample comes) approximated more closely the older system of yeoman and cottager small-holdings well into the nineteenth century. West Riding farms were not only relatively small, most under fifty acres, but were also farmed by their owners or by occupiers with firm tenancy. Similar was the case in the North Riding. Thus the farmer-employers were not materially much better off than the agricultural laborers they employed, a homogeneity less common in the south. In addition, the system of the tied cottage—the laborer occupying at nominal rent, so long as he remained on the job, a cottage belonging to his employer—was not prevalent in Yorkshire. Instead, a true "living-in" system prevailed—not so much the barrack-like "bothy" system of Scotland's northeast, but a lodging and boarding with the farmer's family in the farmhouse itself.[83] Also common, instead of the weekly wage or piece-rate system of the south, was a seasonal or annual contract, which guaranteed workers a wage and gave permanence and a sense of mutual enterprise to both farmers and workers.[84] All these practices that continued to be common in the north resulted in a familial relationship within farming communities that was characteristic of the older patriarchal peasant society.[85]

At one level, therefore, the sign quotient of the poetic world views is high; poetic conceptions "reflected" the pragmatic world views. But one of our assumptions about folk poetry is that, by definition, it also has a connotative component to it that signifies an abstract ethos of a higher logical type than the concrete and perceivable realities of the daily experienced world. In getting at this extra signification we may at the same time logically interrelate the four conceptual models to discover a coherent world view of *the* local song as a genre. Let me work up to arguing for a particular ethos by considering what a modern "optimistic" historian has to say about the Industrial Revolution and, by extension, its intimate companion, the urban environment:

> The Industrial Revolution . . . was more than an expansion of commerce, more than a series of changes in the technology of certain industries, more than an acceleration of general economic growth. It was a revolution in men's access to the means of life, in control over their ecological environment, in their capacity to escape from the tyranny and niggardliness of nature. . . . The uniqueness of the historical Industrial Revolution is that it opened the road for men to complete mastery of their physical environment, without the inescapable need to exploit each other.[86]

As a purely hypothetical statement of an ideal world, this proposition is exemplary; unfortunately nature's physics have proved that man's environment is not infinite in its resources and thus not entirely open to "complete mastery," while the history of human behavior has shown that despite the Industrial Revolution human beings continue to exploit each other. But the key concept in the quotation is "control"; industrial society could supposedly control its "ecological environment." Notice, however, how this hypothesis directly contradicts the one advanced by the maker of "The Factory Bell," a song espousing a positive feedback conception of Self/Other relationships; the rural worker, it said, far from being controlled by the "tyranny and niggardliness of nature," was on the contrary quite happy at his labor, "uncontroll'd" either by man or by nature, while the factory worker was very much controlled, not only by others, but also by the environmental artifacts of the Industrial Revolution—especially the factory bell.

While rural workers would hardly have subscribed to a descriptive (as opposed to poetic) definition of themselves as "toiling gaily" at spade and plough and "roll[ing] amidst pleasures"—especially while on the job—they would have understood, I think, what the maker of "The Factory Bell" signified at a deeper level by the notion of "uncontroll'd." Consider the case of a category of worker who in the last century existed betwixt and between these two poles of rural and urban environment in the village of Baildon, which sat astride the boundary between the industrial center and the rural north of the West Riding. This was the handloom weaver, undergoing at this period a transition from the old to the new. The older pattern was one of domestic industry and self-employment; what the weaver produced he used in part, sold in part, supplementing his income with occasional farm work and poaching, while the newer pattern was a sixty-odd hour week in-factory employment. The Baildon weaver, however, though still self-employed at home, had to meet certain externally imposed schedules to fill orders from factory middlemen on time; but the older pattern of variable work schedules still maintained a psychological hold:

The hand-loom weavers were often poachers, and many of them devoted the first three days of the week to this pursuit. In consequence they had to work "all hours" for the rest of the week so as to "livver" on the Saturday. All day Friday and often until daybreak Saturday the weavers would be what the fraternity called "pent" at their looms owing to time lost in poaching. . . . In Baildon there was a poachers' song which, according to an old resident, ran somewhat as follows,

Monday i't morning hour of delight,
I'll go and see if dog's in form for a fight,
Tuesday i't morning no right to begin,
My time should be spent in the living brought in.
Wednesday i't morning to go to mi work
I scarcely can abide.
I'll go to the fields to get some fresh air,
And see if the dogs are in quest of a hare.
Thursday i't morning it is time to begin,
My time's getting short and my money's getting thin.
Friday i't morning my looms getting slack
All it will say "a day ta lat."
Saturday i't morning it's a poor living to bring in.[87]

We see in this account of the handloom weaver the same contrast that so struck the poet of "The Factory Bell"; the difference is that here the contrasts exist within the same occupation and worker. On the one hand, there is the "delight" in a match between man's "natural" rhythms-cum-inclinations and certain Other agents in his environment—the morning, the fields, the fresh air, the dogs, and the hare. On the other hand, however, we have not a match but an asymmetrical relationship of one-way control between the worker and "time," the need for money, and even the looms, whose unnatural rhythms admonish the weaver and keep him up at nights— "naturally" a period of rest and sleep—working. As E. P. Thompson has pointed out; the construct "time" is crucial in the above account, for this is *industrial* or *clock* "time," like "money" reified into a commodity that one "spends" to one's loss, whereas natural time is "passed" according to the fluctuating rhythms of *both* nature external to *and* nature internal to humans.[88]

In short, it is the abstract idea of the structure of control-relationships between Self and Other that lies at the core of what the seemingly diverse world views of rural and urban songs signify. To put it another way, the basic premise of local songs appears to be of the following order: that a rural environment allows one greater powers of control within one's context-of-action, either by allowing the reciprocity of equality between Self and Other (the match model) or by containing within its established structure resources that allow reciprocity to be reestablished should the balance become skewed by one agent's taking on too much control vis-à-vis others (the negative feedback model). In urban environments, on the other hand, the usual case is an imbalance; control is innately vested in one or a few agents and flows in one direction—even *must* flow in one direction, as the "either us or them" syndrome indicates (the positive feedback model). Finally, in contradistinction to rural environments, reciprocity of control relationships in urban milieux cannot be gained from resources within the system but must be imported from outside so that the very definition of the system is transformed into something of quite a different reality (the transcendence model).

There is an interesting difference between the handloom weaver's context for match and the contexts that display match in rural songs; the weaver's rhyme envisages the equilibrium within a context that makes no significant distinction between "work" and "play"—poaching. To the vast majority of nineteenth-century rural dwellers, however, "work" and "play" were not so delightfully intertwined, and while in "play" songs—the numerous hunting pieces, for instance—the countryfolk had no difficulty envisaging match, in the "work" songs things were not quite so harmonious, as "The Old Yow" and "The Country Lad" make clear. But at least negative feedback was possible in these circumstances, a give-and-take between Self and Other that evened out the flow of control in the long run. Work contexts in urban songs, however, displayed overwhelmingly the positive feedback model. And even in their match songs that took place in primarily leisure-time activities, everyday occupational roles of the rural participants still adhered, as in "Hunting in Flyingdales," "Li'l Jackie Beresford," and "Song of the Glaisdale Harriers." So while work and play were not the same, as they were in the handloom weaver's idealistic notion of poaching, at least they were not that discrete, and both, moreover, allowed consensus as their ultimate state. But in urban songs work and play are mutually exclusive. In the work contexts of "The Factory Bell" and "Poverty Knock" among others, only unequal control relationships and positive feedback obtain. Those urban songs that allow consensus in negative feedback and transcendence conceptions are almost all "play" contexts—but not the countryman's and countrywoman's play, with its fairly close relationship with the world of work; instead, the urban play contexts are rare, occurring once a year (as in "Wibsey Fair"), once in a lifetime (as in "Praise of the Rejoicings at Rothwell," "Opening of St. George's Hall," and "Queen's Visit to Leeds"), or in a context quite artificially cut off from everyday life (as in the song of the York debtor's prison). In fact, many of these songs so separate work from play that they entirely invert normalcy, the logic of capitalism, the Protestant Ethic, and "clock time":

> Her sweetheart is a snob [cobbler], who swears In spite of
>   wind and weather,
> He'll sell his lapstone and his wax, Likewise his hemp and
>   leather:
> He swears that he will sell his cloak, And little pigs and all,
> They mean to strike upon the day They open St. George's Hall.

> There is another verse I'll sing to you, You never heard the like;
> The lasses that are in the Town, For Wages mean to Strike
> They say they'll have a better price, Or else not work at all,
> They mean to strike upon the day They open St. George's Hall.

> The Masons and the Carpenters, And Builders too, likewise
> Upon that day, I mean to say, A Tool they will not rise.

The Counter Jumpers, Barbers, Clerks, and Factory Lads and
    all,
Will have a Spree upon the day, They open St. George's Hall.

On this once-in-a-lifetime occasion, in other words, the natural instincts and rhythms of the Self's libido will assert (or should we say
reassert?) control over one's own actions and over the agents in one's
immediate environment that normally control one. And as a final
note to these work/play relationships, I may point out that the only
two rural songs that display unequivocally a positive feedback conception are poaching songs from an era in which the logic of industrial capitalism was being vigorously asserted in the countryside
in this particular sphere of rural activities, the sphere of hunting
and gaming.[89]

No rural system, of course, in Yorkshire or anywhere else, exhibited anything approaching "real" equality in districts with large
landowning squires like the "Honourable Aislbre" and the occu-
pant of Camerton Hall. But the powers of control that flowed from
higher to lower classes in villages and parishes with longtime resident landowners were sanctioned by tradition as well as balanced
by reciprocal duties of higher toward lower to countervail those
"rights" of control.[90] And in intraclass relationships the need for
reciprocal controls to maintain equality and at least apparent consensus was an extremely important ethos of *the* rural world view
and subject to constant and active monitoring. Working-class wives
in Lark Rise, for instance, "had an almost morbid dread of giving
offence and would go out of their way to be pleasant to other
women they would rather not have seen. As Laura's mother said:
'You can't *afford* to be on bad terms with anybody in a small place
like this.' "[91] This fear of the overassertion of control by a single
agent existed in both the potential offender and offended; parents
showed no pleasure when their children distinguished themselves
in school, for instance, while neighbors were quick to render sar-
castic comments on the children of others who did so excel.[92]

This concern for interpersonal equality within a social class is
consistent with many rural English behaviors, though observers
assign diverse causes to those behaviors. One Suffolk farmer, for
instance, commented on the countryman's dislike of being questioned, on his "reluctance to come down definitely and make any
kind of overt stand"; he is secretive about his own business and
especially about personal good fortune, which he will conceal "at
all costs."[93] The speaker himself ascribed this hermeticism to a reluctance to tempt either fate or the landlord's greed (he might

raise the rent); but it is equally possible that the additional fear of rising above his social Others contributed to his reticence. A newcomer to Akenfield, also in Suffolk, attributed his neighbors' strange behavior to yet a further personality trait, "innate cruelty" and lack of human kindness. He leased a local farm that was in abominable condition, and few thought he would make a success of it. But neighboring farmers, unasked, contributed help that, to the recipient, quite contrasted with the streotyped notion he had of Suffolk country people (as well as, we might add, with their proverbial mistrust of newcomers).[94] But as soon as the new farmer, contrary to expectations, began to make a small success of his farm, the neighbors withdrew, becoming cold, distant, and no longer helpful.[95] Evidently he had by his success become a threat to the balance of power-relationships.

This ethos is still prevalent today in English village culture, as a recent ethnography of Hennage in Norfolk indicates.[96] Indeed, it may be related to a deeper ethos that many "peasant" societies display, the "image of limited good" mentioned earlier—the notion that only very finite resources exist in the ecosystem and that one person's fortune inevitably means another's misfortune.[97] Thus while most of our ethnographic examples above come from the south of England, particularly from its most studied region, East Anglia, there is strong reason to suspect that the generalizations are applicable to most "marginal cultivator" rural regions, including Yorkshire.

An intimate corollary of the rural ethos of control-relationships-in-equilibrium is an acute awareness that outside forces might disturb this traditional structure. The countryfolk's suspicion of outsiders moving into their region has already been referred to; this suspicion was especially pronounced when the newcomer lacked clear social and, consequently, role-power definition.[98] But especially mistrusted were representatives of governmental institutions whose authority flowed from agencies entirely outside village control. In the nineteenth century the most prominent such agent in the village was the policeman. This was, of course, the modern bobby, not the earlier parish constable who had been a local man elected by the village landowners themselves. Yet even though the Victorian village policeman himself might be a local man, by all accounts the person who occupied the role was the loneliest and most avoided person in the community.[99] The same is true in more traditional rural districts even today.[100]

In the urban districts of Yorkshire, of course, such external agents of control—ranging from legal institutions to factory machinery—were not only far more numerous and far more powerful than those in rural districts but also were relatively new products of culture and experience, and were without the longtime sanction of tradition behind them. The urban experience was an extreme manifestation of a general change that the Industrial Revolution had for some time been bringing more slowly to the countryside as well, though not so thoroughly to rural Yorkshire: "Instead of the village community (as symbolized by open fields and commons) there was now enclosure. Instead of mutual aid and social obligation, there was now the Poor Law, administered exclusively by the rulers of the countryside. Instead of family, patronage or custom, there was now the straightforward cash nexus of wages. . . ."[101] But while the rural dweller could still call upon available resources of control, the urban dweller could at the very best legitimate the new industrial experience by calling upon external analogies that were idealistically *like* older orders of reciprocity—the closed village, the community festival, or the royal court.

Despite the overwhelming pervasiveness today of industry and the socialist state, the ethos of personal control is still evident in English village culture. Clement Harris discovered that the core quality of a "real" Hennage villager was "competency"—the ability to efficiently manage one's own affairs without calling upon outside agencies or even other villagers' help. One "real" villager lessened her status considerably when her daughter became involved in a scandal at school. No stigma was attached to daughter or mother by the facts of the scandal; the mother lost face by being unable to manage her own daughter, and then compounded this offense by later calling in the police to control her daughter's continuingly difficult behavior. "To call in outside help is to attack the moral and emotional self-sufficiency of the group," and even in village contexts wider than that of the family, deviations from the norm of match must be handled by the internal self-regulation of negative feedback, rather than by redefining the situation by calling upon outside help.[102]

Today, in towns and cities industry is no longer a "revolution" but the taken-for-granted ground of normal experience, just as the agricultural village community was the ground of normalcy against which new experiences were so often measured in the last century. The modern-day industrial working class has its own institutions like labor unions to assert reciprocal controls vis-à-vis environmental Others. But in the personal sphere, "Bradford in the Sun," the most modern item in our sample of an urban song, represents local perceptions of one major area of antagonism in today's city. "Bradford in the Sun" envisages the logical end of an extended positive feedback relationship; self has lost so much control in relationships with the environmental Other, who flourishes while we become impoverished, that the only alternative is for Self to depart the ecosystem entirely.

These four models, we must not forget, are selected representations and idealized expressions of meaning, not simply photographic reflections of day-to-day life itself. Urban man had his mates, his family, his pub, and his church where he could and did experience match in real life.[103] And tensions and disagreements there were aplenty within rural communities. Perhaps one really important difference of the "causal" sort between the two environments was that the culture of the ordinary countryfolk provided them with a greater number of traditional expressive devices to mitigate disagreements as well as with the opportunity to themselves participate in performing those devices—activities like the men's ceremonial (or "mummers") displays, traditional pranks and tricks, and of course satirical verses.[104] Occasionally, in fact, there may even have been a distinct role-slot available in the rural social structure for the satirist, for someone licensed to be both part of the community yet welcome to show individuals their foibles and aid in maintaining Self/Other balances of power. The blind fiddler of the East Riding, Thomas Mercer, may just have filled that slot in his day and district:

> There was one . . . of thoughtful and somewhat melancholy countenance, who only smiled quietly, and sat looking apparently on the floor. "What's the matter, Massey?" cried my neighbour.
> "Nought. He's a fool that's no melancholy yance a day," came the reply, in the words of a Yorkshire proverb.
> "That's you, Tom! Play us a tune, and I'll dance."
> "Some folk never get the cradle straws off their breech," came the ready retort with another proverb.
> "Just like 'n," said the other to me. "He's the wittiest man you ever see: always ready to answer, be 't squire or t' parson, as soon as look at 'n. He gave a taste to Sir Clifford hisself not long ago. He can make songs and sing 'em just whenever he likes. I shouldn't wunner if he's making one now. He's blind, ye see, and that makes 'n witty. We call's Massey, but his name's Mercer—Tom Mercer. Sing us a song, Tom!" . . . With a voice not unmusical, rhythm good, and rhyme passable, he rattled out a lively ditty on the incidents of the hour, introducing all

his acquaintances by name, and with stinging comments on their peculiarities and weaknesses. The effect was heightened by his own grave demeanor, and the fixed grim smile on his face, while the others were kicking up their heels, and rolling off their seats with frantic laughter.

"Didn't I tell ye so!" broke in my neighbour, as he winced a little under a shaft unusually keen from the singer's quiver.[105]

In their small way, Tom Massey's songs contributed to the internal self-regulation of his rural society, assisting an equilibrium the urban visionary would have to artificially and passingly import from outside.

4

AN
ETHOS
FOR A
REGIONAL
CULTURE

The
Poetry
of
Martha
Bairstow

Most of the urban song-poetry discussed in chapter 3 was local to the central area of the West Riding, Yorkshire's most heavily populated and most industrialized region. Here, textile manufacturing and coal mining have been historically the predominant industries, just as working-class people have always made up a large percentage of the population.[1] While today in such urban (or, for that matter, rural) milieux songmaking and singing at the local level is just about nonexistent—except in a few very select contexts—poetry making and sharing, by recitation as well as through print, flourishes. This is principally poetry made by ordinary working-class men and women about matters in their own primary environments.

This "domestic" or "occasional" verse interprets the world-within-manipulable-reach to those who have a practical and emotional investment in the facts that the poetry takes as its topic. Consequently, just as the poetic interpretations tend to be extremely normative ones, so do the form and language tend to be conventional. These characteristics align the modern-day genre with traditional song-poetry and make it amenable to the analytical techniques of folk studies. In both this and the following chapter we shall examine some examples of contemporary working-class poetry in this light, discovering in the process how it can share code-structure, world view, and messages—in short, meaning—with older song-poetry. We shall also see the ranges that local poetry of whatever sort can cover, from the exhibiting of a strong community voice and the striving for ends rhetorical and practical on the one hand, to the quest for more private, individualistic, subjective insights on the other. The former is clearly of greater interest to the folklorist and is common in working-class poetry; the latter is more common in middle-class poetry. We shall also see, however, that such diverseness may apply within the work of a single poet, depending on personal development through different experiences. Nevertheless a consistency of world view is maintained by the working-class poet so that the *social* quality of his or her work is seldom suppressed.

To these ends, therefore, we shall study in this chapter the life history of one such working-class maker of local poetry, while in chapter 5 we will examine a series of poets, both working and middle class, and their poetic visions of the same subject matter. The subject of this chapter, Mrs. Martha Bairstow, lives in the central West Riding's conurbation of industrial cities, towns, and villages with its significant amount of interspersed meadow and farmland.[2] Her home is in the small town of Millington—a short bus ride from the city of Bradford—with a resident population of about thirty-five hundred.[3] Like her predecessors whose work we encountered in the preceding chapter, this Yorkshirewoman writes poetry on topics from her immediate milieu, poems that, in her words, are always "founded on fact."

Mrs. Bairstow was born in the village of West Hartford, two miles away from her present Millington home. Her mother, Mrs. McNeil, came from a lower middle-class Derbyshire family that had fallen upon hard times; consequently, the young Derbyshire girl was forced to enter domestic service as a teenager, first in Scotland and later in the West Riding. But she was not as badly off as she might have been, for she was in service to a baronet, which itself carried a higher status, and she had had more exposure to "high culture" than is usually the case with girls born into the working class. She was musically knowledgeable, for instance, and played the piano. She was also familiar with great literary figures, and even today her daughter is fond of quoting the "quality of mercy" speech from *The Merchant of Venice,* proudly attributing her familiarity with it to her mother. Mrs. Bairstow also stresses that her mother never failed to inculcate into her children lessons on the importance of good grooming, deportment, address, and speech, and indeed Mrs. Bairstow is testimony to the effectiveness of her mother's training.

Most conspicuous evidence for this is her speech, which, even though she was born and has lived all her life within a very small district of the West Riding, is much more influenced by "refined" Standard English than is usually the case among Yorkshire working-class folk, who are extremely proud of their regional culture and its dialect. Trained by her mother therefore to see beauty and value in the "higher" culture a middle-class ethos espoused, Mrs. Bairstow's early ambitions were to become either a newspaper reporter or a governess, both, along with schoolteaching, stereotypical middle-class occupations.[4]

But it is at this point that a tension in Mrs. Bairstow's home environment may be first noted, for her father dismissed peremptorily any such aspirations in his daughter. He thought them "highfaluting," pretentious, unattainable, and even unnatural, since they involved professions above the appropriate reaches of their own working-class status. "Work," to her father, was synonymous with manual labor and quite the opposite of intellectual endeavor like news reporting or soft labor like that of a governess. In this Mr. McNeil espoused an ideology not uncommon in the working class of his day, with its mixture of conservatism and pride. He had other attitudes and habits many observers disapprovingly and stereotypically believe are endemic to the working class: he drank too much, would not hold a steady job, and treated his wife with uncommon roughness.

Mrs. Bairstow is quick to attribute her father's less likable behavior to his difficult life, however. William McNeil was a former career soldier who had already fought in World War I when he married Mrs. Bairstow's mother. A Scotsman, he met his future wife while she was in service in his home country, he having had to retire from the army because of poor health brought on by wounds received in the war. He moved to Yorkshire to marry the young servant girl, by then resident in the West Riding, and the two set up house in poor lodgings in West Hartford. Mr. McNeil worked intermittently as a laborer, chiefly for the local Corporation on road construction. But the irregular and low-paying work that made poverty a constant reality for the household, his proclivity for drink, and his harshness toward wife and four children made for an unstable home. Mrs. McNeil herself was constrained to work as the village charwoman, a job of significantly lower social standing than that of her previous domestic employment, and her husband's behavior, his nationality (Scottish), and his religion (Catholic), while they would not have made much difference in the larger city of Bradford or even the nearby towns of Morley, Batley, and Cleckheaton, marked the family as socially marginal in the village of West Hartford. "We were the colored people, we were the Pakistanis," explained Mrs. Bairstow with an analogy to the most visible social distinctions applicable in today's West Riding society. Nor did moving into a different home when Martha was still a young girl markedly improve the McNeil's social or material standing, for the cottage they could afford was as humble and disrepaired as the lodgings they had formerly suffered. As for Mrs. Bairstow's school life, the family's low social status carried over into her relationship with her own peers, with attendant teasing, bullying, and ostracism. Yet, she vividly recalls, training from her mother stood her in good stead when the Inspector of Schools would make his annual visit; Martha would be the one chosen by her teacher to recite a poem for the government man, since her affection for fine literature and her speech, which more closely approximated Standard English than did her classmates', gave her the best qualifications for such a performance. The reader will shortly see both this family home, Moorside Cottage, and Mrs. Bairstow's public recitation for the Inspector of Schools made the subjects of poems much later in her life.

Like most working-class children in the 1930s, Martha left school at fourteen for fulltime employment. She first went to work in a printing shop, as close to her dream of newspaper reporting as she could get and as her father would allow. This job lasted for two years, but its distance from home finally forced her to change employment to mill work nearer home; she thus at sixteen became part of the industry for which the Industrial West Riding is best known, textiles, though her job as winder was in a silk mill rather than in the much more common woolen and worsted factories. At twenty she married a local man who at the time, World War II, was in a commando unit of the British forces. She lived with her parents for the first two years of her marriage, seeing her husband on his periodic leaves. Subsequently, the young couple moved into yet another bit of substandard housing, a one-room cottage in nearby Millington. But life was getting no easier for Mrs. Bairstow. In fact, the reverse was true; her soldier husband proved to be as erratic in his behavior as her soldier father had been, the upshot being that he deserted her soon after the war and the birth of her third child. They had been married for five years.

If anything, circumstances became more difficult for Mrs. Bairstow with the departure of her husband. For six years she lived in the one-room cottage raising three children a scant five years apart in age, managing chiefly on social security payments that allowed the barest subsistence. She began a series of parttime jobs when her youngest child turned four—serving in the school canteen, as a charwoman, as a harvest worker in summer and fall, and on the assembly line at a large Batley biscuit factory. The family's living quarters improved substantially when she was allotted a council house in Millington, a two-up, one-down rowhouse quite superior to anything she had lived in so far. She eventually took on fulltime factory work when her youngest child reached adolescence, later switching in 1966 from the biscuit factory to a wire-making one. By the late sixties her now-adult children had all left home, and in 1968 she married again. Her new husband, Richard Bairstow, a fellow worker at the wire factory, was considerably younger than she, but had a strength and stability of character that the two principal males in her life so far had lacked. Since 1968 Mrs. Bairstow and her husband have lived a very quiet and contented life together in her Millington council house, although she retired from work in 1970 because of chronic if minor thrombosis of the leg. She is today a vivacious, creative, intelligent, and contented woman, and she and her husband are a model of domestic happiness.

Mrs. Bairstow's life history may seem to be an atypical one, but I doubt this is the case. Her experiences with her father, with her first husband, and later as a single mother are chiefly a function of poverty, and poverty has been a frequent companion of the factory system that has dominated the Industrial West Riding for the last hundred-odd years. The region's same factory system has always attracted "colonial" immigrants into its low-paying and low-skilled jobs—the Irish in the nineteenth century, West Indians in the 1950s and 1960s, and Asians in the 1960s and 1970s. The results have often been general social antagonisms of the sort that characterized Mrs. Bairstow's formative years in West Hartford. What is perhaps unique to Mrs. Bairstow's experience is that her family was a microcosm of the larger Industrial West Riding culture: her father, in behavior and ideology, represented the working-class poor; her mother, the potentially upwardly mobile middle class, with its "refined culture" ethos.

Mrs. Bairstow wrote her first "real" poem in the summer of 1968, two years after she had begun working at the wire factory. She had always been fond of artistic expression, was quite a storyteller, and was in all ways a striking speaker. She had previously tried her hand at verse while working on the shop floor of the wireworks, composing single-quatrain rhymes on fellow employees and on occasional events of the work day for some time before she attempted her first extended composition. These earlier "ditties," as she calls them, were humorous comments on the immediate setting, and she would compose them in short order while working at her machines, jotting the rhymes down on bale labels and passing them around the floor for her colleagues' amusement. These verses she considered an inconsequential way of passing the time, but they did give her something of a reputation as a poet; consequently, when in the summer of 1968 a most unusual and severe storm suddenly struck the district during working hours, the event was so startling and unique that one of her mates urged her to capture the moment in a poem. Mrs. Bairstow, as awestruck as everyone else, and under the powerful influence of the novel experience ("it was like the night Christ was crucified"), composed what she considers her first "real" and "serious" poem:

THE STORM[5]

The hour was dark then black as night,
It was nearly too dim to see.
Even with the power of electric light,
'Twas just like eternity,
Flashes of lightning broke up the black,
The thunder sounded with such a crack,
We all thought that doomsday had come,
The hail came down like sharp razor strikes
Beating on glass like the sound of a drum
Getting louder and louder till at last,
Nerves were sent reeling, women were screaming
Into our works the water was teeming.
One could not escape from this onslaught of fear
It would have been easy to shed a tear,
Our foreman was steady but he'd never seen the likes,
Neither had we, not in our little life,
Surely that roof is going to come in,
Let's run for it, how terrifying the din,
Then suddenly it grew lighter and it won the day,
As usual, Mother Nature had her way.

Mrs. Bairstow was so pleased to discover that she could combine an extended set of verses into a whole poem and on a serious subject to boot that even today "The Storm" remains one of her favorites, and she considers it one of her best productions.

The making of a local folk poem is often stimulated by the immediacy of a real experience; it is also poetry made with a social goal in mind. These and related restrictions of language, conceptual models, meter, rhyme, and length all constrain the poem texts. Thus an interpretive analysis must not be cast at too concrete a level of diction, but at a level of major signifiers and their structure. With this in mind, we can see that "The Storm" contains the following premises: (1) nature can be unpredictably violent; (2) so powerful is she in her violence that normally dependable cultural artifacts like electric light, a building's walls and roof, and authority figures like foremen are incapable of resisting her force; (3) nature may even cause normally rational, calm, and competent people to lose control and themselves become violent and disordered; (4) people are, in fact, in many ways structurally and functionally *like* nature, even if punier—nature's teeming water, for instance, is duplicated in human shedding of tears in terror, her noise by human screaming, her blackness by human inability to see; (5) that very nature, finally, also has the ability to bring life-supporting order to humans, for she possesses nonviolent counterparts of her violent properties—life-giving water, silence and stillness, and sunlight. (In "The Storm," only this last, sunlight, is explicit, but we shall see those other qualities of nature in her orderly role in Mrs. Bairstow's other poems.) The nature/human analogies are strengthened in the poem by the conventional designation "Mother Nature." In the poem's closing line, this signifier is most clearly associated with nature's nurturing, rather than destroying, role. But nature's power and unpredictability is not thereby eliminated, for she "had her way" in bringing disorder and destruction as well as order and life.

"The Storm," Mrs. Bairstow's very first poem, contains a basic world view that will not change significantly as we examine her repertoire of poetry (which, as far as I could discover, numbered twenty-two compositions by the late summer of 1973, when I last interviewed her). One thing that is unique to "The Storm"—though not structural—is that this poem has no marked social ethic to advance, which is not surprising given the topic and the circumstances of its composition. The majority of Mrs. Bairstow's later poems, however, contain clearly intended social messages, and some, accordingly, give more weight to the causal power of culture than does "The Storm." Whether her poems refer to contexts of domestic life, occupational life, the outdoor landscape, regional culture, society at large, or even, occasionally, the supernatural and celestial, the tensions between the relative dominance of disorder (the "natural" in *both* nature and man) and order (the "cultural" in man and nature) structure her poetic representations of the topic at hand. The code that informs the structure of her poems, in fact, is very similar to that of the symbolic songs in chapter 2, even displaying a parallel mediator, which in Mrs. Bairstow's case is most often "home," in both terrestrial and celestial affairs. But none of these realms—domicile, workplace, outdoors, or cosmos—are distinct separabilia in Mrs. Bairstow's poetry; for not only is there traffic between them, but the structure of each maps onto others, within the two major paradigms of disorder and order.

The best way to present an analysis of Mrs. Bairstow's poems is to follow chronologically her progress as a poet from 1968 to 1973 and to show how, despite changing circumstances in her own life and despite certain concomitant changes in her poetry making, a consistent substratum of meaning remains. To this end, I follow a natural division suggested by what I know about the poet: a first period of poetry making spans her last three years at the wire-making factory, 1968 to 1970; a second period dates from her retirement to 1972, a period when she was not in the best of health and lived a relatively inactive, isolated, and homebound life; and a third period corresponds to the first eight months of 1973, when she began once more to take an active interest in wider regional affairs. Let us examine each of these phases in turn.

From 1968 to 1970 Mrs. Bairstow wrote six poems, five of which treated topics from the wireworks and were intended for an audience of her fellow employees. The first of these is "The Storm"; its composition and much of its content are set squarely in the context of the factory itself, and its dissemination was similarly confined until the poet was persuaded to offer it for publication in the then *Cleckheaton Guardian*.[6] A second poem is a jocular satire, not entirely without serious intent, called "The Battle of the Pie." It was stimulated by a complaint on the employees' part about the shortage of food in the company cafeteria at lunchtime. The seriousness of the actual affair is indicated by the workers' forming a delegation, of which Mrs. Bairstow was a member, to present their grievance to management. In the poem, the meat-pie conflict is represented in a battle allegory. Since the squabble was also an interemployee one between those who came early enough to get food and those later ones who did not, "The Battle of the Pie" depicts the alienating effects of a military enterprise on all participants; one hides alone in one's "dugout" (foxhole) to escape unkind words, which "fly like bullets"; one lines up in the "long, long trail awinding" (a reference to a popular World War I song) to await one's destiny at the lunch counter. The chief signifying oppositions are not between people, however, since everyone is depicted as being under attack, but, on the surface at least, between the rewards of a "nice warm pie" and the punishment of cold tea only. More fundamentally, they are between the satisfying of human needs for tasty and nourishing food on the one hand, and the inability of bureaucratic machinery to adequately satisfy those human needs on the other. In contrast with the chaos of the battle, the "long, long trail awinding"—the rigid order that bureaucracies impose on people (the lining up to be served in turn)—signifies the fundamental opposition between order and disorder. Here it is not satisfactorily mediated, not even by the "dugout": while that refuge does protect individuals from the fray, it isolates them at the same time from their fellow men. The function of resolution in this conflict is performed not by a textual signifier, therefore, but by the poem's jocular approach, which redefines the events and injects humor into a situation in which ill-feeling has prevailed.

Two other occupational poems from this period, however, pose stronger resolutions within the texts' manifested signifiers. One, "Manly Mac," satirizes a young tough who worked on the shop floor and treated the women workers with arrogance and disrespect:

MANLY MAC

Young Mac he is a rotter,
At forty he will totter
He cares for nothing, no not he
The clever young blighter he be
It's get lost this and get lost that
He thinks everybody's as blind as a bat
If you're forty, to him you're a bag
He's forgetting that someday he'll be an old lag
His Motto, "Do as others do unto you"
His vengeance enough to turn the air blue
He sticks out his jaw and opens his mouth
Showing razor sharp teeth, his words are uncouth
That flat cap he wears holds his hair on
He says he's got brains but they don't last for long
Brags of his muscle power then bends a nail in two
I'd love to see someone give him the toe end of their shoe
He's as hard as that nail, don't expect sympathy
But if he's sick he wants all one's pity
He's trying to sing now with that Irish twang of his
Don't we get 'em at the Wireworks
Gee WIZZ.

Mac makes a point of almost reveling in those human properties that, as "The Storm" illustrated, are like nature's negative aspects:

he is overpoweringly strong; emits the most dissonant of sounds in his swearing, bragging, and singing; and, like the storm's "sharp razor strikes" of hail, "sticks out his jaw and opens his mouth / Showing razor sharp teeth." Sharpness and violence in culture, however, can be put to positive ends to counteract Mac's negative use of these attributes; thus, the poet would "love to see someone give him the toe end of their shoe." Mac's youth is a negatively valued signifier in relation to his middle-aged victims, whose age deserves respect. Finally, there is the mediator, a very important one in Mrs. Bairstow's poetic world view, but unfortunately one that Mac lacks —a certain kind of reasoned use of the mind. Thus "he says he's got brains but they don't last for long." This lack is paralleled in the image of "blind as a bat," for in Mrs. Bairstow's poetry the signifier "seeing" is intimately related to rational, humanitarian behavior.

The other work-related poem is "Man Lost," which addresses a real love affair between a married foreman and a female shop-floor worker:

MAN LOST

And he fell into the web of fire,
Seeing only her offered desire.
Finding of late he loved her less,
Yet struggling with full knowledge of the mess,
Pitting his strength against his weakness of heart,
Knowing full well that from her he should part,
But the serpent's head arose high in the sky,
And with the wings of evil did he have to fly,
Far away in the distance was his home,
But tempted by she from this did he roam.
Her conquests are many but her jewels are few,
Losing old loves and starting anew,
His star on the horizon beckons him home,
To love, contentment and all of his own,
He'll need all the help from the angels above
Or feel the sharp points as the devil with fork does shove,
No time for regrets in his quick lime,
Just a few thoughts in hand could save his lifetime.

Here, the "fire" of passion and the sharp fork of Satan have overpowered the lover and propelled him into his disastrous liaison, while in a celestial opposition, the beckoning "star" shows the approved way. The depths of his degradation are assisted by those evil companions of the Tartarean realm, serpents, while the contrasted heights of propriety—higher than the rearing of the serpents' heads and the wings of evil that bear the man into sin—are those neighbors of the stars, angels. In the terrestrial realm the major thematic opposition is between the locus of the liaison (away from home) and the locus of grace (in the home), intimately associated with the cosmological pushing and pulling. A further homology is thus proposed between the cosmic battle of heaven and hell on the one hand and the social conflict of appropriate versus inappropriate behavior on the other. The terrestrial ideal of the home can only be achieved by active thought and decision making, not just by passive knowledge, for the man already is cognizant of doing wrong; only reflection and decisive action can properly counter the rule of the heart's "natural" passions.

The fourth poem in this group was written upon Mrs. Bairstow's retirement from the firm; it focuses on the opposition between the "turmoil and strife" of factory work and the also-present "hours of fun" during which the workers "made the rafters ring" with cheer and song. A similar opposition lies in the work/home nexus; work was routinizing and confining, recalls the poet, home provided "rest" and "release." At the same time, however, home is, like work, ambiguous, for its peace and calm can be somewhat dull, and one's thoughts now fly back to the thrill of the occasional joys and excitements of work. The poem resolves these paradoxes within the home/work domains by philosophical means, by appealing to thought: "New patterns must form, changes be made." It ends on a cheerful note with a *folk* musical refrain:

FARE THEE WELL
Goodbye to [Jason Farnsworth] and Sons
To daily labours and hours of fun
Away from routine, turmoil and strife
Parting from friends, maybe for life
Long hours spent together in this mill
Struggling in summer and thro' winter's chill
Wond'ring if ever that clock would go round
To the hour of release, then homeward bound
Away from it all, now I'm having a rest
Yet my thoughts fly to work and I'm at my best
Though my body lies here, on my pedals I fly
Upon that bike for eight o'clock I do try
Then I roll over and know it's all gone
I've shed some tears but life still goes on

New patterns must form, changes be made
Perhaps for the best, old worries will fade
Remembering the days we made those rafters ring
Cheerio my friends—Hey ding a ding ding.

In these five early poems it is not difficult to discern a consistent code structure. The greatest antitheses, which appear only in "Man Lost," are between the Tartarean world of the Devil (disorder) and the celestial one of God (order). These represent two extremes of value. There is a less extreme antithesis between nature and culture in the terrestrial realm. But properties of both nature and culture can display order and disorder; nature is ordered when "culturized" in her sunlight, for example, while culture is "naturalized" in the rude and violent behaviors of people. Thus both nature and culture have negative and positive properties, but those properties are distinct; nature's lightning is not the same as nature's sunlight. The single images that do contain paradoxically conflicting values of positive and negative are primarily man-made habitats: the dugout, the workplace, and the home. It is this last, the home, that is a dominant symbol and preferred mediator of oppositions in Mrs. Bairstow's poetic world view. The other commonly used signifier of resolution is thought, motivated by sensibility and the analogous "seeing." But these properties are positively valued only (and opposed to the insensitive "rationality" of bureaucratic "thought"), and thus display a negative feedback relationship with their contrasts, rather than the dialectical one that "home" does. As we move on to consider more of Mrs. Bairstow's poetry we shall see that as more semantic domains and more signifiers are added, and emphases are shifted slightly along the nature-culture axis, the basic code-structure and its major premise do not change.

Her second phase covers the years 1970 to 1972 and is prefigured by a poem, "Paul," which Mrs. Bairstow wrote while she still worked at the wire factory. This two-year period was in one important sense a difficult time for our poet, for she was in bad health, was experiencing difficulty with her oldest son on a number of fronts, was having to face the fact of now being middle-aged, and was still adjusting to her recent marriage. With a newly restricted social life, physically inactive, and house-bound to a large extent, she became extremely introspective and sought topics from her childhood reminiscences, from private and personal experiences of the moment, and from her immediate family. Accordingly, the "home" signifier and its complements become particularly promi-

nent in her poetry, as do semantic oppositions between such concepts as the past and the present and health and affliction.

Take "Paul," for example, which chronologically belongs to
her first period but semiotically to this second. In keeping with the
usual purpose of Mrs. Bairstow's poetry making—to return to equilibrium events in her environment that are out of joint—the circumstances of "Paul's" composition were as follows. Paul was the
illegitimate son of the poet's neighbor and had an unfortunate home
life, his mother being a generally flighty and undependable woman.
She considered her son a burden and was in fact about to surrender
him voluntarily to child welfare authorities. This was so out of keeping with Mrs. Bairstow's own ideology of the importance of family
and home life that she thought a poem putting Paul in a new light
would change the mother's mind. In the poem, the child is "sent
from heaven" and needs to be protected from the real world's
"trouble and strife," which he will later "know" in abundance. But
for the moment his childhood innocence should be preserved by his
everyday-world benefactor, "Mother Nature." In the poem, the
world of children and innocence fits the popular fairytale stereotype: Paul's environment is a landscape of "toadstools," "flowery
dells," "mossy paths," "grassy banks of green," and "long rushes,"
its inhabitants "pixies" for playmates, "fairies" for protectors, and
(quite harmless) "witches" as representatives of danger. A similar
poem on another real child in Mrs. Bairstow's network is "Helen
Louise," about her granddaughter. The poem smooths over the
child's public tantrum in a Bradford shopping center, an acute
embarrassment to her accompanying grandmother. "Helen Louise"
in its internal action follows the model of negative feedback rather
than the transcendence of "Paul"; set in the everyday world of the
shopping center, with neither pixies nor witches, it indicates that
children are not entirely pure innocence. As in "The Storm,"
"Manly Mac," and "Man Lost," Helen Louise allows unbridled
nature to rule her behavior and has to be reprimanded with a dose
of thought, of consideration for others, and of cultural self-control
in general.

"Paul's" fairytale frame of reference far predominates in the
poems of this second period, however. And though their *dramatis
personae* include realistic figures—the socially marginal and the an-
tiquated—these figures are quite compatible with the fairytale: children, old folks, a gypsy witch, and a tramp. Paradoxically, while the
poems' contents are more "traditional" in this sense, Mrs. Bairstow's
poetry making is less of a social activity in this phase than it was
during the other two. Between 1970 and 1972 her principal imme-

diate audience is herself and her kin, her vision a more personal and introspective rather than social and extrospective one, and the functions of her poetry making more emotive than rhetorical. These features all fit her changed circumstances—retirement, restricted social contact, ill-health, and relative confinement.

Four of these poems deal with personal memories from her childhood, and she herself is a prominent actor in them. "Moorside Cottage" tells of children coming unexpectedly across a deserted cottage hidden in a copse on the village moor. The cottage clearly belongs to an earlier age, "built in a village far away from the town," and contains secrets and memories that delight the children who clamber over the roof and peek through the windows: "Feeling excited, we'd wished for the key / To unlock the door, then, secrets we'd find, / Like books you read, adventures of a kind." But the cottage in the final analysis is brokendown and no longer used; it belongs to the preindustrial past in which fairytales are set. Thus it is cold, with no fire in the grate, only long-dead cinders. Soon the sky gets dark, the air goes chilly, and the children race back to the safety of home. This poem presents an idealization of Mrs. Bairstow's own childhood home, Moorside Cottage, and is subtitled "A Childhood Memory." Another poem, "A Childhood Fantasy," also treats of an image from Mrs. Bairstow's childhood, an eccentric village woman popularly known as Gypsy Jane, reputed locally to be a witch. Its structure is similar to "Moorside Cottage," the innocent children at play venturing into Jane's fairyland preserve: "Wearing long clothes, all shabby and black, / Carrying a bag more like an old sack, / Tall battered hat well down on her head. . . . Black beady eyes, her skin very brown, / Big boots on her feet, making no sound," a description we must not take as a literal depiction of what the woman really looked like. To this fairytale creature, who is much closer to nature than to culture, the children respond ambivalently, "feeling excited, and yet feeling scared." As in "Moorside Cottage," they eventually escape and return to the safety of the present-day real world, the symbolic "home."

Just as "Moorside Cottage" and "A Childhood Fantasy" take their impetus from single childhood images, so "A School Poem" builds on Mrs. Bairstow's early experiences reciting for the school inspector. The landscape here is also of the older world, but not the fairytale woods; it is a realistic pastoral setting with a fine house resting on a hilltop. The rural landscape is contrasted with "the town," from which it is "far away." The poem's ending couplet once again asserts the power of thoughtful determination to achieve the ideal of this "home":

A SCHOOL POEM

I stood in school with chin up high,
And gazed out at the cloudless sky,
To say a poem, 'twas called, "My Will,"[7]
And classmates sat there, oh! so still,
Rememb'ring then the words so clear
Yet full of meaning in my ear,
I heard my voice from far away,
Say words and verse in bright array,
Mingling with emotions strong,
They then cascaded into song,
Of flowers and beauty everywhere,
A large fine house was centred there,
Upon a hill of purple bloom,
I almost smelt the sweet perfume,
I heard the music of the stream,
As it splashed thro' fields of green,
Linking hamlets here and there,
Picturesque pathways, views so rare,
Fresh the breeze on this lovely down,
Peaceful, serene, far away from the town,
Now I know that it is "My Will,"
To live in this house, on a Yorkshire hill.

Another poem on a childhood memory, "founded on fact" as all Mrs. Bairstow's poems are, is "The Two Runaways." Here the socially marginal, "natural" role is filled by the quite realistic figure of a wife who is running away from home. The setting is the familiar pastoral one of nature and innocence—children playing in the rural outdoors with their pet mouse. Moved by comparison of her own caged state to that of the mouse, the fleeing woman stops to address the children. She opens the door of the mouse's cage, and the creature, like the woman herself, escapes from culture. Both woman and children now enter fully into the realm of childhood play, chasing the mouse until it is recaptured. But real life with its social obligations intrudes, and the woman's pursuers arrive to take her back to home, husband, children, and duty. Tensions between conflicting values are prominent in this poem, for the free innocence of nature is contrasted with the incarcerating aspect of culture. The poet cannot take an explicit ideological stand against the wife's captors, for "home" is an important mediator in Mrs. Bairstow's poetic ethos. She escapes this ideological dilemma not by appealing to thought but by taking throughout the children's point of view and interpretive frame of reference: it is all play, innocent "jolly good fun," and the youngsters laugh at this real-life analogue of a catch game. They focus their reading of the affair on the metaphorical mouse, which, caged, is "culturized nature," as pets are, and thus a kind of resolution: "We laughed and we found this jolly good fun / Caught like our mouse, she'd had to go back."

The fourth poem of this group of early memories is " 'Friendly' the Tramp," a poem about a real-life figure of a type quite common in England up to about World War II. In the conventional community world view, tramps were, like Gypsy Jane, socially marginal and figures of fear. To Mrs. Bairstow, however, the tramp represents the old fashioned, as do fairytales, rural environments, and natural freedom; the poem discourses sympathetically on how his type is now at odds with modern urban life ("Highways have changed"). Mrs. Bairstow tempers the tramp's "natural" qualities, however, by assigning him a cultural identification, the cognomen "Friendly," her own creation. Thus the signifier here mediates the dichotomies of nature and culture.

Another poem from this second phase treats the present rather than the past, though the idea of the past is still signified by implication. Mrs. Bairstow originally wrote this poem about herself, titling it "Me and My Dog," but later changed the title to "[Richard] and His Dog" and presented it to her husband. As she explained to me, Richard unfortunately did not share her own poetic perceptions of nature; she hoped that a nature poem, purporting to be from his point of view, but actually espousing her own, would allow him to see things in the same light. The poem's imagery is quite representative of the very real rural landscape that pockets the district of the Industrial West Riding in which Mrs. Bairstow lives. As in "The Storm," however, nature is not an idyll of fantasy only; she is to be enjoyed, but in moderation—one has one's "fill" of it, as come evening darkness and cold descend. These dichotomous qualities are starkly expressed in the line, "Nature is cruel but she can give such joy." Once again it is the home that provides a resolution of these two poles, with a fire in the hearth that is not the purely natural "lightning," but the natural fire controlled by culture. The domesticated dog at one's feet, the analogy with the innocent properties of the "boy," and the retained memory of the rural landscape that will "last until I am old," all allow a coexistence within the "home" matrix of natural and cultural properties. But note that the cultural quality of the home is not immaculately perfect, for it lies in town, where the narrator "has" to make his home:

Once more in the street where I have to live
To the warmth of my hearth, the fire does give
My dog lies contented asleep at my feet
After running thro' woods as if on winged feet
Nature is cruel but she can give such joy
I'm relaxed and happy as when once a boy.

Two further poems deal primarily with supernatural phenomena, and, says Mrs. Bairstow, also treat real personal experiences. Both take place during the dangerous night, but in the relative safety of one's bedroom at home. The first encounter is with (Sir Francis) "Drake's Ghost," a frightening but not terrifying experience. However, as in "The Storm," nature brings equilibrium back to the occasion that has been disordered by the ghost's visit; morning light breaks through the very window that had mysteriously vanished from sight at the ghost's first appearance. The other visitation, in "Phenomenon," is by the shade of Mrs. Bairstow's "Scottish grandma" on her father's side. While the narrator is afraid, the ghost of her recognized kin is not as threatening as was Sir Francis Drake's, though its appearance is accompanied by the loss of cultural light—the turning off of the gaslamp. The rekindling of the light, and again the breaking of daylight, mark the ghost's departure and the return to normalcy.

Kin and old age are features of both "My Mother" and its sequel, "Her Passing." The first is an affecting ode to Mrs. Bairstow's favorite parent, at the time dying in a Bradford hospital. Her mother, who in life had been in part the epitome of culture and self-improvement, of "thought," is now however quite the opposite, lacking the ability not only physically to see but to perform ordinary motor activities such as feeding herself. She is entirely a victim of raw (as opposed to "Mother") Nature. But she has passed her fine qualities on to her daughter: "She was so strong, in her I could hide, / Giving me strength, sweeping troubles aside." Now it is Martha's turn to exercise sensibility's thought and control: "My troubles she shared, now it's my turn, / I'll do my best, her love I'll return." In "Her Passing," Martha's mother is released from the tyranny of nature to the rest and security of a celestial home with God:

Released from all pain, both night and day,
Her spirit is freed, and stealeth away,
Triumphantly soaring to heaven's abode,
Casting its shackles of earthly load,

Now she's at rest in God's house above,
In a new land of light and love.

Similar is a poem on an old man who was a patient in the same
hospital and who died just before Mrs. McNeil did. The poem, "An
S.O.S. to God," is in the form of the old man's prayer that he be
released from his condition, a condition similar to Mrs. McNeil's in
that he could no longer control his own motor activities. "Let me
come home," he prays, and soon he too "rests in heaven with the
above one and all."

Although during this second phase Mrs. Bairstow's poetry making was less of a social and, correspondingly, less of a "folk" activity
than was the case in her first phase, during these years 1970 to 1972
it seems clear that she was exploring more deeply, through introspective poetry, the foundations of a value system and world view
more instinctively and less reflectively expressed in her very first
poem, "The Storm." One indication of this introspection is, of
course, that childhood memories constitute so many of her topics.
She appears to have been searching her past, which bore for her
many unhappy memories, almost therapeutically, seeking to recon-
stitute it into a good Gestalt, one that would make more whole the
ambivalences she felt toward its many disjunctions. Accordingly,
the oppositions in poems of this second phase are not as extreme in
their semantic values as was the case in "The Storm," "Man Lost,"
and "Manly Mac." The disordered pole of natural phenomena is
represented by some quite benign images—the childhood innocence
of Paul and Helen Louise; the tumbled-down cottage; old Gypsy
Jane; the harmless tramp; the ghosts of that Elizabethan English
hero, Sir Francis Drake, and her Scottish grandmother; and the old
age, which comes to us all, of her mother. Similarly, the ordered
pole of cultural phenomena displays certain negative qualities—the
readiness of Paul's mother to deposit him with a child welfare
bureaucracy, the modern town that opposes the tramp and the Yorkshire country house, the duty from which the runaway wife is fleeing. Thus mediation is not as difficult to accomplish in the world
view of these poems, since their poles are not too distant in value.
The poet is still apparently ambivalent toward her favored mediator
of "home," however.

By the beginning of 1973 Mrs. Bairstow's health was restored,
and she began to reassert an active interest in matters outside the
home. The domestic friction that had resulted from her oldest son's
living in for three years disappeared with his departure, and she
and her husband settled into a now peaceful and happy life. Her

role as a poet became more important to her, especially as several of her poems had already appeared in the newspapers of her own and of neighboring towns. Consequently, she began to write poetry on more regional, more culturally generalized topics. "The 1972 Winner" is a poem, chronologically, from her second period (it was written in the summer of 1972); but in spirit it is of this third phase, and it is also, in a sense, related to the first period, since it deals with her former employer. Its topic is the wireworks float's taking first prize at a local show. Modern industrial society, which so far in Mrs. Bairstow's poems has been represented as "overcultured"— as in contrast to older village and country milieux, or in its inability to solve the problems of meat-pie shortages—is here an approved setting for the topic. "The 1972 Winner," however, presents technology in its aspect equivalent to human "thought"—that is, not just the mechanics of technology, but humanized technology; the firm's entry, an airplane, is "a fine artistry of wire." But nature is not entirely forgotten, for "The sun came out from behind the clouds, / As they won 1st PRIZE with an overall win."

Another poem, "The Appeal," is set in the heart of the city, Bradford, and in the same St. George's Hall whose opening was celebrated in the 1853 broadside we encountered in chapter 3:

THE APPEAL

The blind man stood upon the stage,
    With guide dog standing by,
I looked down at my programme page,
    And humble tears were nigh.

Behind him there in bright array,
    Was the Black Dyke Band,
To sponsor his appeal this day,
    With music great and grand.

John Foster's name on banners blue,
    Written there in gold,
This name, this band, so very true,
    Its wonders to behold.

This setting in St. George's Hall,
    Bradford's Festive Place,
To have our eyes and see it all,
    Should be our thankful grace.

The military frame of reference we saw used for its alienating characteristics in the earlier spoof, "Battle of the Pie," is drawn on once more (and will be again in the next two poems), though this time for its qualities of spectacle and nationalism. This is not solely artifice on Mrs. Bairstow's part but selectiveness, since the band she speaks of (a nationally and even internationally known brass band sponsored by the Foster family's local textile complex, the Black Dyke Mills) adopts military motifs in both uniforms and music, as do most other sponsored working-class brass bands. The benefit concert, with the band's smart uniforms and banners and mastery of ensemble music, represents working-class cultural music coming to the aid of people whom nature has robbed of one of their most important human abilities. These blind also rely for help on "cultured" nature—trained dogs. (The concert was held to raise money to purchase such seeing-eye dogs.) There is also a message for the audience: those who do have eyes should use them for thought, should see that the blind need the help of people more fortunate than they. Finally, the poet also gives way momentarily to nature's approved emotions, losing control and crying through those very eyes in sympathy with the plight of the blind.

The controlling of disordered nature by human thought and creativity is also thematic in "Ode to a Famous Nurse," a poem on Florence Nightingale stimulated by a current event, a strike by hospital workers. In one way, the poet was trying to remind the strikers of their heritage and duty, which should supersede such fragmenting concerns as labor/management disputes. Like the ambiance of "The Appeal," "Ode to a Famous Nurse" is full of military imagery—banners flying in the sun, salutes, colors of red and white and blue, medals, soldiers, and fanfares of trumpets, again all quite historically appropriate since Florence Nightingale first made her mark in the Crimean campaign. The human "new knowledge" and resulting "cures" that Florence Nightingale inspired are eulogized for controlling sickness and pain. A pun on the famous nurse's name prevents nature from complete consignment to the realm of the destructive, however, for "Without nightingales"—birds that sing culturally approved music—"our world will never die."

Mrs. Bairstow's final poem up to the time I ceased my work with her was written in May of 1973. Its topic is English football's annual nadir, the Football Association's Cup Final at Wembley Stadium—in 1973 regionally significant because one of the two finalists was the West Riding's own Leeds United, the other from

Sunderland in County Durham. Again the military and nationalistic ambiance is foregrounded:

WEMBLEY'S 1973 F.A. CUP FINAL WINNER

Spectators swarmed the stadium bright,
    Soccer's final day,
Queen's guards with band, so fine a sight,
    The crowds began to sway.

All homage paid, "Abide with me,"
    Bright flags and banners high,
Then like a great tumultuous sea,
    Up went a deafening cry.

'Twas mighty Leeds and Sunderland,
    Captains,—wee Scots men,
Who faced the throng in Wembley's stand,
    Upon the soft turf then.

No shining knights in armour bright,
    For gallant Leeds today,
As Sunderland with wondrous might,
    Chased all their goals away.

They used their bows of burning gold,
    Their arrows of desire,
This scored their goal, then Sunderland "Bold,"
    Rode chariots of fire.

"Hozannahs" long, rang loud and clear,
    And mingling with the rain
From loyal fans, fell many a tear,
    Of happiness,—and pain.

This national spectacle takes its tropes of transcendence in part from William Blake's "Jerusalem," which has the status of an anthem in contemporary English culture. Three major milieux in Mrs. Bairstow's cosmology are represented here. The celestial is represented by "hozannahs" and the hymn "Abide with Me" (which is *the* anthem—but in a distinctly secular sense—of soccer fans, especially northeastern ones; interestingly, its singing at center field by a professional performer, Frankie Vaughn, to open the ceremonies had been scheduled by officials in hopes of dampening the "natural" rowdiness that many soccer fans are famous for). The terrestrial of society is represented by the main topic, the football game itself, though chiefly in military imagery from both medieval and Biblical sources. The terrestrial of nature, less well represented, is signified primarily by the rain; in this case, the rain is a mediator that soothes the heat generated by the human emotions as well as by culture's artifacts—bows and chariots—of "burning" gold and "fire." The rain also mediates the polar opposites that its human equivalent, tears, signify—"happiness" and "pain"—and thus brings equilibrium to the human universe.

In keeping with the expanded topics of her third phase as a community poet, Mrs. Bairstow's last four poems accept mediators less ambiguous and of wider scope than the domestic "home" of her earlier work. The cultured technology of the wire airplane is of this sort, for instance, as are the cures of Florence Nightingale. Yet natural mediators are still more than evident, as in the case of the sun in "The 1972 Winner," the rain in "Wembley's 1973 F.A. Cup Final Winner," the nightingale in "Ode to a Famous Nurse," and the cultured nature of seeing-eye dogs in "The Appeal." The playing down of "home" as a mediator is evidently a function of her maturity, in three senses: first, in her accepting the more positive aspects of culture as a suitable *media via*; second, in her becoming more convinced of the rightness of her belief-code and thus choosing mediators with less personal ambiguity than the home; and third, in her widening the scope of her topics to more regionally relevant concerns. But all her signifiers of resolution fall into a paradigm of mediation between disordered nature and ordered culture—or, more precisely, of a synthesis of the two: "culturized nature" (like sunlight, gentle rain, nightingales, seeing-eye dogs) or "naturalized culture" (tears of pity, folk and brass band music, a fine home in a rural setting).

We see, therefore, that Mrs. Bairstow did not remain static over her five years of poetry making; she changed her types of topic, enlarged the scope of her semantic domains, and emphasized a little more the positive qualities of the cultural pole. But the fundamental code-structure of the world view, and its major ethical premise about society, remained constant. One result of this consistency is that her poems can be adapted to fit situations in her world within manipulable reach, situations that the poems were not directly written for. In her first phase, while she worked at the wireworks, the pragmatic immediacy of her poetry making as a social activity cannot be questioned. For example, young Mac made a daily habit of insulting the older women on the shop floor, creating tension and conflict. Expectedly, Mrs. Bairstow's poem, "Manly Mac," was greeted with instant acclaim by fellow sufferers of Mac's insults, though Mac's initial reaction was hardly as laudatory. He threatened our poet with a rhetorical "I'll kill you" and tore up the paper with the offending poem when he got his hands on it. But Mrs. Bairstow had foreseen that possibility and topped him yet again with a triumphant "I knew you'd do that. I've got a copy." The end result was that within a few days Mac tendered an abashed apology to the ladies, particularly to Mrs. Bairstow. In fact, she and Mac soon became "quite good friends," and harmonious relationships were established on the floor. "Man Lost" also succeeded in correcting a social deviation within Mrs. Bairstow's immediate occupational group, though not directly; the manager saw the poem, realized that the love affair was causing internal dissension among the women, and summoned the machines foreman and his mistress into the office for a lecture. The couple broke off their liaison; the affair was satisfactorily resolved. "Battle of the Pie" redefined the real events through analogy and parody, thereby helping to soothe ruffled feelings and restore camaraderie between the haves and the have-nots, while "Paul" attempted to transform the mother's attitude toward her illegitimate son, with the hoped-for result that she would feel proper maternal love for the boy and not give him up for adoption. All these poems, along with some from her second period, like "[Richard] and His Dog" and "Helen Louise," are clear cases of folk poetry's "conative" (or rhetorical) function, of its attempt to perform a corrective service on real conditions in the immediate environment of the poet's Social Others.

But the consistency and generality of Mrs. Bairstow's world view permit her also to put to active social use the more personal poems of her second phase. Take "Moorside Cottage," for instance, which to some extent transformed into a fairytale "cot" the reality of the hovel in which she had spent her childhood. Three years after composing the poem Mrs. Bairstow sent it to her local newspaper, relating it to present-day events with an accompanying letter—printed in the *Spenborough Guardian* along with the poem—lamenting the recent spate of building activity in the district that necessitated the tearing down of attractive, older homely dwellings like "Moorside Cottage" in order to erect modern houses that few working-class people could afford and that had, moreover, little aesthetic appeal.

Somewhat similar was the case of certain poems in her third period whose topics in real life would seem remote from the poet's manipulable reach. The most insightful example of such a poem used for immediate social ends is the "Ode to a Famous Nurse." I have already mentioned one equilibrating purpose of this poem in a social context somewhat at the edge of the poet's sphere of influence: to communicate to local hospital workers the harmful effects of their strike by presenting the example of Florence Nightingale, an English culture heroine who had risen above petty personal and material interests to follow a higher vision of altruism. But there was yet another set of related circumstances; her close friend and neighbor had just been admitted to a Leeds hospital with glaucoma, was for all intents blind, and was about to undergo an operation to restore partial sight. It turns out that Mrs. Bairstow was in fact very much put out with her friend when she wrote these verses, for she herself had put much time and effort into taking care of the sick woman, running her errands, doing her housework, and acting as nurse, but had not received what she thought was sufficient appreciation for her own sacrifices. During one interview with me while her friend was still in hospital, Mrs. Bairstow inveighed at length against her friend's family background, personal habits, overreaching pride, and lack of Christian values. Yet she had just composed "Ode to a Famous Nurse" and had sent it to the hospitalized woman to cheer her up. Thus the poem was aimed at three audiences as a message of proper behavior: at the hospital workers, suggesting that they not neglect their rightful duties; at her friend and neighbor, to cheer her and to mend the rift between her and Mrs. Bairstow; and at the poet herself, with the aim of resolving her own conflicting emotions, as she herself, much like Florence Nightingale, had undergone personal hardships and sacrifices for others with little assistance and reward, but knew that she should continue in her endeavor, guided by a higher moral purpose than mere self-interest. "The Appeal," also about the physically afflicted, and composed at the same time, served three very similar ends, save that it was directed not to hospital staff but to those generalized Social Others who could contribute toward welfare for the blind.

On the other hand, a personal element of the sort seen in the making and purpose of "Ode to a Famous Nurse" and "The Appeal" is also relevant in several other poems which seem to be wholly Social and Other-directed. Take "Man Lost," for instance, which appears to be speaking solely for the group and not for interests unique to the poet; but there is an obvious association between incidents in this poem and incidents in Mrs. Bairstow's own history, for she herself had been the victim of a deserting husband. Similarly, her recurring concern in her post-1970 compositions with harbingers of death, like old age and sickness, must be seen alongside her own ill health during those years, a period when she thought she might soon be "leaving this fair world behind," as she put it. Ultimately, however, this personal association in Mrs. Bairstow's topics strengthens the quality of community that is so integral to working-class poetry making as a folk phenomenon. The Social Self of the poet has experienced the same problems her Social Others have; they have experienced what she has. The linkages in both fact and affect parallel the linkages in contact, common habitation, and shared culture.

All these aspects of bonding between the poet, her experiences, and her audience inform her selection of suitable topics for poetry, since they lend themselves to the world view and ethos that Mrs. Bairstow so consistently maintained in her chosen genre. This world view, structured on a paradigmatic opposition between "natural" signifiers of lack of control and "cultural" signifiers of too much control, the opposition mediated by an ethos that draws dialectically from each opposing paradigm to form a *media via,* is clearly similar to the world view structure of the symbolic model of traditional songs on lost love analyzed in chapter 2. The similarity even extends to the symbolic nature of the signifiers, with the important difference that Mrs. Bairstow's major symbol is her mediator, the home, also a mediator but not apparently symbolic in the love songs. Of course, Mrs. Bairstow *has* experienced "home," while the girls in symbolic songs never knew that ideal in reality.

It is not difficult to relate Mrs. Bairstow's poetic world view to her life experiences, for the very same oppositions obtained within the structure of her early family and domestic life. At the pole of order was the "culture" of her mother's middle-class heritage, values, and teaching; but this heritage was at odds with Mrs. McNeil's real and ignominious role as the village charwoman with a no-good husband. At the pole of disorder was the "nature" of her father's real persona and behavior; but this reality was at odds with his former role as an epitome of ordered culture—a soldier who had fought for his country. Mrs. Bairstow often speaks of her father in a "mythical" sense, as both a warrior and a Scotsman whose lineage included Robert the Bruce and Robert Burns. (That the captains of the two teams in "Wembley's 1973 F.A. Cup Final Winner" were both Scottish was one personal element in the poem's composition.) These two real and polar personalities, mother and father, could not, however, achieve a synthesis, and their marriage and home was not a happy one; their failure may have influenced in part Mrs. Bairstow's slight ambivalence toward that particular mediator.

After Mrs. Bairstow married and set up her own home, she experienced but a recapitulation of her earlier years. Like her father, her husband had been wounded in the war, had emotional problems, was not a good provider for his wife and children, and eventually abandoned them. It was at this point that her mother's example served Mrs. Bairstow well. Constantly poor, she was forced to provide for herself and her children through a series of low-paying and menial jobs. But unlike "Paul's" mother, she was a "good girl," says Mrs. Bairstow, and with justifiable pride points out that she never let self-interest guide her, never fled the confines of home and its duties to "enjoy" herself as so many others in her position did and do. Yet, she confesses ambivalently, she did let her "youth slip away." The sacrifice was worth it, however, for she maintained her home intact, raised her children, and did her duty. Now in middle age she has finally achieved that ideal equilibrium of a settled and stable home life with her new husband, a just and deserved reward. Her new expressive form of poetry making is the medium for a compact synopsis of the value system she has lived by over the years and can now proudly justify.

Mrs. Bairstow's *media via* between nature's "energy" and culture's "information" is particularly appropriate for modern-day Yorkshire and its post–World War II generation, so many of whose parents were miners and textile operatives but who themselves have greater opportunities of upward mobility in the freer structure of postwar society. Upward mobility for the children of prewar working-class parents has been, of course, available to all English men and women; what is specific to certain regions like Yorkshire, however, is that this upward mobility has had to be integrated with the strong tradition of a distinctive regional culture, whose most notable features in Yorkshire's case are working-class society, a distinctive dialect, and a host of personality traits implied in their traditional cognomen "tykes."[8] The factory worker who won a huge sum of money on the football pools in 1973 tersely encapsulated this principle of change-while-not-forgetting-your-roots when he asserted that "I'm a Yorkshireman. I know how to handle brass and I'll be giving nowt away."[9]

Mrs. Bairstow's father represented certain aspects of those roots: a traditional conservatism (in not allowing his daughter to aspire to "high-faluting" professions) and stereotypical working-class traits of intemperance and immediate gratification. But he was not a Yorkshireman. The poet's mother mirrored the newer, more national ideology of bettering oneself, of assimilating official British culture through the works of famous literary and musical artists, of displaying refinement in everyday behavior. But she was not a Yorkshire woman. Mrs. Bairstow, who *is* Yorkshire born and bred, realizes that neither the older paradigm (epitomized in the more "natural" and more northern Scot) nor the newer (epitomized in her more "cultured" and more southern Derbyshire mother) provides the best ethos for one's center, one's "home." The narrator's "will" in "A School Poem" perhaps most literally exhibits the ideal: a Yorkshire home that is neither a townhouse nor a Moorside Cottage but an eminently livable home in a sylvan setting. The home in this poem is one of that signifier's few nonambivalent representations.

The similarity of this world view to that of the symbolic model of love relationships is clear; but the two also differ in an important way that acknowledges the years separating them as flourishing and applicable conceptions. For the symbolic code legitimizes a view of human behavior by naturalizing it, while Mrs. Bairstow legitimizes a view of nature by culturizing it; the one is a proposition of what nature is, the other is about what a regional culture properly should be.

5

LOCAL
POETRY
AND
MODALITIES
OF
EXPERIENCE

The
Lofthouse
Colliery
Disaster

On 21 March, 1973, an event occurred in the West Riding that took foremost place in local public consciousness for a week and that continued to capture much attention over the succeeding two months. While, on a strictly objective level, this event was but a local affair, it evoked strong reactions from people all over the Industrial West Riding and the northern coal region, which stretches south from Rothwell (just east of Leeds) to Yorkshire's coal-producing neighbors Nottinghamshire and Derbyshire. These three counties form a single coal region, geologically and even to some extent culturally, as the first four lines of "Safety First," a poem by a former coal miner, Ephraim Mugglestone, indicate:

> For many years I worked below, in the bowels of the earth
> My father and grandfather did, long before my birth,
> In the coal fields of South Yorkshire, Notts; and Derbyshire as
>   well,
> And very many stories of tragedy I could tell.[1]

The event of 21 March stimulated composition of several poems by residents of the area, and it is these, along with two poems by Mr.

Mugglestone of Nottinghamshire, that I shall examine in this chapter.

The core event itself was an accident underground at Lofthouse Colliery, whose pithead is in the central West Riding's Stanley Urban District. First opened in 1873, the colliery has its headquarters and pithead at the twin villages of Outwood and Lofthouse Gate, and its underground workings extend south and southwest for about one and three-quarter miles as the crow flies. In early 1973 coal was worked from a total of five "faces," or working areas on the coal seam. One of these, the South 9B face, was the scene of the accident in the early hours of that Wednesday morning of March 21. Let me sketch the facts of the accident and its aftermath as reported by local and national news media.

A team of fifteen men were working the night shift in the face area of South 9B. Some were advancing the two tunnels (or "gates," maingate and tailgate, parallel to each other, at right angles to the face, and some 210 yards apart) into the coal seam; some were working on the conveyor, a moving belt that carried the cut coal from the face and down the maingate for eventual removal aboveground; and some were busy at the seam itself, in the smaller passage, with a working space about two feet deep by three feet high, that ran horizontally along the seam, joining the main and tail gates across the 210 yards separating them. These last were the colliers, a five-man team on the night of the accident; their job was to remove from the seam the coal, cut and loosened chiefly by the mechanical coal-cutter (or "trepanner"). With the help of shot and pick, the colliers removed the coal and loaded it onto the conveyor belt immediately behind them, propping up the ceiling of their passageway as the coal was extracted and as they accordingly advanced into the seam.

At about 2:30 A.M. a deluge of water suddenly burst through a point in the face close to the maingate end. Those men in the region of the face were either immediately surrounded or in imminent danger from the flood, and whoever was able waded and ran down the main and tail gates back toward the entrance. Since each gate was about twelve feet wide by eight feet high, the fleeing miners' movements were relatively unhampered; but the men in the passage along the seam itself were in a more difficult position, since this passage was not only a lengthy 210 yards from gate to gate, but of such meager dimensions that the men were in kneeling or lying positions. Because of its small total area and because it was the immediate region of the emerging water flow, this passage filled up too quickly for those working in it to reach the gates in time by crawling on their knees, and when those escaping had finally traveled the full three and a half miles of underground passageway to the surface at Outwood, they found that seven of their original number were missing. A rescue team was quickly formed, redescended the mine, and coursed back along the various tunnels toward South 9B, but over a thousand yards from the face it found further advance blocked by water and rubble.

The face passage of South 9B was on a gradient, higher toward its north end, where it joined the tailgate; consequently, those aboveground hoped that the junction of face passage and tailgate would be above water and that the subsequent air pocket—if the trapped men had managed to reach there in the first place—would sustain life for forty hours or so. Unfortunately, the entrance to the tailgate was itself blocked by the water that had inundated the maingate, coursed through the "crossgate" running at right angles to the maingate and parallel to the face a thousand yards away, and filled up the "sliproad" that joined this crossgate—and thus ultimately the maingate—to the tailgate.

By the following day—Thursday, 22 March—massive rescue operations had been set in motion: the boring of an air hole down to the trapped and, it was hoped, alive men was started; pumps worked full-time to remove the water from the inundated area; several rescue teams arrived from nearby Yorkshire collieries so that attempts to get through the blocked tunnels underground could be carried out around the clock. The greatest hope was pinned on the National Coal Board's brand-new team of frogmen from Staffordshire, who were just completing their training; this team, in fact, had been scheduled to undergo one more practice session before becoming operational, but the task at Lofthouse became both their final practice and their first real operation.

It was soon obvious, however, that both gates to the face were blocked not only with water but also with impenetrable mud and silt and the twisted wreckage of mining apparatus and thus were rendered impassable to anything but heavy dredging equipment. The pumps were worked without pause, but for some time there was no perceptible drop in the water level; evidently the flood was still pouring through the original break, and the process of draining, it appeared, would be a lengthy one. But time was short if the trapped men were to be reached before the available air gave out. Sidney Haigh of Outwood, age fifty-eight, a miner for forty-four years, development foreman at the pit, and father of one of the trapped men, twenty-year-old Alan, conceived a daring plan; he would lead the digging by hand of a small two-by-three foot tunnel through the rock above the existing but blocked sliproad to the point where the first of two wooden ventilating doors in this road should have stopped the back-up of mud and water into the tailgate.

For days the pumps worked constantly, the frogmen made unsuccessful forays, the rescue tunnelers hacked their tiny passage through the solid rock, and officials and technicians aboveground revised their estimates of available air in the chamber, holding out hope for the men's survival long after the original forty-hour period had passed. By Saturday, 24 March, the continuous pumping was at last beginning to take effect, and the water level was visibly dropping. By Monday the rescue workers were able to advance through the crossgate and into the entrance of the maingate.

But it was in the tailgate that the men were expected to be, and there, meanwhile, the tunnelers had reached the first of the ventilating doors behind which they had hoped to descend into the open sliproad; they found, however, that the door had been ripped off of its hinges by the force of mud and water and that the road was therefore still blocked beyond that point. They continued their tunneling toward the second ventilating door not far beyond. Fortunately, this door had held, and on Monday the tunnelers broke through the ceiling down into the sliproad. As had been expected, the road contained a considerable amount of water but was passable; into the tailgate they waded and forward to the face, the water gradually becoming less of a problem as it petered out in some places, rose only knee-high in others. But less than three hundred yards from the face they began to encounter increasingly concentrated obstacles of rubble and mud, and after another fifty yards came to a point where their progress was completely blocked by a solid wall of muck, still some two hundred yards or more from the face. Not only did they find none of the trapped men, but after six days the air had turned foul; even if the men had been there, they would not have survived. The bitter news was conveyed to the pithead, where a National Coal Board official was forced to announce to the waiting crowd of relatives, friends, helpers, rescue workers, and newsmen that the seven miners were to be assumed dead.

About noon that same day rescue workers at the maingate end had sighted a body close to the entrance of that passage, a body they recovered and brought to the surface later that evening. It was Charles Cotton, who had been working not at the face itself but in the maingate. He had fled with the others after the initial flood, but Cotton, who was to have celebrated his fiftieth birthday on

22 March, had tired in running the thousand yards to safety and been overtaken by the water not far from his goal.

The attempts to rescue the men now became attempts to recover the six remaining bodies, and an appeal was launched to solicit contributions toward assisting the widows and twenty-two children that six of the seven dead miners had left behind. Named the Lofthouse Colliery Disaster Fund (even though, according to National Coal Board policy, the accident was not technically a "disaster," since at least ten men must be killed in an accident to warrant that designation), it was to be administered by Stanley Urban Council, in whose district Outwood lay. On Thursday, 29 March, eight days after the accident, the Coal Board announced officially that the seven Lofthouse miners were dead.

Throughout April and May the Fund grew, with donations from Yorkshire and all over Great Britain, eventually more than doubling the £75,000 mark set as the cutoff point by the Charity Commissions. Fears of the dangers of old and uncharted mine shafts in the Industrial West Riding proliferated. It was assumed that one had been broken into unknowingly by the Lofthouse miners, thus releasing the water that had collected over the years of its disuse. Calls were made for more thorough surveying and charting of these and for filling them up more thoroughly than had been the usual practice. Work was halted at Gomersal Colliery in nearby Spenborough, as an uncommon amount of water had been appearing at the face there for some time, and the decision was eventually made to close that pit rather than risk another Lofthouse. All these reactions are illustrative of the heightened public consciousness of coal mining and its dangers that was generated by the Lofthouse Disaster. At Lofthouse Colliery itself meanwhile, as recovery work went on, production resumed at the remaining four coal faces on 2 April after a poll of the colliery's workforce had been taken and agreement reached to resume work, providing that the recovery efforts continued unabated. After another fortnight or so, however, the work of clearing the blocked gates became so laborious and dangerous that a further referendum of the colliery workforce was held to decide whether recovery operations should be continued or stopped, the face sealed, and the bodies left where they were. The men voted on 28 April to adopt the latter course, and this was eventually carried out.

On 30 May an official inquiry into the accident opened in Wakefield Crown Court. A total of sixty-two witnesses were questioned over ten days by the Inquiry Chairman, by representatives of the Department for Trade and Industry, and by National Union of

Mineworkers officials. The Inquiry's finding as to the probable cause of the accident was that South 9B face had been unknowingly advanced into long-abandoned but uncharted nineteenth-century workings in which water had collected over the years. The particular culprit was the workings from the old Bye Pit shaft, some seventy yards from the current South 9B face. This shaft, according to National Coal Board records, had been sunk only to the Haigh Moor coal seam, some 420 feet below the surface; since the Lofthouse miners were working the Flockton Thin seam, about 730 feet down, the old workings had been considered no danger. However, information discovered just before the Inquiry in the field notebooks, housed at the Institute of Geological Sciences in Leeds, of a nineteenth-century geologist, A. H. Green, revealed that the Bye Pit shaft had in fact been sunk deeper than thought, to the Flockton Thin itself. The National Coal Board surveyors had missed this datum when planning the Lofthouse workings.

The then acting secretary of the Yorkshire Area of the National Union of Mineworkers, Mr. Arthur Scargill, who led the questioning for the N.U.M. at the Inquiry, stressed three main areas of neglect on the part of management that had contributed to the fatality: first, adequate precautions would have included boring test holes ahead of the face to check for the presence of water, especially since it was known that there were old workings in the vicinity; second, though the men had been complaining for over a fortnight of a "rotten-egg smell" at the face, this warning, along with others, like a small increase in water collecting on the floor and a strange humming noise coming from the face, had not been sufficiently heeded as danger signals; and, third, inadequate research by insufficiently trained Coal Board surveyors had resulted in their missing the information in the Geological Institute archives that would have given a clue to the actual depth of the nearby abandoned shaft. Mr. Scargill put forward a twenty-five-point plan, worked out by his union team, which he suggested should be implemented by the National Coal Board in the interests of future mining safety.

I have recounted the objective "facts" of the affair as taken chiefly from newspaper, radio, and television reports. Such "facts" consisted of natural occurrences that were largely outside human control as well as the goal-directed and practical responses of those actively involved in the occurrences. But there were other facts that, though they did not have a base in the physics of nature and of practical action but only in human conception, were only a little less real for all that. I am referring, of course, to conventional interpretations that cultural norms place on experience, human impositions like "social class," which, while they have very real effects in the physical world, are not as predetermined by it as were the objective facts of the Lofthouse events and their aftermath. The important aspects of these cultural facts of the Lofthouse affair—or "social constructions of reality"—are of the following order.[2]

First, miners are traditionally a distinct cultural subgroup with unusually well-defined and well-maintained boundaries. Though this is changing, it is still true to a significant extent that miners not only tend to live in "mining communities" but also see themselves as possessing high self-definition and as being a relatively closed group; they are viewed in a similar light by those of other occupations and especially of other social classes.[3] Miners are not generally as visible as are, say, construction workers, uniformed service workers, or other working-class people whose homes are more separated from their workplaces than is the case with miners.

Second, mining is not generally conceived to be a highly valued profession. Miners are working class, not well paid (at least as of 1973), and have dangerous occupations; thus they do not rate highly as marriage partners, for instance. Mining itself, moreover, is a physically demanding and unpleasant job, which makes it unattractive as a potential career; even miners themselves, while they may not particularly question their own lot, frequently express the fervent wish that their own children take up different occupations.[4] As the miner-poet George Wainwright, of Newmarket Colliery near Leeds, said to me, "It doesn't come as an asset to you to work down the coalmine, you know." In general, the relationship between mining society and nonmining society, particularly from the viewpoint of the latter, is one of little mutual contact, knowledge, or wish to exchange places.

The third "socially constructed" fact is that the Lofthouse event was considered in public consciousness at large to be a tragedy, a disaster, and all that implies affectively, regardless of the National Coal Board's official index of terminology. No one to my knowledge saw it as a fit topic for humor, satire, parody, personal gain, or indifference. These three social "facts," therefore, must take their place alongside the more objective facts as intrinsic to the Lofthouse Colliery accident, insofar as general perception of West Riding inhabitants would have had it.

Given facts of both the objective and the intersubjective kinds, we can visualize a range of personal responses to these stimuli that form a continuum from the instrumental to the expressive. The instrumental pole refers to responses that were structural and functional matches with the facts themselves; responses that were little mediated by introspection as to abstract implications of the facts but that instead accepted their prevailing and given definitions (objective and socially constructed); responses that put the minimum and necessary means into play to attain well-defined and singular ends; responses that interpreted the facts univocally; responses that, in short, were literal, objective, practical, and predictable from a knowledge of the facts. The expressive pole, on the other hand, refers to responses opposite to the instrumental: responses that were distanced from the immediacy of the fact-stimulus by personal introspection, by reflection upon abstract and more encompassing meanings that one could infer from the facts; responses that were nonutilitarian in their cause-and-effect relationship with the external world; responses that interpreted the facts multivocally; responses that put maximal means to work to achieve unarticulated goals; responses that were connotative, subjective, ideational, and unpredictable.

Of course, these are analytical constructs; few acts would be either one or the other of these two ideal types. But the continuum is useful for comparative purposes; let me illustrate with some examples of responses that were made to the Lofthouse Colliery affair and with a discussion of their possible strands of relative instrumentalness and expressiveness.

First we may take the common reaction of thousands of individuals and organizations, from all over Great Britain but especially in Yorkshire, to the tragedy; they donated money to the Lofthouse Colliery Disaster Fund for the families of the dead men. The donor who wrote a check or who collected contributions from fellow employees at his job site and bought a postal order was reacting chiefly in an instrumental way; there was practical need of financial assistance among those families who had lost their principal source of income. We could point to a minor expressive aspect in such an action, a feeling of pity, or of empathic awareness of how the giver would feel if such a tragedy had befallen him or her; but the response seems dominated by the instrumental element in that it exhibits a close and immediate fit with its purpose—to satisfy a basic physiological requirement for survival.[5]

The second example is of the two men at Wombwell, near Barnsley in south Yorkshire, who staged a benefit boxing match in the courtyard of a local inn. The pugilists, neither a professional boxer, but a bricklayer and a steel erector by trade (the latter won in the fourth round), collected over £50 from the onlookers and donated the receipts to the Fund.[6] Here, the instrumental element also seems dominant, but the expressive aspect is more pronounced than in the first example, with the additional mediation between event and response of the boxing match. We could discern signification in the display of fisticuffs—as an act of empathic physical suffering, for instance, a subconscious identification with the pain the dead men must have experienced. The act may also be interpreted as a silent display of strength and masculinity, as an analogy with a conception of miners that, we shall later see, is central to several poems on the Lofthouse tragedy. But like our first example, the raising and donating of money appear to constitute the primary motive of this pugilistic response, and there are the additional possibilities that, first, fisticuffs were the best resources for fundraising the two had to offer, and second, that fisticuffs is not entirely out of place in a pub's immediate environment (a "socially constructed" reality).

In a third example, the expressive and the instrumental may be evenly proportioned. A public house in Outwood, where the colliery was headquartered, changed its name from the Drum and Monkey to The Rescuers, having commissioned a new sign, a painting of a rescue team advancing to the pithead in order to descend on their dangerous mission. The sign was the work of a professional artist, Mr. Irving Pugh of Harrogate, north of Leeds, and was based on press photographs of the Lofthouse rescue operations. The figure in the sign's foreground is a clear likeness of Keith Stone, a fitter on the fatal shift who fled for his life from the flood and who gained acclaim by immediately donning rescue gear and redescending with the very first team of rescuers. A Mr. Howe, a representative of the brewery that owned the pub, told the news media that "most of the dead men used this public house. This sign is not intended as a reminder, but a symbol. I don't think any of those who survived the disaster will ever need reminding of it."[7] This symbolic aspect was probably intended to glorify and immortalize the bravery of the men in a permanent work of art, to assert the notion that their bravery was something special and would never be forgotten. Yet it would seem that the iconic nature of the sign, which representationally depicts the miners, and its physical proximity to where the events occurred militate against the sign's having inherently high symbolic value. It would indeed be probably as much a reminder, a univocal and referential sign—and thus instrumental—as it would be a symbol. As for the artist and the brewery, we can have little idea of the expressive nature of their actions, but should take into account that the artist was commissioned and (presumably) paid to do the work, and that it may have been in the back of the brewery's mind that such an action might increase sales, though I doubt such was the case.

Finally, a fourth example, one with the expressive quality dominant, is the action of an anonymous man who planted a memorial garden to the dead near the pithead. According to the news report, he did not wish his name known, and it was one of the Lofthouse rescue workers who told the press about him. The only information he himself would give was to say that one of the dead men, Frank Billingham, "had once done him a big favour."[8] The garden's expressive value is strengthened by its nonlikeness to its referent; the garden "refers" to a set of concepts and associated values rather than to objective "things," signifying the idea of the cemetery plot, for example, of a laying to rest in a peaceful and Edenic setting that the colliers, suffering violent deaths and permanently entombed in mud and coal, were never able to attain. In addition one could point to the life-image of the growing plants and flowers that landscaped the memorial garden, suggesting perhaps that in the midst of life we are in death, and vice-versa, or that life itself is cyclical.

This discussion reveals the difficulty of attempting to discern and measure expressive aspects when only very limited information on two constructs, the major stimulus and a portion of the response, is available. While some insights can be gained from knowledge of these data combined with some knowledge of the culture's conventions, interpretive possibilities would be greatly enhanced by more complete knowledge of the actors and the circumstances surrounding their acts. While such information is not available for all cases of the making of poems on the Lofthouse Colliery Disaster, it is available in enough instances to reveal a pattern that permits wider inferences where data are lacking.

And it is, of course, the local poetry stimulated by the Lofthouse Colliery Disaster with which this chapter is chiefly concerned. Poetry making is, by definition, a significantly expressive act; but folk poetry is also, by definition, significantly instrumental as well. In our analysis we shall see clearly how folk poetry differs from nonfolk poetry by means of a not entirely unexpected pattern in the data; that is, the closer the individual poet was to the reality of the Lofthouse event, the more instrumental his poetic response and the more folkloric his poem both as a product and as a social act; the farther the poet was from the reality of the event, the more expressive and the less folkloric his poetic response. I will discuss each of the nine poems in the order of instrumental to expressive, an arrangement that represents a primitive ordinal scale.[9]

First is a poem by Mr. George Wainwright, a pumpman at Newmarket Colliery in Rothwell just east of Leeds and just north of Lofthouse. Mr. Wainwright had fifty copies of his poem printed on broadside by a nearby Morley printer and presented copies to workmates, fellow working men's club members, and personal friends. (A photographic reproduction of the broadside is given on the next page; the actual size is 9⅛″ x 5″.) Mr. Wainwright, who was sixty-two years old in 1973, was born in Castleford in Yorkshire's coal region. He first went to work at fourteen in a local glass bottle works, and throughout his youth engaged in a succession of jobs ("I've done various jobs in me time; I've even had a bash at digging twelve-foot sewers"), including mining, before joining the army. He enjoyed military life but his wife did not, and at her wishes he left the army in 1950, after twelve years of service, and returned to the mines. He has worked at Newmarket since then, and for the last six years has lived in the Holbeck area of south Leeds.

Mr. Wainwright is sometimes called by his workmates the "Robert Burns" of Newmarket Colliery as well as "the Pit Poet," and has composed several poems about mining in general and about Newmarket in particular. His favorites are the two he wrote as tributes to the colliery's first-aid team, copies of which hang on the walls of the ambulance room at the pit. Mr. Wainwright is thus known as a poet within his occupational network, and while he says that there is no particular increase in status attached to that role, the role itself helps create situations in which he is called upon to compose. In fact, his poem "The Lofthouse Disaster" was in a sense commissioned by one of his colleagues, although he says the idea had already occurred to him independently:

> It would be about a fortnight after the disaster at Lofthouse happened. And it were a deputy at our pit called Derek Garsides. And he said to me . . . one night, you know, he says "George, it's time you got pen to the—pen and paper out." And he says " . . . write about this disaster at Lofthouse." And then . . . I started. . . . Started it right away after Derek Garsides asked me. You know, and it took me about a month to compose it up together.

Mr. Wainwright followed the details closely in newspaper and television accounts as the events at Lofthouse were currently and retro-

THE LOFTHOUSE DISASTER

The night shift proceeded quite normal,
  On a face that had been pretty good;
When suddenly without any warning,
  The men were engulfed by a flood:
They rushed from the scene to find safety,
  In that grim watery Hell-hole below;
It was reported that eight men had escaped,
  But that seven men were trapped was a blow.

Then emergency calls were sent out,
  To colleries both distant and wide;
For rescue teams to come with haste,
  To battle with the underground tide:
The response to the call was tremendous,
  With real speed they were soon at the Mine;
Each a super-fit man with the skill and the grit,
  All endowed with a spirit so fine.

With lightning speed the momentum grew,
  As gallant men went down below;
Frogmen were brought to the tragic Mine,
  To search in that grim icy flow:
But alas these brave men were defeated,
  Their efforts were really in vain;
They employed all their skills to get to the men,
  But to lose brought them sadness and pain.

Giant pumps were then brought to the pithead,
  To lower the great depth of the flood;
For a while there was massive excitement,
  When reports of their progress was good:
For the water with speed was receding,
  Could it be that success was in sight?
As unrelenting toil was endured,
  Throughout each day and night.

Then another new bid was embarked on,
  Just one of so many more things;
With no time to lose in the rescue,
  They turned to the top of the rings:
With speed they all worked in relays,
  The gallant rescue teams went in;
For almost a week undaunted they toiled,
  Spurred on with the spirit to win.

Then came a dramatic announcement,
  That a team had got through to the gate;
But alas there was no one to be seen,
  How they cursed the mad water with hate:
Their efforts to find their mates alive,
  Now turned to remorse and fears;
In this great epic rescue attempt,
  Their bravery will live through the years.

The search carried on unabated,
  In the grimness so deep underground;
When news was received at the surface,
  That Charles Cotton's body was found:
It now seemed certain it's sad to relate,
  That the other six miners were dead;
Caught up in those horrible waters,
  In conditions of terror and dread.

For six long weeks the work went on,
  In the water and sludge in the gates;
Until all hope was finally abandoned,
  With no sign at all of their mates:
And so all the toil and valour of men,
  All ended with grief and distress;
To all those who helped those sadly bereaved,
  We say thanks to you all, and God Bless.

                    G. WAINWRIGHT, Newmarket Colliery.

spectively reported, and over the course of the month "gradually built it up" to complete his poem. Another of the deputies at the pit admired the result enough to take a copy into the offices of the *Wakefield Express*.[10]

What was the poet's chief motive in making these verses? "Well, my main theme were in, you might say, in writing it, were to express my feelings about all the valor that went on in trying to rescue the people." The poem clearly illustrates this topical emphasis on the rescue attempts, for its narrative is structured sequentially on the history of the six-day ordeal, mentioning in addition far more individual details than do any of the other poems—for instance, the digging of the new tunnel above the sliproad in verse five and the finding of Charles Cotton's body in verse seven. Both the strict narrative sequence of the story as it is dramatically told as well as the attention to concrete detail make Mr. Wainwright's "The Lofthouse Disaster" somewhat of a documentary record in verse. Another important feature is the poet's mentioning of the bereaved families and thanking all who helped them, especially with donations to the Lofthouse Colliery Disaster Fund. This attention to the practical, and the obedience to concrete facts and temporal logic, are instrumental components of the composition, linking the poetic response closely to the structural demands of its referent's facts.

But Mr. Wainwright himself emphasized his expressive motive in the exegesis quoted above, and two of his poem's elements in particular strike an expressive note: the image of the rescuers and that of the underground environment. The former are "super-fit," "gallant," "endowed with a spirit so fine," and participating in a "great epic rescue attempt." These are not characterizations miners normally place on either themselves or their work; we shall shortly see some evidence of this. Still, even in miners' own experience, the Lofthouse affair was not a normal occurrence, but an unusually dramatic accident, and poetic response to it did demand an unusually expressive tone. But note that even so Mr. Wainwright counterbalances this expressive image by assigning a further characteristic to the rescue workers—a high degree of quite normal emotion. Thus the "super-fit" actors in the "epic" drama also feel "sadness and pain" about their lack of success, experience "remorse and fears," and end their unsuccessful attempts in "grief and distress," while their dead colleagues had suffered conditions of "terror and dread." As we shall later see, these emotions are also untypical of a miner's response to conditions of danger and of failure, and are thus also expressive; but in the poem these kinds of lay emotions counterbalance the men's more "epic" potency, resulting in a portrait of whole humans, realistic in their multifacetedness, though in an intensified manner that poetry, the real drama at Lofthouse, and the poet's certain degree of distance from the events all demand. Ultimately, Mr. Wainwright's miners are like you and me, if more blessed in their share of our common human characteristics.

The image of the underground workplace is also treated with a degree of figurativeness: it is a "grim watery Hell-hole"; the water flow is "icy" and even "mad." Again, these are special intensifiers as befit the unusual intensity of the actual event; but again, like the image of the miners, this scenic imagery is counterbalanced by the prosaic description of underground in the opening lines of the poem: the night shift was "normal," the face "pretty good." The net result is, again, intensification but within the bounds of conventional interpretation. In sum, the potential frame of reference of epic battle is not sustained throughout as an encoder of signification, only alluded to in places; the interpretive ground of "The Lofthouse Disaster" is chiefly the account of a historical event and associated praiseworthy actions by participants.

As for the social aspects of Mr. Wainwright's poem, he was in part clearly fulfilling his existing role as a poet and the expectations such a role engendered in his community. He was asked by a workmate to capture the events and their significance in verse, and he went to considerable effort to communicate the results. The poem's most instrumental feature is clearly marked by its place in the closing couplet: those who contributed money to the bereaved are thanked.

The second poet is Mr. Ephraim Mugglestone from Langold, a village in Nottinghamshire half a mile from the Yorkshire border. Mr. Mugglestone, sixty-four years old in 1973, had been a miner in the region from the age of thirteen to fifty-eight, with a five-year break for service in the forces during the Second World War. In 1967 he finally left the mines to become a porter at the Victoria Hospital in Worksop, five miles from his home. Mr. Mugglestone made two poems on the Lofthouse tragedy, both of which, like Mr. Wainwright's, were disseminated on broadside. There was a more pronounced instrumental element in Mr. Mugglestone's printing of his verses, however, in that it occurred to him while composing the first poem that he might use it to raise money for the Disaster Fund. Accordingly, he had two thousand copies printed by a firm in Dinnington, just across the county border in Yorkshire. (A photographic reproduction appears on the next page; the actual size is 10" x 8".)

In Memoriam

The Aftermath of the Lofthouse Disaster
By E. MUGGLESTONE
11 Church Street, Langold, Nr. Worksop, Notts.

Never again will they see the light of day;
And their loved-ones can only kneel down and pray,
For the six poor souls in the Lofthouse mine,
On whom the sun no more will shine.
As their flesh lies rotting and their bones turn to dust
In the heat of the mine their bodies must rust
Behind seals built by men, who had given their "all"
In the rescue attempt, when they answered the call.
No coffin or shroud to cover their skin
No flowers from friends, only tears from their kin.
What a terrible end to those lives in their prime,
What a price for the coal, we get from the mine!
And too soon all forgotten in this hustling world,
With the flag at half-mast, for a time, then unfurled.
Their loved ones will remember, for many a long year,
And suffer in silence and hide many a tear.
But the world will go on with its daily routines;
And more coal produced with those ugly machines;
So let's play 'Safety First' and have no repeats,
Of the Lofthouse Disaster - shout it aloud in the streets.

Mr. Mugglestone was born ten miles from Worksop in the Nottinghamshire village of Langley. His grandfather, father, and several brothers (there were thirteen children in his family, twelve siblings and one cousin) were miners, and in the tradition of mining families as well as in consequence of the social and economic conditions of the 1920s, it was almost inevitable that he should go into the mines himself upon leaving school at thirteen:

> I left school at thirteen years of age and it was the only thing I
> —I mean at that time if your father was a miner *you* were a
> miner. You never thought about going in for anything else.
> It's a funny thing, but you were brought up to mining.

Most of his life has been spent in the area around the coal region of south Yorkshire and its neighboring counties.

Like Mr. Wainwright, Mr. Mugglestone has for some time been known as a poet within his occupational network, in this case, the Victoria Hospital. In fact, only since he began working there has he turned to writing poetry. A few years earlier, a two-page pamphlet of his poems ("The Hospital Porter's Poems") had been printed and sold under the aegis of the institution where he works—in particular, its branch of the Royal College of Nursing—to raise money for the nursing college; another of his pamphlets, again with three poems, had also been sold to raise funds for the continuing battle against spinal bifida, a condition from which his only grandson died at the age of seven. Not only had Mr. Mugglestone been writing poems for some time, therefore, but he had also printed and sold some for charity; thus a precedent both for a public role as poet and for using his skills for charitable purposes had already been established at the time of the Lofthouse Colliery Disaster.

Such an instrumental purpose in his first composition about the Lofthouse Disaster was accomplished with remarkable success, for money from the sale of his broadsides resulted in the poet contributing over £133 to the Disaster Fund. "The Tragedy of the Lofthouse Colliery Disaster" also expanded his role as poet within another important social network, the local working men's clubs:

> I've only recited it once and that was in a working men's club.
> A miner's working men's club, one Sunday night. And one chap
> came up to me straightway, says, "Can I have three hundred
> copies of that." And he took three hundred copies. And he sent
> me sixteen pounds seventy, like.

It was this expansion of his poet's role, in fact, that contributed to the making of his second poem on the events at Lofthouse. In May, after the decision had been made to entomb the bodies, Mr. Mugglestone was approached by another local club, which was organizing a concert to raise money for the Fund, and asked whether he would contribute for sale some copies of his first poem. Instead, Mr. Mugglestone wrote another, "In Memoriam: The Aftermath of the Lofthouse Disaster," and had five hundred copies printed in time for the concert. (See the following page; the actual size is 8″ x 5″.)

Mr. Mugglestone's "The Tragedy of the Lofthouse Colliery Disaster" is similar in several respects to Mr. Wainwright's poem; in fact, when I showed Mr. Wainwright the poem by his fellow miner from Nottinghamshire, he preferred it to the five other Lofthouse poems I had in my collection at the time, saying, "It's impossible for an outsider who don't work at the pit to have wrote like that." It is the realism of Mr. Mugglestone's poem that attracted the Newmarket Colliery poet; in its narrative technique, the poem matches the real chronology of the rescue attempts. Realistic details of the topic are also abundant in "The Tragedy of the Lofthouse Colliery Disaster," though they are details more of mining in general than of the Lofthouse events in particular, which Mr. Wainwright's poem so concretely depicted. For instance, the locating of the face "three miles from the 'pit-shaft,' " the mentioning of the trepanner, and the specifying of the water as¹ originating in "old mine workings" all tie Mr. Mugglestone's poem to this particular historical event. These are signs that do not come from the poet's craft per se but from the topic's facts.

Mr. Mugglestone's image of the rescuers is more instrumental than is Mr. Wainwright's. They are the more ordinary "Brave Men"; they are "*like* Heroes"; they respond primarily to human motives quite common among miners, like comradeship. Mr. Mugglestone himself in his years underground took part in rescue attempts—one to succour his own trapped father, in fact—and he generalizes such an experience quite pragmatically: "You go in and get him out . . . any miner would. . . . Where you're praising these particular rescue men, well, it doesn't matter whether it happened at Lofthouse or where it happened, you'd still have that same thing. Everybody would go in." The opening lines of another of Mr. Mugglestone's poems—this time on a Derbyshire mine disaster—emphasize this normalcy: "They were real live human beings, just the same as you and I."

A further instrumental feature of Mr. Mugglestone's poem is

ENGLISH FOLK POETRY

This Poem, composed by Mr. E. Mugglestone, 11 Church Street, Langold, an ex-miner, and now a porter at the Victoria Hospital, Worksop, is intended as a tribute to all those brave men who assisted in trying to rescue the seven miners, who lost their lives in the Lofthouse Colliery Disaster.

Mr. Mugglestone guarantees that every penny raised by the sale of this poem, will be donated to the "Relief Fund" for the dependants of the victims, and thanks everyone for their contributions.

PRICE 5p. per COPY.

THE TRAGEDY OF THE LOFTHOUSE COLLIERY DISASTER

They were working on the Night shift, on the "coal-face" underground,
Some three miles from the "pit-shaft", where no daylight's ever found,
The machine was tearing at the "coal", and all seemed right until,
There was a sudden "cracking" of the coal, and a "gap" they could not fill,
And all at once the "water" from old mine workings they had "struck",
Poured through that "gap" in torrents, like a "raging sea" - Bad Luck!
They made a dash for "safety", and one or two of the men got through,
But seven "poor souls" were left behind, and for them grave "fears grew",
The scene was Lofthouse "Coal-mine", and soon the grave news "spread",
Quite soon a crowd did gather, all around that dark "pit-head",
Then very soon all "Britain", heard about it on the "News",
And waited patiently, and prayed - in homes, and in "Church-Pews",
There was no shortage of "Brave Men, to go down underground,
To search the "mine" for any sign of "life", that might be found,
But the water had "cascaded", barring the way of these brave men,
And there was "little-hope" for those poor souls, trapped down below, but then,
These "rescuers" would not give in, and for days they "battled" on,
And worked like mad, - with miles of pipes, - until the pumps did run,
Whilst all the time the "Relatives", tried hard to keep back "tears",
And prayed for "miracles" to happen, and so allay their "fears",
Not a single stone was left "unturned", by the men far down below,
And round the "clock" they battled on, to make the water "flow",
The courage of these men must be, a lesson to us all,
And thank "God" for the "comradeship", as they answered to the call,
At last they found a "body", and then all hope was lost,
Of finding anyone "alive" - seven more "lives" to the"cost",
Of "winning" coal to keep us "warm", Oh! what a price to pay,
With human lives, that ne'er again, will see the light of day,
So when the task of these "staunch-men", is finally "complete",
And the bodies all "recovered" - from the "water", "silt" and "heat",
We'll say "Well Done, God Bless you all", from the bottom of the "heart",
You gave your "ALL" like "HEROES", and each one played his part.

****

the mentioning of certain facts that were inseparable from the whole event—for example, the grief suffered by the dead men's families. Though the poem refers only to the emotional side of the families' circumstances, not to their practical need for financial support, the poet added this further instrumental component to his action by selling the poem to raise funds for those families.

So far "The Tragedy of the Lofthouse Colliery Disaster" appears from the discussion to be more instrumental than Mr. Wainwright's poem; one characteristic that raises its expressive quality, however, is the hint of victimization in lines 26–28:

> . . . seven more "lives" to the "cost",
> Of "winning" coal to Keep us "warm", Oh! what a price to pay,
> With human lives, that ne'er again, will see the light of day.

An economic image is adumbrated here; "we" are the consumers who pay too dearly for the product coal in the currency of miners' lives. But the figure is not extended to include the fourth component of an economic transaction, the exploiting—and thus profiting —"seller" of the product; nor does it explicitly suggest that we victimize the miners by casually using them as currency for our own self-indulgence. The victimizing image is thus only a potential one, for two reasons: first, running throughout the poem is a dominantly thematic conception of equal reciprocity in social relationships (the comradeship of the miners, the fair exchange between the bravery of the rescue workers and the gratitude we render them in return) that is contradictory to the theme of exploitative relationships; and second, Mr. Mugglestone's normative world view accepts dangerous work and the need to mine coal as given features of the real world. He does not question that state of affairs, only the particular methods of some of its operations.

These premises emerge clearly in Mr. Mugglestone's second poem, "In Memoriam: The Aftermath of the Lofthouse Disaster," which also raises the notion that the economic transaction is grossly unfair: "What a terrible end to those lives in their prime, / What a price for the coal, we get from the mine!" However, the poem goes on to pose not only a solution to the problem, but a solution that draws upon existing resources rather than upon change: the solution is to intensify safety precautions. (This is an ongoing concern of Mr. Mugglestone's; he has written a whole poem on the topic, "Safety First," the first four lines of which are quoted in the opening paragraph of this chapter.) Thus, the existing interpretation of the system is not up to question, only some of its mechanics, and the implications of the economic trope are not pursued; the instrumental in the response prevails.

One obvious difference between the first two poems and "In Memoriam" is that the latter is in a lyric mode, not a narrative one. But this mode also matches the reality of its topic, which is not the rescue attempts, as in the preceding poems, but the deaths. And unlike the rescue attempts, the deaths were not a sequence of events over time but an indivisible occurrence at a single point in time. The static mode of contemplation and sentiment that is the lyric manner thus matches the structure of the real topic. A further realistic element is the forthright sentiment of sympathy for the dead men's kin, embedded in an affecting description of their sorrow. And once again, of course, there is the use made of this poem to satisfy basic human needs; Mr. Mugglestone raised an additional sum for the Disaster Fund with its sale.

The most expressive thread in this text is one that reminds us of the significations implied by the memorial garden the unidentified man planted aboveground. The dead miners are deprived of sunlight, of proper encasement in sheet and coffin, of strewn flowers about them, and of repeated visits from loved ones. Instead, they lie alone in the turbulence of consuming heat, their unsecured bodies merging with surrounding earth, never to be in close physical contact with visiting kin but separated by massive "seals built by men." This distaste at abandoning to nature one's own dead where they fall, whether it be on a battlefield, in the ocean, or underground, is not peculiar to miners nor to British belief systems. But Mr. Mugglestone goes further than simple and conventional distaste; somewhat in the manner of Mr. Wainwright's "hell-hole," the final home of the Lofthouse dead is clearly analogized to Purgatory in an expressive set of signifiers.

A poem that combines in equal proportions a narrative technique in telling of the rescue attempts with a lyrical technique in dealing with the deaths is one by Mrs. Mavis Walsh Proud of Thorpe, a small village in Rothwell Urban District and right next door to Lofthouse and Outwood. Mrs. Proud was born about two miles away from Thorpe, in Morley, but has lived in her present home for the last thirty years. Like the two poets we have considered so far, she comes from a working-class background. She left school at age fourteen to work in the mills, and today works parttime in the canteen of the local school. As she described herself to me in a letter of 19 May, 1973: "We are just ordinary folk who live in a terrace house here in Thorpe." She is also a long-time resident of this mining district; in fact, her husband comes from a mining family and went into the pits himself straight from school, but after a year and a half "got out," as he says, at his father's insistence, to work on the railways. Since 1967 he has been a bartender in Wakefield.

Both Mrs. Proud and her husband stressed to me the local and the our-community aspects of the Lofthouse Colliery Disaster. They can see the pithead from their home; they know personally many who work there and their families; and because of their proximity, the drama of the events was all around them over the week-long period of the Disaster. But she talks of it quite pragmatically: "It was just a local disaster that happened around us," she said, "and I just wanted to put it down in my book. And I put it down as a poem."

The poem shows this sense of personal involvement, this closeness between herself and the topic, both in its first-person, semi-participant-observer device, and in the affecting sadness of its tone:

LOFTHOUSE MINE DISASTER[11]

A great tragedy has struck us, and our eyes are filled with tears,
A terrible disaster at our mine, which has worked for many
    years.
Our hearts are filled with sadness, and our bodies numb with
    shock,
To think about those miners, entombed down there, with rock,
And a tremendous depth of water, and all that silt, and slime,
You've got to have a heart of iron, to work down in a mine.
Day after day, night after night, the rescue still goes on.
Will they reach those men, who have been down there so long.
And yet a greater call goes out, to try to reach those men,
People come from far, and near, to help to get to them.
But days go by, and all hope, now begins to fade.
Their time is getting shorter now, more effort must be made.
By now the people realize, all efforts were in vain,
Let's hope they did not suffer, or die of any pain.
Our thoughts go out to relatives, and friends, of those brave
    men,
We all share in their great sorrow, and try to comfort them,
No one knows the parting, nor what the parting cost,
Only God in His great Mercy, has gained what they have lost.

Like the two other poets we have so far considered, Mrs. Proud concentrates to a large extent on a literal rendering of the facts of the event, mentions the plight of the relatives left behind, and shows concern that the dead men's final resting place was entombment in "rock. / And a tremendous depth of water, and all that silt, and slime." Whether because of her sex, or because she was more personally involved with the victims of the disaster—or a combination of the two, perhaps—her poem is a more emotional and sentimental piece than the generally "tougher" and more pragmatically sympathetic poems of Mr. Wainwright and Mr. Mugglestone. A further expressive aspect is its undertone of fatalism: Mrs. Proud's rescuers do not attack their task as energetically as was the case in our first two poems; the poet-observer asks whether, rather than asserts that, the men will be reached; there is an implication that the rescue efforts were predestined to fail ("By now the people realize, all efforts were in vain"); and only God truly knows and truly gains.

While her poem does not display the degree of Lofthouse-specific detail that the miner poets' narrative poems do, and is thus more expressively generalizable, Mrs. Proud does particularize her topic by placing herself in close social conjunction with the victims and their families and with the mine itself, which is "our mine." Accordingly, the miners are far more the everyday humans that most people are; they are "brave men" but it is their "hearts" that are of "iron" rather than their bodies, as in Mr. Wainwright's and Mr. Mugglestone's poems. Even a signifying homology that the poem constructs is in the realm of everyday feelings rather than in the realm of the more remote economics; just as the miners are "frozen" in rock, so are we "frozen" in shock. This is not transformation but similarity across semantic domains at the same qualitative level, and further accentuates the participatory empathy between the miners and us. Mr. Mugglestone's very favorable reaction to Mrs. Proud's poem when I showed him a copy is instructive: "It's more down-to-earth; it's much on the same line as that of mine, ain't it? ["In Memoriam"] . . . it means the same thing, really." However, influenced perhaps by the apparently more emotional tone of Mrs. Proud's work, he added perceptively, "I would say he's either a miner himself or it's his wife that's written that."

While Mrs. Proud, like the two miner poets, shows practical concern for the plight of the widowed and orphaned survivors, she only hints at a concern with the unsuitability of the burial environment—"entombed down there with rock." Such a hint appears in a poem by yet another miner, but in a more complex, perhaps sublimated homology. The author of this poem is Mr. Danny Hampsey of Dinnington Colliery in south Yorkshire, a colliery where Mr. Mugglestone himself was once employed. I was unable to contact Mr. Hampsey, and so most of my information comes from a newspaper item, the complete text of which I quote:

A MINER'S POEM FOR LOFTHOUSE[12]

An area which is as dependent on mining for as many jobs as ours still is, always feels for the people involved in such tragedies as the recent one at Lofthouse in a special way.

Mr. Danny Hampsey, himself a miner at Dinnington, wrote the following poem which was read at a memorial service for the Lofthouse victims at Dinnington Parish Church.

"No more for them the song of birds,
The smell of new mown hay,
No more will they see a wide green hill,
Or watch young lambs at play.

They cannot hear their children cry,
Or console their grieving wives,
They went down the mine to provide for them,
And there they lost their lives.

Jesus paid the price of sin,
On Calvary by His blood,
These men paid the price of coal,
In the Lofthouse slime and mud.

We can help by prayer to meet their God,
The men who gave their lives,
We must try to help with material things,
For their children [an]d their wives."

We can infer from the reporter's introduction that, in general, the same cultural considerations applicable to our first two miner poets probably apply to Mr. Hampsey as well. The expressive signifiers verge on the symbolic, however, in Mr. Hampsey's semantic projection of the dead miners into the domain of religion: Jesus is to sin as the Lofthouse miners are to coal. The implications of this homology's analogic extensions are far-reaching: Jesus died of course not for his own sins but for ours; thus the Lofthouse miners must have died not for their own coal but for ours. By further extension, therefore, the miners were our scapegoats, an extension more strongly implied here than in Mr. Mugglestone's economic trope.

Three things in Mr. Hampsey's text mitigate the extremity of this interpretation, however. First, the poem does not explicitly point the finger at us, the nonminers of its audience; in fact, our sin could not be too extreme because the penance is not very severe—consisting only of praying for the miners and of making some material contribution to their families' welfare. The second mitigation is that verse two centers the miners' motivation not in the social system at large, which includes us, but in the very narrow matrix of the family. It was for their own families, to provide them a living, that the miners faced danger; if anything the text more explicitly "blames" the families for making scapegoats of the Lofthouse victims. A third mitigation is that the Biblical frame of reference is not sustained or developed as a ground for interpretation; it is but one motif.

In the absence of a native exegesis we must depend chiefly on such textual analysis. We are helped somewhat by our knowledge of working-class poetry, however, and such knowledge suggests that the transcendent extremity of the scapegoat interpretation is only partially and subliminally applicable here. We are also helped by knowing that this poem was read at and probably composed for a church service; thus the occasion and the associated setting may have contributed more to the religious motif than did a transcendent vision of abstract meanings of the Lofthouse tragedy. Certainly, the closing couplet is firmly situated at the instrumental pole of response-meanings.

There is another element of the expressive in the opening verse, which reminds us once again of the ideal burial place that the dead men, it was so painfully evident, were never to enjoy. Here, of course, the reference is to what the victims will miss in life, not in death, but the two images are not that far apart when we place them in a larger set; just as the muck of the flooded mine-tomb is to the peaceful beauty of a conventional gravesite, so the ugliness of the underground work environment of living miners is to their aboveground off-work environments. Despite the live-miners element in Mr. Hampsey's homology, however, as a signifier it still is highly expressive, for not only are miners' underground milieux not seen by miners themselves to be all that ugly, but also their home environments are not usually of such pastoral qualities; row-houses and slag-heaps are more the norm. Of the five poems we have examined so far, therefore, Mr. Hampsey's is clearly the most "poetic" in the sense of expressing an interpretive vision rather than one determined by the reality of the stimulus event—even though his closing couplet does lead us firmly back to empirical facts. A further realism is found in the lyric mode, which, as I have said, matches the "lyric" reality of death as an atemporal state.

A sixth set of verses on the Lofthouse Colliery Disaster comes from a song composed by Mr. Walter Greaves of Crosshills, near Keighley, about eight miles northwest of Bradford and on the outer edge of the textile area, bordering on the agricultural Dales region. Sixty-six years old when I met him in 1973, Mr. Greaves has been a blacksmith almost all his life, as his father was before him. He described his background and his contact with mining culture:

> He was a blacksmith who became a quack doctor, was me dad, and I used to go to markets with him . . . Castleford . . . a lot of mining markets . . . this is where I've made me contacts with miners. . . .
>
> I've worked with miners—I've never been a miner, but I've worked with miners. I've worked on markets at Barnsley, I've met them, I've raced with them as a racing cyclist, and—you know, I felt—I really felt that I'd like to do some little thing, express my feelings and that.

Here is the text of Mr. Greaves's song as recorded in performance by the maker himself.[13]

The Lofthouse was a happy pit
Lofthouse men came from far and near
Miners made from Yorkshire grit
They seemed to know no fear
As coal they got from out the earth
At what cost in blood and tears
How can you say what the coal was worth
They'd won these hundred years?

Two weeks before the fateful night
They reached their highest goal
That century never more had seen
Twelve thousand tons of coal
But just as though their pride must fall
The sound of bubbling water
Came frightening through the South 9B wall
Chilling hearts of men so brave.

Two tiny pumps the experts said
To cope with the water seeping
Despite the warning small heed was paid
And their comrades now lie sleeping
To have made test bores would have wasted time
Our production must not slacken
Coal dust they measure in pounds and pence
To these people nothing else matters.

At half-past two o'clock and then
Angry torrents of floods broke through
Tossing gear, machines, and men
Helpless they were as storm-flung leaves
"Run for your life, get out, get out,"
It was every man for himself
No time, no chance to help your mates
The waters would not wait.

Six days we pumped to get them out
An air pocket might have saved them
The news we dreaded came at last
The pocket it was empty
Not one had reached the precious air
And in coal-black mud now they lay
No more their families' lives to share
No more see the light of day.

It's no disaster the Coal Board said
Only seven were not spared
At least ten miners must be dead
Before disaster can be declared
So when these miners are picketing again
Let us hope it will not be soon
Remember heroes do not change
The newspapers change their tune.

The demand for traditional blacksmithing not being what it once was, Mr. Greaves has been in recent years far more involved with producing artistic than utilitarian metal work. To further this end, he attended classes at the Dewsbury and Batley Technical and Art College a few years ago and there came in contact with local folksong revival participants. Since then he has become very much involved both as a performer and as a follower in the West Riding folksinging network, and in fact advertises himself as the "Singing Blacksmith," specializing in songs and monologues.[14] A further related factor in Mr. Greaves's attraction to the folksong revival is the strong leftist orientation of some of that movement.[15] Mr. Greaves has been an active member of the British Communist Party for some forty years. We must consider his song in this wider framework, therefore; he was attracted to the folksong revival and to the folksong model as a culture form in part because of certain ideological characteristics both of the movement and of certain types of folksong.

The formal features of Mr. Greaves's verses display in the

main nonfigurative language and the conventional meter, rhyme, and stanzaic form of traditional folksong, all of which have also characterized the other five poems. Similarly, he situates his topic in its real environment with a certain concreteness of detail specific to this event. Like our other poets, he shows distaste for the nature of the final grave, mentions the bereaved, if somewhat tangentially, and exhibits a strong sense of personal identification with the miners by switching to the first person "we" when telling of the rescue attempts. The miners, particularly the rescue workers, are "heroes" in the final stanza, but mortal and fallible heroes, especially when confronted with intransigent natural forces; the flood, for instance, destroys the usual comradeship of miners and creates the unnatural circumstances of "It was every man for himself / No time, no time to help your mates"—though this is a hypothetical reconstruction of events that few miners would accept as factual.

We can see, however, that Mr. Greaves has incorporated into his verses other aspects of the Lofthouse affair that, though real, we have not encountered in the previous compositions. Moreover, he takes a strong ideological stance on those aspects. For instance, he criticizes the authorities for not boring precautionary test holes, suggesting that their negligence was due to materialistic considerations at the expense of humane ones; he chastises them for not heeding the warnings of the seeping water that had been going on for some time before the accident; he accuses them of other "establishment" behavior in general with his ironic barb at their denying "disaster" status to the accident on quantitative grounds; and he gets in a dig at the protean nature of the establishment press's ideology, which changes depending on its holder's vested interests of the moment.

Certainly, much of this detail is instrumental in directly reflecting real events in the physical world; even the inferences Mr. Greaves draws from these facts—inferences about the Coal Board's motives and philosophy—are to a credible extent rational ones. But how well do his interpretations fit the conventional frame of reference that West Riding cultural norms usually place on these things, the prevailing "social construction of reality"? It is instructive to hear our working-class miner, Mr. Mugglestone, give his opinion of Mr. Greaves's song; saying "I've no time for folk like that," he elaborated:

> I don't think it's fair criticism. Because, I mean, take me, for instance; who am I to criticize the Coal Board? I wouldn't know what the Coal Board is doing. Until a proper inquiry has been

made by the people who understand these things, I don't think it's fair to criticize.

When I told Mr. Greaves this opinion of his verses, he lamented the lack of "class consciousness" on the part of the critic and asserted that miners in the more militant Barnsley area, the center of Yorkshire's coal mining activities, would certainly be in sympathy with his point of view—though, in fact, Mr. Mugglestone has worked most of his life very close to the Barnsley district. At first glance, Mr. Greaves's rebuttal gains support when we recall that one of the specific criticisms leveled against the Coal Board by the union's official representative at the inquiry, Mr. Arthur Scargill, was its failure to dig test bores at South 9B face—the same charge Mr. Greaves levels in his song. But Mr. Greaves's dismay at Mr. Mugglestone's disapproval ignores the different perceptions he and the retired miner hold as to the nature of the genre "poem," for one, and of proper role conduct, for another. As a genre, a poem to Mr. Mugglestone—and indeed, to most working-class poets in my experience—is a proper vehicle for factual "truth," for tribute or lament, and for dwelling on the spiritual and emotional qualities of its topic; there are other genres of expression more appropriate for attack. Accordingly while Mr. Greaves's attitude and substance were matched by those of Mr. Scargill of the N.U.M., not only was it Mr. Scargill's proper role to analyze and find fault, but the genre of the inquiry was the appropriate context for social ideology and disputation, whereas poetry making was not. Witness a public statement Mr. Scargill himself made shortly after the disaster: miners all over the country were in the process of conducting a strike vote when the tragedy occurred at Lofthouse, and Mr. Scargill pleaded with his constituents that they not let the affecting nature of the disaster sway their vote; in other words, he asked them to be ruled in their decision on the practical topic of the strike by rational considerations, by a realistic weighing of the facts, not by any sentiment that the Lofthouse events may have aroused.[16]

In sum, while Mr. Greaves is more realistic in some of his references than are our other poets, he uses this instrumentally determined content for highly expressive ends by interpreting these data within a Marxist frame of reference that challenges the normative frames of reference—informational, pragmatic, and humanitarian. Only briefly does the songmaker adopt the alternative definition that our other poets have suggested: the economic cost equation between coal and life (stanza one). He also eschews the self-correcting solution favored by our previous poets, preferring instead a model of adversary relationships. According to the dictates of this model, working-class miners are in unnegotiable conflict with the bourgeoisie that includes both management and newspaper editors. The working conditions of coal production create alienation even among workers themselves; when, through the fault of management, disaster strikes, each man must ignore his mate to fend for himself in a battle for limited resources. The system that stresses high production as a desideratum not only causes tragedy by slighting safety precautions but also seduces the allegiances of the worker, to his own ultimate detriment; witness stanza two, in which the miners have been led into the sin of hubris (overreaching pride at their record production), a sin that literally causes the tragic catastrophe of the inevitable fall.

Within Mr. Greaves's microsocial environment of the folk revival clubs, of course, such a song and its frame of reference would not normally be considered inappropriate, in part because of the intellectual and leftist orientation of many folk revival participants, in part because many of the industrial folksongs of the nineteenth and twentieth centuries that portray management/labor conflict are popular as performance items and prominent in favored folk revival chapbooks, like A. L. Lloyd's *Come All Ye Bold Miners*.[17] Mr. Greaves acknowledges influence from other popular songs about mine accidents, particularly "The Ballad of Springhill" and "The Gresford Disaster."[18] For example, his source for the tune to which he set his words was a recent issue of *English Dance and Song* magazine; there the traditional air was used to carry the words of a recently composed song, "The Silkstone Disaster," on an 1838 Yorkshire mine disaster. That song, too, was potential grist to the mill of sociopolitical protest, since many children had been killed in the disaster, but its author, like our other Lofthouse poets, instead wrote an elegaic lament for the dead children. Mr. Greaves criticizes "The Silkstone Disaster" for missing the opportunity to incorporate ideological protest into its text. "The Gresford Disaster," on the other hand, does lay specific blame on authority and, moreover, incorporates the highly unusual (for folksong) device of irony in its final verse:

> The Lord Mayor of London's collecting
> To help both our children and wives
> The owners have sent some white lilies
> To pay for the poor collier's lives.[19]

The similarity between this and Mr. Greaves's ironic last verse in his mine disaster song is obvious; "The Gresford Disaster," he says, "has influenced me, quite clearly."

Thus even within the folk revival's own definitions, Mr. Greaves's Marxist interpretation is not fully shared. His song's acceptability within this setting is ultimately more attributable to its emphasis on working-class *dramatis personae* and on the regional, culture-specific nature of its topic (his is the only Lofthouse poem that specifies regional identity—"miners made of Yorkshire grit").[20] On the other hand, its lack of significant popularity with local audiences and other performers is likely attributable to its strong ideological stance toward a *local and current tragedy*. Certainly, within the much larger macroenvironment of West Riding culture norms, his frame of reference is highly expressive and significantly removed from the "facts" of his topic.

I have spent an unusual amount of exegesis on Mr. Greaves's song because it is in certain ways the most unique of the nine Lofthouse poems. The first five poems more visibly constitute a set, as do the next three, while Mr. Greaves's stands by itself. The first of our three remaining poems is concerned almost entirely with the most dramatic aspect of the Lofthouse affair, the rescue attempts. I was unable to interview the poet, and so most of my information comes from the poem itself and its introductory note, as printed in the *Dewsbury Reporter*. The poet lives in one of Dewsbury's satellite industrial villages:

HONOURING THE RESCUERS[21]

Those who followed the news of the Lofthouse Colliery Disaster were no doubt greatly impressed as I was by the sheer heroism of the rescue teams.

As an amateur poet, I have expressed my feelings in verse and send you a copy herewith in case you feel that your readers may be interested.

> Roy Blakeley,
> Spen Valley Road,
> Ravensthorpe.

LOFTHOUSE COLLIERY MARCH 73

Did you see how they flocked here to the rescue
    With grim resolve in every manly stride
As they marched in single file towards the pit head
    Half fearing what they'd find down there inside?

Did you wonder how these men could find the courage
  To struggle in the bowels of the earth
To grapple with the odds all laid against them
  To give the waiting children second birth?

Did you know how much they placed themselves in danger,
  How they toiled until exhaustion took its toll
How they fought to find their mates and give them succour
  Forgetting self to reach their worthy goal?
Can you understand the hell they had to face there,
  The mud and cold and cramp and silt and slime
The distress of one road closed after another,
  The desperate need to struggle through in time?

Can you forget these great lads' glorious efforts
  Although they very sadly came to nought?
In the end they found their struggles unavailing
  But God knows how courageously they fought.
We can never pay the debt we truly owe them
  But we'll remember till the very end of time
That those men who earn their living at the coalface
  Are imbued with a courage that's sublime.

Although "Lofthouse Colliery March 73" is the fourth poem to concentrate on the rescue efforts, in contrast with the other three—Mr. Wainwright's "The Lofthouse Disaster," Mr. Mugglestone's "The Tragedy of the Lofthouse Colliery Disaster," and Mrs. Proud's "Lofthouse Mine Disaster"—Mr. Blakeley's poem does not let the flow of actual events dictate a narrative mode to his presentation; instead, the poet has distanced his composition from those facts and conceived of them statically in the contemplative lyric mode. At the same time he pays greater attention to poetic form in conceptualizing his topic, with the result that a set of "artificial" conventions are drawn upon to structure the images—in this case, a tightly-knit series of rhetorical questions: did you see? wonder? know? understand? forget? and so forth.

This distancing of poem from topic through the mediation of the introspective self and that of poetic form is also displayed in the poem's depiction of social relations. Mr. Blakeley's introductory note delineates three distinct categories of social actors: himself, the "amateur poet"; his audience, the "your readers" of the *Dewsbury Reporter*; and the members of the rescue teams. The poem throughout most of its text maintains these distinctions; the audience is addressed directly in the second person ("Did *you* see," etc.), the miners are referred to in the contrasting third person ("how *they*"), and the author is implied as first-person speaker. These three categories are reduced to two in the last stanza, the "we" and the "they," as the poet collapses his reading audience and himself into a single social category "we" in debt to the miner "them."

This we/they contrast is particularly marked in the image of the miner Other. We have seen the miners eulogized in our other poems, but by intensification rather than by transformation. Mr. Wainwright's "super-fit" men, for instance, also displayed counterbalancing intensity of ordinary emotions, and Mr. Mugglestone's miners were *like* heroes. Mr. Blakeley's subjects, however, are less human and less fallible; though they are "half fearing," feel distress at failure, and tire physically, their dominant qualities are more transcendent ones—they "struggle in the bowels of the earth," have the potential to "give the waiting children second birth," and "are imbued with a courage that's sublime." These images are chiefly informed by an interpretive frame of reference that is religious-cum-military. The military connotation is expressed in the image of marching in single file to "struggle" and "fight" against superior odds in an environment of high and formidable danger, the religious in the image of the rescue workers as saviors both of their trapped mates and of the potential orphans. These men are "sublime" to the extent that they do not just preserve but practically create life—"give the waiting children second birth." Such sublimeness is beyond the ordinary knowledge available to "us." We can at best "remember"; only God, to whom the miners are closer than we are, truly "knows." A distinct hierarchy is set up here, then; at the highest level is God, at the lowest are the ordinary poet and his audience, in between are the mortal but transcendent miners, whose relationship to us is one of creator-givers to receivers. The implicit analogy between miners and Christ, while not as overt as in Mr. Hampsey's poem, is more thematically sustained here. Interestingly, one of Mr. Mugglestone's reactions to this poem was that the author "sounded more like a parson" to him.

We should note also that Mr. Blakeley's poem does not mention two "facts" most of our other poets have included: the unsuitable nature of the victims' grave, and the grief or needs of the bereaved. And as far as we know, no instrumental use, such as selling the verses for a donation to the Disaster Fund, was made of the poem.

The eighth poem is by Mrs. Margaret Watford of West Ardsley in Morley Municipal Borough. Mrs. Watford lives quite close to where the shaft was sunk in a vain attempt to provide air to the possibly still alive miners until the underground rescue teams could reach them. She drove by this scene every day for a week on her way to and from work in Dewsbury; thus she experienced a daily, visible reminder of the Lofthouse Disaster. She sent her poem along with an explanatory letter to the *Morley Observer,* which published them as follows in its Batley affiliate:

SEARCHING FOR BLACK DIAMONDS[22]

The recent tragedy at Lofthouse Colliery, has moved me to write a poem, in remembrance for the men who lost their lives. Perhaps it may be of some little comfort to those who knew them.

> If I had the poet's magic pen,
> I would write a glorifying sonnet, to the men
> Who live their whole existence down the mine
> Cleaving out, black diamonds as they shine
> In the dark wilderness these Giants grow to love
> Such love can only be a mystery, to those who spend their
>   little lifetimes up above.

> So being an outsider, it is hard to understand
> That pride of home, and weariness, and land,
> The happiness, and the endurance of these men
> Who turn for tormented hours, their heads
> Their backs, and all their beings, downwards from the sun,
> To sweat and strain, until at last their GOAL
> Is seen—reclining in its regal setting—COAL!!

> > Margaret Watford
> > 4[1]5 Westerton Road,
> > West Ardsley.

After I had made her acquaintance, Mrs. Watford confessed to me that she had not been telling the truth in the letter above. She had, in fact, written the poem in 1943, when she was nineteen. While the poem's sentiments had resulted from an admiration for the miner similar to one aroused in her by the events of Lofthouse, the poem's composition was not stimulated by a specific circumstance such as a mining accident. I include her poem in this analysis because she considered it an appropriate response to the Lofthouse Disaster and because she communicated the poem to her local audience as being such a response.

I may give some brief background information on Mrs. Watford: she was born in Keighley, Mr. Greaves's hometown, but has lived in Dewsbury and Wakefield most of her life. She comes from a middle-class family (her father was regional manager for an insurance company) and received formal education up to the age of seventeen. Her present occupation, since being widowed in 1970, is collecting and collating data for computer operations of the Dewsbury Hospital Management Committee. She is very much involved in local women's organizations, youth programs, social work, and the Morley History Society. She is very creative, and has written many unpublished poems as well as the occasional short story and skit, among other things.

Since Mrs. Watford's poem is not directly "about" the Lofthouse events, she of course makes no mention of either the accident or the rescue; her poem is a conception of the miner in general. Formally, the content and structure is determined to some extent by the conventions of the sonnet genre rather than by the realities of its topic; thus besides the conventions of line count and rhyme pattern, the sonnet form also determines the poem's movement from a relatively specific problem to its relatively general solution. As in Mr. Blakeley's poem, however, the most striking aspect of Mrs. Watford's "Searching for Black Diamonds" is its view of the social relationships between Self and Other and its dominant semantic frame of reference. Thus the "we" of Mrs. Watford and her non-miner audience and the "they" of the miners are even more clearly distinguishable than are similar social categories in Mr. Blakeley's poem. First, there is a strong contrast in the spatial domain; they live their hyperbolic "whole existence" down below, while we live "up above" them. Second, we are lighted by ordinary sunshine, they by the excessive brilliance of "black diamonds." Third, their environment is composed of extremes, both of wilderness and of the rich brilliance of the precious fossil, while ours is presumably characterized by the ordinary of our own "little lifetimes." Fourth, they are Giants, while we are "little"; and finally, they are a "mystery" to us, while we ourselves are, evidently, easily comprehended.

The relationship between the ordinary "we" and the extraordinary "they" is thus structurally similar to Mr. Blakeley's. But Mrs. Watford's frame of reference is certainly not a military one and only by a stretch of the imagination a religious one (for example, if we equate the notion of wilderness with Christ's experience). Perhaps the closest I can come to characterizing its signifying frame of reference is to call it "mythological" (but not necessarily the Giants of classical mythology); the miners are seen as a race apart of physically larger and stronger beings whose shape only is that of men, a race whose sole environment is a treasure-filled underground cavern.

Clearly, the poet's "magic pen" is conjuring up a fittingly "magical" set of motifs that depict a coherent otherworld quite "a mystery" to "outsiders" like herself and her everyday newspaper-reading audience.

Her miners' more mortal characteristics—especially their love of their working wilderness and of the regal nature of coal—are, of course, not miners' own conceptions of these things, nor are they meant to be; my point is only that the poem is greatly removed from the facts of the topic-stimulus and is an almost entirely expressive response. Mrs. Watford, aware of this, incorporates an instrumental element into her letter: "Perhaps it may be of some little comfort to those who knew them." This is an attempt to topicalize her poem to Lofthouse, but it is also a restrained and oblique reference to something that many of our other poets—especially Mr. Hampsey, in his plea for material donations—have been quite explicit about: an expression of sympathy toward the bereaved. In part, of course, social decorum forbade Mrs. Watford's being more explicit, since she does not know personally any of the dead miners' kin or friends. But also, in part, the lack of explicitness is an indication of the poet's extremely introspective and subjective reaction to the Lofthouse implications.

The ninth and last poem on the Lofthouse Colliery tragedy is by a reporter for one of Britain's larger provincial newspapers, the *Evening Post* of Leeds. The poet, Mr. Gordon Pickles, spent long hours at the pithead covering the story of the rescue attempts for his newspaper, which later published the following:

We MUST NOT Forget[23]

This verse was written by GORDON PICKLES, a member of the Evening Post's reporting team at Lofthouse Colliery during the abortive rescue attempt.

> They were seven.
> More than men, they worked for our
> Fires, until a time set its seal upon them, pinched out
> Their flame and stole them away from us.
> That same time will dry the mothers' tears and strengthen
>   their
> Growing young.
> Time will make some of us forget—their headlines
> Will go as cold as the freezing frenzy which flushed their
>   lives away.
> But to some, the sweat-oiled machines who tunnelled to

That coal cavern grave, a black pain will remain.
They will not forget the price. They will not forget the life
Giver turning, betraying its mountain burble and retching
Ugly, spewing out of a black rock face.
Mine men, pit-hardened, spat in that water, bled their
  fingers
On rock for rescue.
That nasty taste, the pain pang of tears, for they were not
  there, men, will take with them every time they go,
  for us,
Down that dark shaft they cannot forget, and nor must
We.

Mr. Pickles allows himself the greatest freedom for expression, since he is constrained neither by the objective facts of the events nor by the formal constraints of a single meter or rhyme, of end-stopped lines, or of highly formal verse models like the sonnet. Instead, his poem is structured predominantly by chosen images and his interpretations of them. In addition, his major signifying units are much closer to the expressiveness of symbols than to the instrumentalness of signs. His two major signifiers are time and water, which connote several meanings within the two semantic paradigms of life and death.

That Mr. Pickles should have conceived of time symbolically is certainly, in one sense, a logical result of the nature of the events; that the men were possibly still alive made time a conspicuous element in the drama at Lofthouse, for in their starkest simplicity, the rescue attempts were a race against time. But our other poets have conceptualized this time as linear and chronological, as the one-dimensional, factual substratum of the flow of events. Mr. Pickles, on the other hand, not only specifies a negative role for time-as-enemy but also enlarges upon this significantly; for instance, time marks the trapped miners as subject to its suzerainty ("set its seal upon them"), eventually carrying its dominion through to the worst possible conclusion—not just determining but indeed causing the deaths ("pinched out / Their flame and stole them away"). The other negative value of time is that it may also "pinch out" the dead miners from our memories. The polar-opposite, positive value of time is that it will help the grieving mothers ease the pain of their loss and give further life to their children ("strengthen their growing young").

The polarized values of the water symbol are that it brings both life and death. Its life-giving qualities are taken for granted, identified in the poem only by being so named ("the life / Giver") and represented only briefly in a pastoral motif ("mountain burble"), the babbling brook of conventional depiction. The negative value of this water is its betrayal as a life-taking turncoat "which flushed their lives away."

While time and water are major organizing symbols relatively independent from each other at one level of abstraction, at another level they belong to the same paradigm of "nature," and contrast with "human." As paradigmatic analogues, both time and water quench the "flame" of human life and "flush" it away. Human attempts to counteract this domination are made with the human analogues of nature's water; the rescuers sweat, spill their blood on the rock, spit defiantly into the flood, and weep. Nature's water responds with human characteristics; it "retches" and "spews" in its fatal eruption. But eventually the pure, more "human" tears of the rescuers, while not saving the doomed men, bring a measure of emotional relief; in addition, tears conquer time by preserving the dead men's memory, for those tears will be perpetually tasted.

Time and water are therefore dualistic in their relationship with humans; they each take as well as sustain life. The dominant homology, of which various permutations are both explicit and implicit, is that water is to life as time is to memory. While, as we have seen, the "is to" relationship has both positive and negative values, the poem's message is that the positive value should prevail; our memory should not give way to the "coldness" of time but should be kept perpetually fresh, just as water should not be a life-taker but a life-enabler. The human portion of this message is encapsulated in the poem's title, "We MUST NOT Forget."

Though time and water are the dominant symbols in the poem's world view, many other signifiers support the opposing death/life paradigms. Death signifiers are these: *below, blackness, coal, cold, time controlling humans,* the *miner-Other,* and *spending one's own human resources* (tears, sweat, spit, blood, life). Their life contrasts are, respectively, *above, brightness, fire, heat, humans controlling time,* the *non-miner Self,* and *spending resources not one's own* (burning coal). The contrasts are in metonymic relationship (the death variables of nature—*coal,* for example—are necessary for the life variables of culture—*fire,* for example), while variables within the same paradigm are in metaphoric relationship (*blackness* and *coal,* for instance). The mediator of these two contrasting life/death paradigms is the signifier of the poem's main message, *memory*; for the living miners, *blackness* will always remain as a mnemonic to keep the dead living in memory, but we who do not experience such blackness must make a more conscious effort to do the same. These signifiers, along with the time and water symbols, constitute the poem's major frame of reference, the best word for which would be "cosmological." Three of the four elements of the cosmos—earth, fire, water—play prominent parts in this poem, as do two of the major parameters of the cosmos, time and space. It is surprising, in fact, that the one missing element, air, is not prominent, since it played such a major part in the real events. It may be that since it *was* such an integral and dominant part of the facts, the poet intended its noticeable absence to speak for its powerful presence; the unspoken *air* versus *no-air*, or the related *infinite air* versus *finite air*, take their silent places quite logically within the life/death code-structure.

One important semantic domain of signifiers in "We MUST NOT Forget" has also appeared in other poems: the structure of relationships between two highly distinguishable social entities, miners and "us." As in Mr. Blakeley's and Mrs. Watford's poems (though here the vehicle for the miner's image is not the religious, the military, or the mythological, but the supermechanistic), the miners are beings quite superior to us in select traits. They are "more than men," "sweat-oiled machines," and "pit-hardened," who ferociously defy nature's overwhelming odds by spitting at it, by bleeding their fingers unheedingly on its rock. Those are predominantly mechanistic qualities. Their superhuman qualities are a memory that even time cannot conquer and their capacity for grief is not of the same order you and I suffer; it is the physical and sensory "nasty taste . . . pain pang of tears," a different sort of intensification from the "sadness and pain," "grief and distress," and "remorse and fears" suffered by Mr. Wainwright's miners. This structural asymmetry between them and us is matched by a functional one most closely related to Mr. Blakeley's "Lofthouse Colliery March 73"; the flow of giving is in a one-way direction from the miners to the coal users, with no reciprocity. "They worked for our Fires" and in the process lost their own. And they will continue to do so *"for us"* (the poet's own emphasis).

In sum, of the nine poems on the Lofthouse Colliery Disaster, Mr. Pickles' "We MUST NOT Forget" is the most subjective, most introspective, most abstract, most expressive, and most removed from the facts of the topic-stimulus. Appropriately, it is the most generalizable (excluding Mrs. Watford's poem, which was written long before Lofthouse). Nothing in the poem's title or text is specific to the actual event, save for the opening line, "they were seven"; and seven, like three, is a formulaic number. We also have no reason to infer instrumental motives on Mr. Pickles' part, only affective and conceptual ones.

I have discussed the nine poems on the Lofthouse Colliery Disaster in the order of their increasing expressiveness or distancing of poetic response from the physical constraints of the fact-stimulus. Certain similarities and differences prominent among the nine poems suggest that they might be further grouped into three broad categories. Mr. Wainwright's "The Lofthouse Disaster," Mr. Mugglestone's "The Tragedy of the Lofthouse Colliery Disaster" and "In Memoriam: The Aftermath of the Lofthouse Disaster," Mrs. Proud's "Lofthouse Mine Disaster," and Mr. Hampsey's untitled "No more for them the song of birds" constitute one set whose members share in general a negative feedback model of Self/Other relationships. The divergences between the miners and their dangerous work environment, between the ideal and the tragically real, between the Lofthouse miners and other folk, between the destitution of the widowed and orphaned and our financial comfort—all these are resolved within the poems by some strategy from the system's existing repertoire of devices, whether it be the sharing of grief, the extending of sympathy, the intensifying of precautionary safety methods so that such a disaster may not recur, or the contributing of money to recompense in however small a way the bereaved kin. Of this set, Mr. Hampsey's vision comes closest to transcending the existing system of interpretations, but his analogy between Jesus Christ and the Lofthouse dead is a brief vignette, subjected to the dominant negative feedback conception of resolving the families' overriding need for "material things."

Each poem is fairly concrete in its references to this unique event and cannot be easily generalized. In addition, each poem is cast in a mode reflecting the mode of the real events; when dealing with the rescue, each adopts the narrative mode, when treating the deaths, the lyric. Each portrays the miner in predominantly human images—as a special person, to be sure, but fundamentally like you and me. Most are concerned in some way about the nature of the final gravesite, very much an improper one. This concern is the most dominant expressive element in the five poems as a group. But this expressive element is balanced by the instrumentalness of the poems' equally high concern that practical requirements for basic survival— the economic security of the kin—be met. Finally, we may note that all four poets are relative "insiders" to the event; the three men are or had been for many years miners themselves, and the one woman,

Mrs. Proud, is not only married to a former miner but actually lives in a hamlet attached to the Lofthouse community, knowing personally some of the people directly involved in the affair.

The second category contains but one member, our sixth poem, the text of Mr. Greaves's song. "The Lofthouse was a happy pit" shares many features with the "insiders'" poems. For instance, some of its content is specific to Lofthouse; his miners are portrayed as basically ordinary people, even though their Yorkshire and working-class identities are unusually highlighted, and their relationship with the nonminer "us" is one of equivalence and shared interests. On the other hand, Mr. Greaves does not stress the unsuitable nature of the gravesite, nor does he in more than a tangential way express concern for the plight of the bereaved. He is also unique in telling of the accident and the resulting deaths in narrative, the details of which he mostly made up himself, but which, save for the each-man-for-himself aspect, are probably reflective of what did happen during those few catastrophic moments. The most striking difference in his poem, however, is its depiction of a society with two fundamentally opposed groups: the miners on one hand and the bourgeoisie represented by management and newspapers on the other. This social structure is one of exploiter and exploited, an adversary relationship that cannot be resolved by means available within the present system without destroying that system. His depicted model is thus the positive feedback one of increasing differences and antagonisms between irreconcilable components-in-interaction.

Though in his song he aligns himself with the miners more than even the "insiders" do, Mr. Greaves's real social persona is not the same as those of the "insiders." While born into the working class and while making his living with hand and tool, he is, of course, a producer of artistic products, a craftsman rather than a laborer. He is also self-employed and formally educated to a greater degree than are the "insiders," through both institutionalized channels like the Technical College and more informal channels like Communist Party organizations, which stress intellectual inquiry. He lives not in a mining district but in a textile manufacturing-cum-farming district on the edge of the Dales. A suitable designation for Mr. Greaves, to contrast him with both the "insiders" and the "outsiders" with whom we shall next deal, is "marginal."

The third category contains the three poems by the "outsiders," Mr. Blakeley, Mrs. Watford, and Mr. Pickles. We know for certain that at least two of them—Mrs. Watford and Mr. Pickles, the professional journalist—are of middle-class status and probably have little direct and sustained experience with mining culture or with mining as a profession. In part, this accounts for their poems' lack of concreteness; only Mr. Blakely situates his topic in the Lofthouse tragedy, and even so only in his poem's title, while Mrs. Watford's poem is general enough that it was in fact transferred from her existing repertoire and applied to Lofthouse with only minor stylistic changes. None of the three poems mentions either the expressive distaste at the dead men's permanent burial site or the instrumental need of the surviving families for money. Each poem eschews the narrative, descriptive mode in favor of the imagistic coherence that the lyric mode allows, even when its topic is the real-life dramatic narrative of the rescue attempts.

These three outsider poets are thus far less constrained by the structure of the real event and by its instrumental demands; consequently, they are motivated more by expressive considerations—like "good poetry," for instance—but especially by subjectively abstract meanings that the events imply. Each poet internalizes the Lofthouse Colliery Disaster and matches it with a frame of reference with which he or she is familiar, but a frame significantly removed from the reality of the events themselves. Appropriate to the devastatingly tragic and extraordinarily noble elements of the Lofthouse events, so striking to any outsider, the systems of meanings that the outsider poets associate with the affair are those of religion, warfare, mythology, cosmology, and automation, all universes of meaning on a qualitatively higher plane than that which coal mining inhabits in customary world view.

The resulting model of relationships is that of transcendence. Miners become, instead of working-class manual laborers, glorious soldiers, Giants residing underground amidst sparkling treasures, and the most powerful of machines rather than men. But each of these reinterpreted poetic worlds also contains the social actors that are we ourselves, who also have a real existence; the difference is that in the poetic redefinition "we" are very much inferior. In their relationships with us, miners are Promethean culture heroes and masters of other extraordinary skills, while the generalized Self is "little," the subordinate recipient of gifts it cannot repay, and unable to hold on to a striking memory for any length of time.

None of the "insiders" among our poets had firsthand experience of the deaths or of the rescue attempts at Lofthouse during that tragic week of March 1973. If any had, in fact, worked at the colliery or been related to any of the lost miners, it is doubtful that he or she would have composed a poem on the events—at least certainly not until a considerable period of time had passed. I could not discover any poetry written by someone in this position, someone "coincidental" with the topic; poetry by definition has *some* expressive component and requires *some* internalization and distancing of self from its subject matter. Mr. Mugglestone, speaking from a miner's perspective, found Mrs. Watford's idealistic view of mining inappropriate: "It don't occur to me like that," he said; "I don't think there's any miner that does, meself." He himself had once rescued his father, buried by a sudden fall of rock:

> He was completely buried, but . . . I'd got to get him out, although there was danger from all those thousand tons of stone falling on me all the time. But I stopped there and I grappled and grappled and grappled until I got him out, I know I'd got to get him out. You forget about these dangers. . . . You don't think about anything else, you think about the bloke that's buried . . . you go in and get him out . . . any miner would. . . .

The conceptual model of self/environment relationships in this kind of practical thinking is match; the reacting self matches the demands of the acting environment.

Mr. Mugglestone's contemporaneous response to the rock fall is no surprise, since no time interposed between stimulus and response to permit reflection and expressivity. But what of a situation in which there is such a period of time for "coincidentals" between stimulus and response? Let us take the example of someone who was perhaps the most coincidental with the Lofthouse Colliery Disaster, Mr. Sidney Haigh of Outwood, miner for forty-four years, a foreman at Lofthouse, father to one of the seven missing miners, and the man who conceived as well as actively led the digging of the new tunnel over the sliproad in order to gain entrance into the tailgate. Mr. Haigh was interviewed in his home by the British Broadcasting Corporation after his brilliant idea had been effected but, to everyone's bitter disappointment, had failed to find any trapped men; how had the tragedy affected his attitude toward mining, he was asked. His reply:

> Well, it's a lifetime's work, you see. It hasn't altered my attitude to mining at all. This doesn't worry me one bit. The only thing that worries me about this, all I'm disappointed about this, is the efforts we put in to try to save lives that's been unsuccessful. This is the part that hurts you.

And how did he feel about his job in particular now?

It's a good job . . . I don't associate mining any more dangerous than lots of other jobs, such as fishing. A fisherman's job, to me, is just as hard as mine. I wouldn't like to go out in trawlers fishing. I'm comfortable down t'pit.[24]

Mr. Haigh did not hesitate to interpret the rescue attempt within its everyday-mining frame of reference; in his words above he does not even distinguish his son from the general population of "lives." But Mr. Haigh's rescue efforts while they were ongoing were widely publicized to the Yorkshire region—indeed, to the whole country— and many an outsider's mind and heart were stirred enormously by his part in the drama. Consider what one such outsider, a reporter for the *Yorkshire Post,* wrote while the rescue attempts were at their height: "Sid Haigh . . . a living legend at Lofthouse Colliery, was contemptuous of the time. [His] grey hair turned white ten years ago when his 18-year-old son, Sidney, was killed in a motorcycle accident . . . waiting miners spoke of him in awed terms at the pithead yesterday."[25]

Mr. Haigh did, however, respond expressively to at least one stimulus during the same interview. We have seen how concerned the insider poets all were that the dead miners' bodies would remain permanently buried where they had died; Mr. Haigh was asked what his response would be should the Coal Board decide that the dangerous work of recovering the bodies be halted. "In *my* mind," he unhesitatingly replied, "if they decided to leave my son in, although I've been in forty-four years, I wouldn't go down t'pit again. I'd pack it up."[26] But this incipient positive feedback reaction did not last long, for as the rescue attempts became increasingly a most dangerous proposition for those underground, management asked Mr. Haigh to inspect the gates himself and give a professional opinion. Soon afterwards, the Coal Board announced that it would petition the Lofthouse workforce to agree that the face and the missing bodies be permanently sealed, a request to which the men did acquiesce on 28 April. After the decision to seek such a mandate from the workforce was announced, Mr. Haigh was again interviewed by the BBC, and again his response to the termination of the rescue attempts was sought. This time, the instrumentally motivated match model reasserted itself:

Well, I traveled both gates on Thursday and having seen the conditions meself I entirely agree. But in my opinion I wouldn't like to ask for volunteers. I would be exposing them to a danger and a risk that's not warranted. So I say, "No, I'll let my lad stay where he is along with the others."

Why this change of mind?

> . . . this of course were a real decision at that particular time. But seeing the conditions of . . . both gates . . . now, I think . . . that for t'few years I've left to work at t'pit that I'd rather pass me knowledge on to other people while I still remain at Lofthouse.[27]

Thus our continuum of responses is complete. Those who were "coincidental" with the stimulus, in that it was a part of their paramount reality of everyday life, within their extensive stock of knowledge and actual reach, envisioned that topic in the match terms of a smoothly operating, monistic system. Those who were "insiders," with less knowledge, or certainly with less direct effect from that topic, since it was not their paramount reality but a secondary one (within possible or historical reach), envisaged some way of manipulating existing mechanisms of the system so that it might correct itself in a negative feedback model. The one "marginal," Mr. Greaves, did not see self-correction as possible. As a social activist and to some extent a working-class man himself, the topic to him with within a remotely potential reach; but he chose to view it conceptually, implying that a suitable resolution could be attained only—in the either/or terms of the positive feedback view—by one of the competing ideologies entirely overcoming the other. The "outsiders," to whom the topic was beyond reach, were forced to go outside the system of interpretations to seek a new definition that could comprehend the topic as an ordered and meaningful whole. Their vision was one of transcendence, in which resolution within the system is achieved not by manipulating elements of that system but by transforming it into something else entirely.

During the first eight months of 1973 three mining accidents claiming a significant number of lives occurred in Great Britain. The first was the Lofthouse flood of 21 March; the second a rockfall on 10 May at Seafield Colliery in Fifeshire, Scotland, in which five men perished; and the third a pit cage malfunction at Markham Main Colliery in Derbyshire on 31 July from which eighteen miners subsequently died. Yet it was Lofthouse that seemed to draw the most concentrated, sustained, and widespread attention on both the local and the national levels. It seems reasonable to infer that one important reason for this was a certain "formal cause"; in contrast with the other accidents, which happened in short order, the Lofthouse events were spread out over a week in an evolving dynamic, as the rescue teams met here success, there failure, as the experts kept revising their estimates of the possible air pocket's size, and as the public waited half in hope, half in fear, for a climax which kept being delayed but toward which events inexorably built. None of the other accidents possessed intrinsically this same form of expressive drama.

In addition, the week-long period allowed for a certain "efficient cause"—a great amount of news coverage, dissemination, and commentary, not only in the mass media but also in everyday conversation and in church services, all permitting a much wider, deeper, and more intense spread of information than was the case with the other accidents. And taking my cue from Mr. Pickles, I might suggest that a "material cause" lay in the fact that central to the physical events themselves were seven of life's most fundamental components: time (which all were racing against), motion (the intense activeness of the race), space (the miners, it was frustratingly obvious, were not far underground and yet were unreachable), earth (where they made their living but were now imprisoned), air (which it was hoped they had in sufficient quantity to keep them alive), water (which was responsible for the accident), and fire (the *raison d'être* of the coal they mined). At least one of these seven informs each of the nine poems in a major way, Mr. Pickles' "We MUST NOT Forget" being articulated by fully five.

But the most "final cause" perhaps was that the Lofthouse Disaster brought into consciousness what "coincidentals" simply took for granted, reserving it for special articulation only in moments of ritual celebration like the annual Miner's Day parade: the idea of *communitas*. The tragedy allowed the "insiders" the opportunity to reaffirm, intensify, and more widely disseminate what they themselves took to be a cultural norm, if not, as with coincidentals, a day-to-day fact of everyday living: that they constituted an almost-primary community with the Lofthouse dead and rescue workers. The "outsiders," however, experienced *communitas* as a revelation, as a new perception—a perception that they themselves, *mirabile dictu,* did indeed participate in an I-Thou relationship with miners. In truth, surely all we outsiders were liable to the full and sudden cognizance of a large class of people living in our very own region, the fruits of whose labor we had taken for granted and used every day, but with whom we had never interacted or, indeed, thought very much about. After all, they normally lived in their own hermetic mining communities, were working-class and socially below us, and worked underground, where no one but they see, and where no one else sees them. Now all we outsiders were shocked into realizing that not far below the spot on which we stood *right then* were miners undergoing terrible suffering. We were now moved to view the coal burning in our comfortable grates at home with a new eye; inevitable was the flash of awareness that in fact we are most intimately involved with men like these.

And, of course, we have seen in the poems to what heights these new conceptions of community grew: the awareness that we had ignored these men and certainly relegated them to lower status (in class, education, wealth, and space), while all the time they had been providing us with material essential for our very lives, led to the interpretation that we had all the time been making the most extreme victims of them—most extreme because they did in fact sacrifice for us *their* most precious possession, their lives. The guilt resulting from this new awareness was conceptually expiated in the outsiders' poems by *entirely inverting* the reality of the everyday hierarchy; they are much above us, we greatly below them. Only by this extreme inversion could the past injustice be canceled and the true equivalence of *communitas* be achieved.

Ultimately, however, it seems that the outsider poets spoke their atonement, at least with any degree of permanence, on their own behalf, not on behalf of their class. For while it would be nice to think that the ideal structure of true community envisaged by the poetic conception was to be incorporated into the code of society's traditional world view to generate a new social reality, such was not to be the case. A scant year later, when the National Union of Mineworkers went on strike for higher wages, the most often used phrase in publicly disseminated opinion was the hoary proposition that miners were "holding the country up to ransom." Thus, in one short year the same men whom our poets had envisaged as blood-giving sacrificial victims and culture heroes were now seen to be blood-sucking victimizers and brigands. In the praxes of middle-class everyday life, poets speak with a solitary voice.

EPILOGUE

Poets speak with a solitary voice, in the praxes of middle-class every-day life. As we move further along the continuum of our Lofthouse poets toward the outsiders, clearly the content, form, and function of artistic expression become less referential, less conative, less pragmatic, more poetic, more emotive, and thus—like Old Thomas's singing of "Lady Isabel and the Elf-Knight" at Lark Rise's Wagon and Horses in the 1880s—less folkloric. The unique Ego and the product become the focus of attention at the expense of the Self/Other relationship and the process of social exchange. By the time we get to Mr. Greaves's song we are hovering at the perimeters of the field of folklore; at Mr. Blakeley's poem we have surely crossed over the field's borders.

In one sense, this assessment is paradoxical. After all, the outsiders did take their interpretations from "traditional" belief systems—the religious, the mythological, and the cosmological. But these belief systems are ones that have lost their contact with everyday reality and are perpetuated by officially legislated institutions like school and church; they do not come from community-generated and-generative ones, as is clearly the case in the insiders' poems. The outsiders chose frames of reference suitable to the ideology of a nation-state, not a community; their definitions, like many of the urban songs of transcendence in chapter 3, are simply too far removed from the realities of life as it is experienced and lived to be generally sustainable. Compare them with Mrs. Bairstow's poems during her third phase, when she too borrowed national frames of reference, but synthesized them with the more localized and everyday to posit a more believable, attainable, socially viable set of premises. Or compare them with her second phase, with its more nostalgic interpretations from a preindustrial milieu; she could resurrect these poems later on for more socially applicable use, since they maintained contact with the fund of conventional experience. In the interplay between the real and the imaginary, between the axiomatic and the fantastic, between the utilitarian and the nonutilitarian, between the at-hand and the remote, between the particularistic and the universalistic, grow the fruits of the field we call folklore.

Structuralism, working-class "folk" poetry—how would Cecil Sharp have reacted to all this? Cecil Sharp thought in systemic ways in his search for order and consistency underlying concrete differentia, just as I do, though Sharp was of the pre–World War I generation and deeply concerned with the mechanics of systems and their evolution over time, while I am of the post–World War II generation and more concerned with how systems are organized in space by the information they carry. Sharp was a pioneer in his day, as he fought to legitimize English traditional folksong and to incorporate it into official school curricula; and I, quite frankly, see myself as a pioneer in attempting to bring contemporary working-class poetry into folklorists' purview. How would Cecil Sharp have reacted to all this? Not ill, I think; our differences are small.

NOTES

INTRODUCTION

1. Maud Karpeles, ed., *Cecil Sharp's Collection of English Folk Songs*, 2 vols. (London: Oxford University Press, 1974).

2. Cecil J. Sharp, *English Folk Song: Some Conclusions* (London: Simpkin, 1907). Opinions differ on the question of our debt to this side of Sharp's work. For a laudatory—if ambivalent—opinion, see A. L. Lloyd, *Folk Song in England* (London: Lawrence & Wishart, 1967), pp. 15–17; for the opposite, see David Harker, "Cecil Sharp in Somerset: Some Conclusions," *Folk Music Journal* 3 (1978): 220–40. Somewhere in between these two views is D. K. Wilgus, *Anglo-American Folksong Scholarship Since 1898* (New Brunswick, N.J.: Rutgers University Press, 1959), pp. 56–64.

3. Sharp, *English Folk Song: Some Conclusions*, p. 18.

4. All the studies of local songs I know about are North American, however. The best of those that treat Anglo-American songmakers are the two books by Edward D. Ives, *Larry Gorman: The Man Who Made the Songs* (Bloomington: Indiana University Press, 1964) and *Lawrence Doyle: The Farmer Poet of Prince Edward Island*, University of Maine Studies, no. 92 (Orono: University of Maine Press, 1971), and one by Henry Glassie, Edward D. Ives, and John F. Szwed, *Folksongs and Their Makers* (Bowling Green, Ohio: Bowling Green University Popular Press, [1971]). In this last work, Ives's study, "A Man and His Song: Joe Scott

and 'The Plain Golden Band,'" pp. 69–146, is a good example of an attempt to establish the criteria I have discussed.

5. For a convenient inventory of common types of variation found in traditional song, see Tom Burns, "A Model for Textual Variation in Folksong," *Folklore Forum* 3 (1970): 49–56.

6. I have been influenced in my thinking here by Dan Ben-Amos, "Toward a Definition of Folklore in Context," *Journal of American Folklore* 84 (1971): 3–15.

7. The only published scholarship of any scope is in the special issue on "Monologues and Folk Recitation" of the *Southern Folklore Quarterly* 40 (1976), edited by Kenneth S. Goldstein and Robert D. Bethke. See also T. M. Pearce, "What Is a Folk Poet?" *Western Folklore* 12 (1953): 242–48.

8. For referential, conative, and other functions of communication, see Roman Jakobson, "Concluding Statement: Linguistics and Poetics," in *Style in Language,* ed. Thomas A. Sebeok (Cambridge: M.I.T. Press, 1960), pp. 350–77.

9. See Kenneth S. Goldstein, "Monologue Performance in Great Britain," *Southern Folklore Quarterly* 40 (1976): 12–14.

10. Local newspapers are usually published once a week, stress news coverage of their own boroughs, are usually between sixteen and twenty-four pages, and are not generally bought by people who live outside the borough.

11. See chapter 1 of Dorothy Marshall, *Industrial England 1776–1851* (London: Routledge & Kegan Paul, 1973), for a discussion of the factors which "turned the majority of [England's] people into townsmen and industrial workers instead of country folk whose income in one way or another depended on the land" (p. 6).

12. This older stratum of traditional balladry is represented by many examples in Francis James Child, ed., *The English and Scottish Popular Ballads,* 5 vols. (1882–98; reprint ed., New York: Dover, 1965). For a representative sample of those Child ballads known to have been popular in England rather than in Scotland only, see Karpeles, *Cecil Sharp's Collection of English Folk Songs,* 1: 1–221.

13. The Yorkshire experience is described in some detail in chapter 3. For the older pattern in North Oxfordshire, as late as the 1880s, see Flora Thompson, *Lark Rise to Candleford,* The World's Classics, no. 542 (London: Oxford University Press, 1954), a semifictionalized account of country life that is surely truer than any objective ethnography or, at the other end of the spectrum, any novel. For East Anglia see Justin and Edith Brooke, *Suffolk Prospect* (London: Faber & Faber, 1963), especially p. 12.

14. Harker, "Cecil Sharp in Somerset," pp. 227–228. Nevertheless, the village setting and the rural working class seem to have been the most important variables in the vitality of folksong traditions, as a list of Sabine Baring-Gould's informants (twenty-odd years before Sharp's fieldwork) suggests. See Bickford H. C. Dickinson, *Sabine Baring-Gould* (Newton Abbot, Devon: David & Charles, 1970), pp. 130–32. See also S. Baring-

Gould, *Further Reminiscences: 1864–1894* (New York: E. P. Dutton, 1925), chapter 15.

15. The notion of "native speakers" used here has its immediate source in Jonathan Culler, *Structuralist Poetics* (Ithaca: Cornell University Press, 1975), pp. 50–51. In anthropology, the primary importance of native speakers' own cognitions is most relevant to the so-called emic approach; see Stephen A. Tyler, ed., *Cognitive Anthropology* (New York: Holt, Rinehart & Winston, 1969), pp. 1–23. Formalist students of literature, on the other hand, would see the extremes of this approach as an example of the "intentional fallacy." In folklore and anthropology, the better scholarly analyses of expressive forms usually combine these two extremes. Victor Turner, for instance, makes the "exegetical" only one of several categories of data; see his "The Syntax of Symbolism in an Ndembu Ritual," in *Structural Analysis of Oral Tradition,* ed. Pierre and Elli Köngäs Maranda (Philadelphia: University of Pennsylvania Press, 1971), pp. 125–36, and his *The Forest of Symbols* (Ithaca: Cornell University Press, 1967), pp. 25–26. See also Clifford Geertz, *The Interpretation of Cultures* (New York: Basic Books, 1973), pp. 3–30.

16. One can find many dibs and dabs of references to each of these matters of ethnographic fact, in personal diaries and autobiographies especially. The only account of any scope that I know of is Flora Thompson's reconstruction in *Lark Rise to Candleford,* pp. 62–69, which I shall describe in some detail in chapter 3. But even that account is of just one occasion—in the pub and with men participants only.

17. These are adapted from E. D. Hirsch, Jr., *Validity in Interpretation* (New Haven: Yale University Press, 1967), pp. 236–38. Cf. Turner's "exegetic," "operational," and "positional" dimensions and his "nominal," "substantial," and "artifactual" bases of symbolic forms in "The Syntax of Symbolism in an Ndembu Ritual," constructs all of which are clearly built on a similar assumption of validity in coherence.

18. Laws numbers that carry letter prefixes from J to Q refer to G. Malcolm Laws, Jr., *American Balladry from British Broadsides,* Publications of the American Folklore Society, Bibliographical and Special Series, vol. 8 (Philadelphia: American Folklore Society, 1957); those with letter prefixes from A to I are indexed in Laws's *Native American Balladry,* rev. ed., Publications of the American Folklore Society, Bibliographical and Special Series, vol. 1 (Philadelphia: American Folklore Society, 1964). Child numbers refer to Child, *English and Scottish Popular Ballads.*

19. These examples of functions are, of course, from William R. Bascom, "Four Functions of Folklore," *Journal of American Folklore* 67 (1954): 333–49. The ideas were pioneering ones, but we have too often taken them to be programmatic rather than—as they were intended to be —stimulative.

20. Two major recent exceptions to this tendency in British scholarship are David Buchan, *The Ballad and the Folk* (London: Routledge & Kegan Paul, 1972), and Robin Morton, ed., *Come Day, Go Day, God Send*

Sunday (London: Routledge & Kegan Paul, 1973). But the first deals with Scottish materials, the second with Northern Irish (it is also nonanalytical). Two interesting recent works that treat urban working-class poetry (not necessarily "folk") are Martha Vicinus, *The Industrial Muse* (New York: Barnes & Noble, 1974) and Robert Colls, *The Collier's Rant* (Totowa, N.J.: Rowman & Littlefield, 1977).

21. John F. Szwed, "Paul E. Hall: A Newfoundland Song-Maker and His Community of Song," in Glassie, Ives, and Szwed, *Folksongs and Their Makers*, p. 149.

22. See chapter 5 of Eleanor Long, *"The Maid" and "The Hangman,"* Folklore Studies, no. 21 (Berkeley: University of California Press, 1971).

23. See John V. Hagopian, "Symbol and Metaphor in the Transformation of Reality into Art," *Comparative Literature* 20 (1968): 45–54.

24. This perspective, insofar as it has influenced me, is best described by Roland Barthes, "The Structuralist Activity," *Partisan Review* 34 (1967): 82–88, and Culler, *Structuralist Poetics*. The particular Structuralist *method* that has contributed most to my own analyses is the one employed by Claude Lévi-Strauss, "The Story of Asdiwal," in *The Structural Study of Myth and Totemism*, ed. Edmund Leach, A.S.A. Monographs, no. 5 (London: Tavistock, 1967), pp. 1–47.

25. Gregory Bateson, *Steps to an Ecology of Mind* (New York: Ballantine Books, 1972), p. 315.

26. For the notion of "quality space," see James Fernandez, "The Mission of Metaphor in Expressive Culture," *Current Anthropology* 15 (1974): 119–43.

27. I borrow the term "semantic domain" from Tyler, *Cognitive Anthropology*, pp. 1–23. "Province of meaning" I have taken from Alfred Schutz, "Symbol, Reality, and Society," in *Symbols and Society: Fourteenth Symposium of the Conference on Science, Philosophy and Religion,* ed. Lyman Bryson et al. (New York: The Conference on Science, Philosophy and Religion, 1955), pp. 135–203. Schutz's analysis, along with the similarly phenomenological approach of Peter L. Berger and Thomas Luckmann in their *The Social Construction of Reality* (1966; reprint ed., Garden City, N.Y.: Doubleday Anchor Books, 1967), has influenced my thinking somewhat, especially in the notion of folksong classification I will adumbrate at the beginning of chapter 3. As I use the terms, "province of meaning" is a larger category than "paradigm" and *its* subcategory, "semantic domain," which itself is a larger category than "signifier." While the interrelationships among these four *as analytical categories* are always the same, the content that fills any of them—or whether any is used—is entirely relative to the data at hand and to the level of abstraction at which the analysis is cast.

For the terms "negative feedback" and "positive feedback" and for a rationale in using them, I am indebted chiefly to Ervin Laszlo, *Introduction to Systems Philosophy* (New York: Harper Torchbooks, 1973). The influence of Laszlo's book, particularly his chapter 4, shows most clearly in the "models of relationships" I will posit in chapter 3.

28. Morphological analysis is best known to North American folklorists through the works of V. Propp, *Morphology of the Folktale,* trans. Laurence Scott, 2d rev. ed. by Louis A. Wagner, Publications of the American Folklore Society, Bibliographical and Special Series, vol. 9; Indiana University Research Center in Anthropology, Folklore, and Linguistics, publication 10 (Austin: University of Texas Press, 1968), and Alan Dundes, *The Morphology of North American Indian Folktales,* Folklore Fellows Communications, no. 195 (Helsinki: Suomalainen Tiedeakatemia, 1964).

29. There are, of course, other implications to the line "As I roved out one May morning," though they would not be of central concern to either Structuralist or morphological analysis. For instance, a performance-oriented analysis might be interested in the line's possible metalingual function as a signal that what follows is a song of love relationships and not some other kind of song, and therefore should be reacted to accordingly. A comparative analysis would be keenly aware of the incipit's historical lineage—probably coming to British folk tradition from medieval French poetic forms of *chansons d'aventure,* themselves probably derived from much earlier classical pastoral poetry.

30. This is one important thesis of the most intelligible account of Structuralism that I am familiar with, Culler's *Structuralist Poetics,* especially pp. 255–65.

CHAPTER 1

1. In this and the following chapter, I abbreviate the titles of source works in order to save space. The abbreviations relevant to chapters 1 and 2 are as follows:

BMNE: Helen Hartness Flanders and Marguerite Olney, *Ballads Migrant in New England* (New York: Farrar, Strauss, & Young, 1953).

BSSN: Elisabeth Bristol Greenleaf and Grace Yarrow Mansfield, *Ballads and Sea Songs of Newfoundland* (Cambridge: Harvard University Press, 1933).

CL: Frank Purslow, ed., *The Constant Lovers* (London: English Folk Dance and Song Society, 1972).

CSCEFS: Maud Karpeles, ed., *Cecil Sharp's Collection of English Folk Songs.*

DBFS: Joan Brocklebank and Biddie Kindersley, eds., *A Dorset Book of Folk Songs* (London: English Folk Dance and Song Society, 1966).

EC: James Reeves, ed., *The Everlasting Circle* (London: Heinemann, 1960).

ECS: Lucy E. Broadwood and J. A. Fuller Maitland, eds., *English County Songs* (London: B. J. Cramer, n.d.).

EFS: W. A. Barrett, *English Folk-Songs* (London: Novello, n.d.).

EFSD: Iolo A. Williams, *English Folk-Song and Dance* (London: Longmans, Green, 1935).

EHFS: Alice Gillington, *Eight Hampshire Folk Songs* (London: J. Curwen & Sons, 1907).

ESPB: Francis James Child, *The English and Scottish Popular Ballads.*

FBI: Peter Kennedy, ed., *Folksongs of Britain and Ireland* (London: Cassell, 1975).

FD: Frank Purslow, ed., *The Foggy Dew* (London: English Folk Dance and Song Society, 1974).

FMJ: *Folk Music Journal* (London, 1969–present).

FSNE: Gavin Greig, *Folk-Song of the North-East* (Hatboro, Pa.: Folklore Associates, 1963).

GG: Fred Hamer, *Garners Gay.* Folk Song Today, no. 2 (London: English Folk Dance and Song Society, 1967).

JFSS: *Journal of the Folk-Song Society* (London, 1899–1931).

MB: Frank Purslow, ed., *Marrow Bones* (London: English Folk Dance and Song Society, 1965).

MFS: Helen Creighton, *Maritime Folk Songs* (Toronto: Ryerson Press, 1962).

SC: Francis M. Collinson and Francis Dillon, *Songs from the Countryside* (London: W. Paxton, 1946).

SES: Bob Copper, *A Song for Every Season* (London: Heinemann, 1971).

SNO: Kenneth Peacock, ed., *Songs of the Newfoundland Outports,* 3 vols., National Museum of Canada Bulletin, no. 197, Anthropological Series, no. 65 (Ottawa: National Museum of Canada, 1965).

TSNS: Helen Creighton and Doreen H. Senior, *Traditional Songs from Nova Scotia* (Toronto: Ryerson Press, 1950).

TTCB: Bertrand Harris Bronson, *The Traditional Tunes of the Child Ballads,* 4 vols. (Princeton: Princeton University Press, 1959–72).

WS: Frank Purslow, ed., *The Wanton Seed* (London: English Folk Dance and Song Society, 1968).

Throughout chapters 1 and 2 song titles are standardized to those in Child, *English and Scottish Popular Ballads*; Laws, *American Balladry from British Broadsides* and *Native American Balladry*; and Karpeles, *Cecil Sharp's Collection of English Folk Songs,* in that order. A song that does not appear in these three works is identified by the title given it in the source work of the version cited.

2. See Laws, *American Balladry from British Broadsides,* p. 237.

3. Broadwood wrote two essays on the subject: *JFSS* 5 (1915): 132–35, and *JFSS* 7 (1923); 36–40. The two quotations are from the earlier essay, p. 133. She mentions "Robes of Glory" because in more than one text of the ballad the maid spies not chains but robes of gold underneath the fisherman's "morning gown." Very few versions, however, specify *his* father's house as the couple's destination; *hers* is the overwhelming choice. Laws may have been unconsciously influenced by Broadwood's thesis when

he wrote his synopsis of this ballad's story in *American Balladry from British Broadsides*, p. 237, for he says that the fisherman "takes her to his father's house"; however, all North American texts available to Laws when he wrote this summary specify, as do most British texts, her house.

4. For the first of these reactions, see *EFSD*, pp. 112–15; Reginald Nettel, *Sing a Song of England* (London: Phoenix House, 1954), pp. 62–63; Cecil J. Sharp, *English Folk Songs*, selected edition (London: Novello, 1920), 2: viii–ix. For the second, see MacEdward Leach, ed., *The Ballad Book* (New York: A. S. Barnes, 1955), pp. 692–93; Laws, *American Balladry from British Broadsides*, pp. 20, 237. For the third, see Wilgus, *Anglo-American Folksong Scholarship Since 1898*, p. 322.

5. Gordon Hall Gerould, *The Ballad of Tradition* (1932; reprint ed., New York: Oxford University Press Galaxy Book, 1957), pp. 33–34; M. J. C. Hodgart, *The Ballads*, 2d ed. (London: Hutchinson University Library, 1962), p. 19. Cf. Laws, *American Balladry from British Broadsides*, p. 56.

6. *EFSD*, p. 112.

7. Nettel, *Sing a Song of England*, p. 64.

8. *SNO*, 2:604.

9. The sample for this study consists of three major repositories of English folksong: *CSCEFS*; *CL, FD, MB*, and *WS*, all edited by Frank Purslow and published by the English Folk Dance and Song Society; and all issues of *JFSS*. When these sources revealed no instance of the relevant signifier, I turned to other sources, in the following order: other collections of English versions listed in note 1 above, Scottish versions in *FSNE*, Newfoundland collections (*BSSN* and *SNO*), Creighton's two Nova Scotian anthologies (*MFS* and *TSNS*), and *ESPB*. Admittedly, using North American versions is not the ideal procedure; but (1) all folksong collection has been a quite haphazard, hit-or-miss affair, (2) traditional folksinging and folksongs remained vital in parts of Scotland and Canada longer than in the mother country, and (3) those same areas were very strongly influenced by English rural culture over the eighteenth and nineteenth centuries.

10. See Kenneth Burke, *A Grammar of Motives* (Berkeley: University of California Press, 1969), p. xv. Burke's fifth category, Purpose, is of a different logical level and so intimate an aspect of each of the other four constructs that it cannot be usefully separated from them.

11. References to examples are for illustrative purposes and are not exhaustive.

12. Cf. "Scarboro Sand" (Laws K18), *CSCEFS*, 1: 265–66, and "Six Dukes, or The Duke of Bedford," *CSCEFS*, 1: 254–55, in both of which the lover has not been murdered but accidentally drowned.

13. One would think that, technically, a "lily-white hand" might be an agency; in English folksong, however, it seldom appears unless it is being taken by someone, and is thus inseparable from that act.

14. See "The Twa Sisters" (Child 10) in *TTCB*, 1:147–48, no. 7, where the murderess is the victim's sister, and "Lord Thomas and Fair Annet" (Child 73), in *CSCEFS*, 1:69–77, where the murderess is the wife of the victim's true lover.

15. For example, *JFSS* 7 (1922): 22: "He took her by the milk-white hand, for it was his intent" and "then he pulled off his morning gown and gently laid her down." In *ECS*, p. 110, we may have a metaphor for sexual intercourse in the following lines:

"I am fishing for a lady gay
Right down the river clear."

He boldly stepped up to her,
And he kissed both cheeks and side;
And he's taen her by her lilywhite hand
And rowed her down the tide.

I doubt it, however. Sexual metaphors in English folksong are usually much less ambiguous than this, as chapter 2 will indicate in some detail. However, see the editor's remarks in *SNO*, 2:604.

16. "The Murder of Betsy Smith" was issued on a broadside by J. Livsey of Manchester but never collected from oral tradition. See Phillips Barry, " 'Fair Florella,' " *American Speech* 3 (1928): 441–47.

17. Almost all examples given so far may be used to support this characterization of the despair/delight poles in maidens' experiences with romance. In fact, note the titles of the song-topic categories in two of the best anthologies of British folksong texts, *CSCEFS* and *FBI*.

18. James N. Healy, ed., *The Mercier Book of Old Irish Street Ballads* (Cork: Mercier Press, 1967), 1:295–96. A traditional text from Nova Scotia is in *MFS*, p. 52. A third British folksong in which a fisherman may be a central agent is "Young Banker" (*JFSS* 2 [1905]: 91–92), in which a maid initially rejects Young Banker's suit, only to change her mind almost immediately. She is too late, however, and he in turn rejects her tardy acceptance. *JFSS* commentators suggested that Banker may have been the young man's name, while the singer herself asserted it was a trade—a hedger (who is normally a ditcher as well). But the name may also be interpreted to mean one who fishes the maritime banks of the North Atlantic; that Young Banker frames his suit to the girl in the words "will you go on deck?" provides some support for this reading.

19. A not unreasonable hypothesis, since in England fishing as a profession (apart from poaching) means deep-sea fishing. Texts of "The Bold Fisherman" often associate the fisherman with the sea as well as with the river: e.g., "Come rolling down the sea" (*CSCEFS*, 1:222 [A], 228 [I]). In *ECS*, he is "a young fisherman / That sails the briny sea."

20. Weak not only in quantity but also, when it is present, as a signifier. Compare the Scottish and English versions of Child 279, "The Jolly Beggar," in *TTCB*, 3:214–16. The Scottish versions emphasize the noble status of the seducer; the English demote his status considerably and promote the girl's. In fact, one English version comes perilously close to being a satire of the poor-girl-weds-rich-boy idea (*TTCB*, 3:221, no. 23).

21. For example, besides "The Jolly Beggar" cited in the preceding note: Child 226, "Lizie Lindsay" (see *TTCB*, 3:365–68); Laws N19, "The

Blaeberry Courtship" (*FSNE*, no. 43); Child 232, "Richie Story" (*TTCB*, 3:380–84).

22. Ambiguous because, first of all, it is not at all clear that she does not recognize his noble status from the very start, and second, because it turns out at story's end that she is also aristocracy disguised—and far more noble, in fact, than he. See *CSCEFS*, 1:129–33.

23. See *SNO*, 3:986–87. This song has never been collected from oral tradition in Great Britain, according to the published record (though "Bold General Wolfe," on the same topic, often has been; see *CSCEFS*, 2:329–33); but "Brave Wolfe" is in every material, formal, and stylistic way a "British" ballad.

24. Compare, as in note 18 above, "Young Banker," *JFSS* 2 (1905): 91–92.

25. Axel Olrik, "Epic Laws of Folk Narrative," in *The Study of Folklore*, ed. Alan Dundes (Englewood Cliffs, N.J.: Prentice-Hall, 1965), pp. 131–41. The article was first published in German in 1909 (p. 129, note). Claude Lévi-Strauss, *Structural Anthropology*, trans. Claire Jacobson and Brooke Grundfest Schoepf (Garden City, N.Y.: Doubleday Anchor Books, 1967), pp. 202–28.

26. Lévi-Strauss, *Structural Anthropology*, pp. 210–11.

27. Turner, *The Forest of Symbols*, pp. 27–28.

28. For example, see W. G. Hoskins, *The Midland Peasant* (London: Macmillan, 1952), pp. 4, 13. Parish boundaries themselves were of great importance to villagers and the focus of ritual activities, particularly "beating the bounds"; see Christina Hole, *British Folk Customs* (London: Hutchinson, 1976), pp. 167–68 ("Rogationtide"). Problems arising from indeterminate land boundaries were probably most severe during the days of open fields.

29. Alfred Williams, *Round About the Upper Thames* (London: Duckworth, 1923), p. 24.

30. Williams, *Round About the Upper Thames*, pp. 8–9. See also pp. 23–24 for a highly symbolic discourse on the same river.

31. On the midwife role, see Thompson, *Lark Rise to Candleford*, pp. 140–141. On layers-out, see Sybil Marshall, ed., *Fenland Chronicle* (Cambridge: Cambridge University Press, 1967), p. 248. Nakedness in daily life was unusual, according to Thompson, pp. 141–42; it was evidently most associated conceptually with birth and death (the standard accounts contain no relevant information on sexual mores).

32. Prayer is most commonly linked to the period just after waking up in the morning and just before lying down at night. Kneeling may also have marked the division between the rest time of sleep and the work time of the day's chores; a woman's first domestic task at dawn was probably kneeling to light the fire.

33. Thompson, *Lark Rise to Candleford*, p. 458.

34. Asa Briggs, ed., *How They Lived Vol. III* (New York: Barnes & Noble, 1969), p. 179.

35. Thompson, *Lark Rise to Candleford*, p. 423.

36. Thompson, *Lark Rise to Candleford*, p. 427.

37. In addition to the texts in *ESPB*, 1, see *TTCB*, 1. For basic North American story-types and for a bibliography of sources of texts as well as analytical studies, see Tristram Potter Coffin, *The British Traditional Ballad in North America*, rev. ed. With a Supplement by Roger deV. Renwick (Austin: University of Texas Press, 1977).

38. See *ESPB*, 1, version H; *TTCB*, 1:167 (no. 54), 183–84 (no. 95). In the ballad's dominant form, the miller simply strips the gold rings from the girl's body.

39. *ESPB*, 3, version R; *TTCB*, 1:151 (no. 22), 174 (no. 71); Arthur Kyle Davis, Jr., ed., *More Traditional Ballads of Virginia* (Chapel Hill: University of North Carolina Press, 1960), pp. 48–49.

40. Snow's version is published in *Sing Out!*, 18, No. 1 (1968): 19. For a discussion of its relationship to other North American strains of Child 10, see Coffin, *British Traditional Ballad in North America*, pp. 213–16. In some North American versions a fisherman rather than a miller draws the girl from the water (see Coffin, p. 33), while in one the lover himself is a sailor (*TTCB*, 1:169, no. 59).

41. See Roger D. Abrahams, "Patterns of Structure and Role Relationships in the Child Ballads in the United States," *Journal of American Folklore* 79 (1966): 448–62.

42. D. K. Wilgus, "A Type-Index of Anglo-American Traditional Narrative Songs," *Journal of the Folklore Institute* 7 (1970): 161–77. Wilgus shows that other scholars have also sensed the relationship between "Little Sir Hugh" and certain well-established ballads of love relationships. A similar intuition may be at work in *TTCB*, 1:181, where the editor prints two fragments of "Floating down the Tide" under the Child 10 rubric (no. 89, no. 90), with the qualifying statement that their kinship to Child 10 "seems very dubious, both words and tune."

43. See *ESPB*, 3, versions G, H. N; *TTCB*, 3:90–91 (no. 35), 91 (no. 36), 93 (no. 40).

44. Instead, "Lamkin" tends to vary in the direction of a bogey-man song for children. See Coffin, *British Traditional Ballad in North America* and its supplement.

45. For the notions of "grace," "transgression," "redemption," and so forth I am indebted to the writings of Kenneth Burke, especially in his *Permanence and Change*, 2d ed., rev. (1954; reprint ed., Indianapolis: Bobbs-Merrill, 1965), pp. 274-94.

46. For texts of "Death and the Lady," see *EC*, pp. 86–87; *CSCEFS*, 1:233–34; R. Vaughn Williams and A. L. Lloyd, eds., *The Penguin Book of English Folk Songs* (Harmondsworth, Middlesex: Penguin Books, 1959), p. 30. Compare with such love songs as "Write Me Down Ye Powers Above," *CSCEFS*, 1:503; "The Shepherd and His Fife," *CSCEFS*, 1:384–85; "Welcome in Young Shepherd," *CSCEFS*, 1:399–400; and Laws P24, "The Butcher Boy," *JFSS* 2 (1906): 158–60.

47. Unlike "Flowery Garden," "The Lily-White Hand" is known to more than a single singer and in more than a single district, for there is

evidence that a similar text was collected in another county many years before (see *FMJ* 1 [1969]: 328, and *WS*, p. 120). This suggests a broadside origin for the text-type; but broadside versifiers were not far from being "native speakers" of the folksong "language" themselves.

48. For example, "The Shannon Side" (*CSCEFS*, 1:651–54); "As I Walked Out One May Morning" (*CSCEFS*, 1:661–62); and "Glastonbury Town" (*CSCEFS*, 1:666–67). For post-coital suicide see "Molly and William" (*WS*, p. 78).

49. Cf. Eleanor Long's "integrator" type of folk artist, in "Ballad Singers, Ballad Makers, and Ballad Etiology," *Western Folklore* 32 (1973): 225–36.

50. See *CSCEFS*, 1:283–85. Some versions of both "The Wexford Girl" and "The Constant Farmer's Son" substitute the phonetically and empirically analogous "stick" as the murder weapon; see *CSCEFS*, 1:294–95, 286–88.

51. See J. H. B. Peel, *Country Talk* (London: Hale, 1970), pp. 38–39; Ralph Whitlock, *A Family and a Village* (London: John Baker, 1969), p. 146. Stakes were also used before the widespread enclosures of open fields in the eighteenth and early ninetenth centuries; see J. D. Chambers, *Laxton: The Last English Open Field Village* (London: Her Majesty's Stationery Office, 1964), pp. 24–25.

52. Ronald Blythe, *Akenfield* (New York: Pantheon Books, 1969), p. 45.

53. Blythe, *Akenfield*, p. 70.

54. Thompson, *Lark Rise to Candleford*, p. 391.

55. Thompson, *Lark Rise to Candleford*, p. 381.

56. Though, we should note, apparently not any *more* common than prenuptial sex among the urban working class of the same period. See Peter Laslett, *The World We Have Lost* (London: Methuen University Paperbacks, 1965), pp. 128–49; Peter Laslett and Karla Oosterveen, "Long-Term Trends in Bastardy in England," *Population Studies* 27 (1973); 255–86.

57. George [Sturt] Bourne, *Change in the Village* (London: Duckworth, 1912), p. 40.

58. Thompson, *Lark Rise to Candleford*, p. 143. Cf. Brooke and Brooke, *Suffolk Prospect*, p. 122.

59. Laslett, *The World We Have Lost*, pp. 141–42. *Vide* the custom of "bundling," as in Enid Porter, *Cambridgeshire Customs and Folklore* (New York: Barnes & Noble, 1969), pp. 3–6.

60. John Nicholson, *The Folk Speech of East Yorkshire* (London: Simpkin, Marshall, 1889; reprint ed., Norwood, Pa.: Norwood Editions, 1977), p. 8. See also R. E. Moreau, *The Departed Village* (London: Oxford University Press, 1968), pp. 148–49; Porter, *Cambridgeshire Customs and Folklore*, pp. 8–10.

61. Sturt, *Change in the Village*, p. 41.

62. W. M. Williams, *Gosforth: The Sociology of an English Village* (Glencoe, Ill.: The Free Press, 1956), pp. 194–95.

63. Thompson, *Lark Rise to Candleford*, p. 145.

64. Thompson, *Lark Rise to Candleford*, pp. 145–46.

65. For summary statements of these kinds of changes, see J. L. and Barbara Hammond, *The Village Labourer 1760–1832* (1911; reprint ed., New York: Harper Torchbooks, 1970), pp. 187–89; E. J. Hobsbawm and George Rudé, *Captain Swing* (New York: Pantheon Books, 1968), pp. 15, 36–37; Harold Perkin, *The Origin of Modern English Society 1780–1880* (London: Routlege & Kegan Paul, 1969), p. 182; M. K. Ashby, *The Changing English Village* (Kineton, Warwick: The Roundwood Press, 1974), p. 174.

66. See George M. Foster, "Peasant Society and the Image of Limited Good," *American Anthropologist* 67 (1965): 293–315.

67. There is even evidence that the older generation of no longer productive grandparents were also treated harshly as drainers of resources; see Blythe, *Akenfield*, p. 199, and E. D. MacKerness, ed., *The Journals of George Sturt, 1890–1927*, 2 vols. (Cambridge: Cambridge University Press, 1967), 1:390–94.

CHAPTER 2

1. Cf. Alfred Williams, ed., *Folk-Songs of the Upper Thames* (London: Duckworth, 1923), p. 16; Sharp, *English Folk Song: Some Conclusions*, pp. 102–3.

2. As will emerge, the categories that result from this first-order classification by language—or, a better term, by rhetoric—have further characteristics differentiating them, like preferred narrative content, distinct messages, perhaps even (I will eventually speculate) appeal to specialized audiences. But classification by surface rhetoric is sufficient, since the other characteristics prove to be redundant with it.

3. There is little doubt that a fourth kind, the *idiomatic* ("obscene" songs of the sort in Ed Cray, *The Erotic Muse* [New York: Oak Publications, 1968]), was also traditionally popular in English rural culture. But there is no published record of such pieces that is of any significant scope. Only one song in our sample approaches this model, "All Under the New Mown Hay" (*WS*, p. 8). See G. Legman, *The Horn Book* (New Hyde Park, N.Y.: University Books, 1964), especially pp. 239–88, 336–426; but see also Lloyd, *Folk Song in England*, pp. 196–97.

4. Maud Karpeles, *Cecil Sharp: His Life and Work* (London: Routledge and Kegan Paul, 1967), pp. 31–32.

5. See chapter 1, note 27.

6. Reeves, *Everlasting Circle*, pp. 17–33.

7. Reeves, *Everlasting Circle*, p. 31.

8. Since I use a large number of textual examples in this chapter, I adopt the same system of abbreviation as in chapter 1. The data sample consists of all songs of sexual liaisons in *CSCEFS; CL, FD, MB*, and *WS; EC; FBI; FMJ; JFSS;* and *JEFDSS* (*Journal of the English Folk Dance and Song Society* [London, 1932–64]). See chapter 1, note 1.

9. It is at this level of signification, the similarity between birds' ac-

tions and people's actions, that we can best talk of metaphor. But as our discussion will show, these signifiers carry far more information than just these one-dimensional similarities.

10. Another image-cliche that may function both positively and negatively is that of gathering flowers (though most often it has a positive value). For instance, the abandoned girl of "Love Has Brought Me to Despair" (Laws P25) runs through the garden plucking flowers and grass for her deathbed; see *CSCEFS*, 1:598–99.

11. There is some irony in this simile, for the *real* criminal, the one who should be bound in chains, is the freely rambling false lover, since it is he who has stolen a heart and robbed you of your liberty. In fact, he is worse than a thief because he will cause your death of heartbreak. See *CSCEFS*, 1:627–28, 172. The image of being emotionally chained in a tragic love affair may appear in a nonfigurative guise, perhaps partly influenced by nonsymbolic narrative songs of love relationships in which disapproving parents lock up their daughters to keep them away from unacceptable wooers (e.g., Laws M15, "The Iron Door"); thus, in a song that is of the symbolic type, "The Loyal Lover" (*FD*, p. 56), the girl whose lover has been shipped abroad is literally chained in Bedlam, having no doubt been deranged by her grief.

12. Indoor action as a significant feature in the song-drama appears most prominently in "The Butcher Boy" (Laws P24), a very marginal example of a symbolic song of sexual liaison. It has a much stronger narrative component and a greater sign-to-symbol proportion than any other symbolic song. But its textual similarity to "A Brisk Young Lover" (cf. Laws P25), which is unequivocally on the symbolic model, and some of its rhetoric, warrant its inclusion in the sample. For specimen texts see *CSEFS*, 1:606–8.

13. Some random examples of common euphemisms for sexual intercourse in English folksongs are "try her," "sleep with," "sport," "toss and tumble," "have a jovial spree," "rifle her charms," "enjoy her," and the rhetorical "what was done there I never will declare." There are many others.

14. The following are the text-types in the sample (identified by standardized titles) and their sources. Titles are in alphabetical order: "The Astrologer" (*MB*, p. 1); Child 112, "The Baffled Knight" (*CSCEFS*, 1:135–46; *FBI*, 414); "The Banks of Clyde" (*CSCEFS*, 2:594–95; *FMJ* 3 [1976]: 166–67); "The Barley Raking" (*EC*, pp. 49–50; *WS*, p. 9); "The Basket of Eggs" (*CL*, pp. 27–28; *CSCEFS*, 2:111–12; *EC*, pp. 99–100; *FMJ* 2 [1973]: 284; *JFSS* 1 [1900]: 46–47); "The Bedmaking" (*WS*, p. 11); Laws M20, "Betsy Is a Beauty Fair" (*EC*, pp. 51–54); Laws P17, "Blow the Candle Out" (*FBI*, p. 396; *WS*, p. 14); Laws Q8, "The Boatsman and the Chest" (*WS*, p. 16); Child 24, "Bonnie Annie" (*CL*, p. 4; *CSCEFS*, 1:32–33; *FMJ* 3 [1976]: 103–4; *JFSS* 3 [1909]: 292–93); "Bonny Kate" (*WS*, p. 18); Laws O9, "Branded Lambs" (*CSCEFS*, 1:390–91; *FBI*, p. 310; *FD*, p. 2); "The Brickster" (*CSCEFS*, 1:457; *MB*, p. 12); "The Brisk Young Butcher" (*MB*, p. 13); Child 43, "The Broomfield Hill" (*CSCEFS*, 1:35–39;

FD, p. 11; *JEFDSS* 9 [1963]: 187–88; *JFSS* 4 [1910]: 110–16; *JFSS* 7 [1923]: 31–32; *JFSS* 8 [1929]: 127–28); "Catch-Me-If-You-Can" (*EC*, pp. 72–73; *WS*, p. 25); "Cold Blow and Rainy Night" (*CSCEFS*, 1:698–700); "The Crockery Ware" (*MB*, p. 19); "Dabbling in the Dew" (*CSCEFS*, 1:437–442; *CL*, p. 80; *EC*, p. 85; *FMJ* 2 [1973]: 287; *JEFDSS* 9 [1957]: 191–92; *JFSS* 4 [1913]: 282–84); "Dicky the Miller" (*CL*, p. 21; *EC*, p. 95); "Down by the Woods and Shady Green Trees" (*WS*, p. 37); "Floating down the Tide" (type 1: *CSCEFS*, 1:300; type 2: *CSCEFS*, 1:301–3); Laws O3, "The Foggy Dew" (type 1: *CSCEFS*, 1:410–17; *FD*, p. 31; type 2: *FBI*, pp. 400–401); "Forty Long Miles" (*CL*, p. 36; *CSCEFS*, 1:419–21; *JFSS* 1 [1899]: 18; *JFSS* 6 [1918]: 19); Child 276, "The Friar in the Well" (*MB*, p. 33); "The Frolic" (*EC*, p. 75; *WS*, p. 44); "The Game-Cock" (*FBI*, p. 457; *JFSS* 8 [1931]: 274–75; *MB*, p. 6); "Gently Johnny My Jingalo" (*CSCEFS*, 1:445); "Glastonbury Town" (*CSCEFS*, 1:666–67; *FMJ* 1 [1968]: 261–62); Laws K41, "Gold Watch" (*WS*, p. 66); "Gosport Beach" (*EC*, p. 126; *FD*, p. 36; *JFSS* 2 [1906]: 262–63); "The Grocer and the Tailor" (*FD*, pp. 38–39); "The Hazelbury Girl" (*CSCEFS*, 1:680–82; *FBI*, p. 404; *MB*, p. 97); Laws K43, "Home, Dearie, Home" (*CSCEFS*, 1: 671–79; *EC*, p. 223; *JFSS* 6 [1918]: 1–2; *MB*, p. 42; *WS*, p. 99); "Horn Fair" (*FMJ* 3 [1976]: 150–51; *JEFDSS* 8 [1957]: 105; *JFSS* 2 [1906]: 204); "The Indian Lass" (*MB*, p. 44); Laws K40, "Jack the Jolly Tar" (*CSCEFS*, 1:694–95; *FMJ* 3 [1976]: 110–11); "Johnny and Molly" (*FD*, pp. 46–47); Child 279, "The Jolly Beggar" (type 1: *CSCEFS*, 1:202–3; *EC*, pp. 215–16; type 2: *CSCEFS*, 1:204–7; *FBI*, p. 419; *FD*, p. 3); "Just as the Tide Was a-Flowing" (*CSCEFS*, 2:558–59; *MB*, p. 48); "The Knife in the Window" (*FBI*, p. 406); Child 110, "The Knight and the Shepherd's Daughter" (*CSCEFS*, 1:129–34; *JFSS* 3 [1908]: 222; *JFSS* 3 [1909]: 280–81); "The Lark in the Morn" (*CSCEFS*, 2:182–83; *EC*, pp. 172–73; *MB*, p. 51); "The Light of the Moon" (*EC*, pp. 136–38; *MB*, p. 52); "The Liverpool Landlady" (*CSCEFS*, 1:706–7); "Low Down in the Broom" (*WS*, p. 70); "The Maid with the Long Birches" (*FMJ* 1 [1968]: 260); "Mary Thompson" (*FMJ* 2 [1974], 349–50); "The Mole-Catcher" (*CL*, p. 61; *EC*, p. 191; *FBI*, p. 463); "Molly and William" (*WS*, p. 78); "My Good Old Man" (*EC*, p. 125; *WS*, p. 81); "Nelly the Milkmaid" (*MB*, p. 59); "Night Visit Song" (*WS*, p. 86); "No Sir" (*CSCEFS*, 1:687–93; *MB*, p. 63); "The Nutting Girl" (*CL*, p. 1; *FBI*, pp. 416–17); "Oh As I Was a-Walking" (*EC*, p. 198); "Oh Yarmouth Is a Pretty Town" (*JFSS* 3 [1907]: 53; *JFSS* 7 [1923]: 52–53, 57); "Open the Window" (*EC*, p. 201; *JFSS* 3 [1907]: 79–80); Laws Q13, "The Oyster Girl" (*CSCEFS*, 2:115–16; *FBI*, pp. 519–20); "The Poor Couple" (*CSCEFS*, 2:7–9; *MB*, p. 71); "Poor Nell and the Chimney Sweep" (*CSCEFS*, 2:100–102); "Portsmouth City" (*CL*, p. 73); Laws O10, "Pretty Betsy the Milkmaid" (*CSCEFS*, 2:61–62; *FBI*, p. 696; *FD*, pp. 6–7; *JFSS* 6 [1919]: 35–36); Laws P18, "Pretty Little Miss" (*CSCEFS*, 1:656–60; *EC*, pp. 41–42; *FBI*, pp. 373–74; *JFSS* 1 [1904]: 230; *JFSS* 3 [1909]: 296–97; *JFSS* 4 [1913]: 281; *WS*, p. 6); "Raking of Hay" (*CSCEFS*, 1:447–48; *JFSS* 3 [1907]: 107; *WS*, p. 51); "Ramble-Away" (*EC*, pp. 93–94; *FBI*, p. 366); "Rap-Tap-Tap"

(*FBI*, p. 468; *MB*, p. 73); "Riding down to Portsmouth" (*CSCEFS*, 2: 117–18); "The Rigs of London Town" (*CSCEFS*, 2:157–58; *JFSS* 8 [1931]: 272–73; *FBI*, p. 423); "Roger and Nell" (*CL*, pp. 78–79); "Rue the Day" (*FBI*, p. 470; *WS*, p. 82); Laws P34A, "The Sailor's Tragedy" (*WS*, p. 101); "Salisbury Plain" (*CSCEFS*, 2: 155–56); Laws Q12, "The Sea Captain and the Squire" (*CSCEFS*, 2:16–17); "The Sentry" (*CSCEFS*, 1:650; *CL*, p. 88); "Seven Months I've Been Married" (*WS*, p. 103); Laws O17, "Seventeen Come Sunday" (*CSCEFS*, 1:422–29; *EC*, pp. 238–39; *JFSS* 1 [1901]: 92–93; *JFSS* 2 [1905]: 9; *JFSS* 2 [1906]: 270–71; *WS*, p. 104); "The Shannon Side" (*CSCEFS*, 1:651–54); "The Shoemaker's Kiss" (*MB*, p. 79); "An S-O-N-G" (*FMJ* 1 [1969]: 330–31; *MB*, p. 82); "The Spotted Cow" (*FBI*, p. 319; *WS*, p. 108); "Sweet Kitty" (*CSCEFS*, 2:106–8; *CL*, p. 67): "Sweet Lovely Joan" (*CSCEFS*, 2: 60; *CL*, pp. 95–96); "The Tailor's Breeches" (*MB*, p. 87); "Through the Woods" (*CSCEFS*, 1:621; *EC*, pp. 186–87); Laws P19, "Tripping over the Lea" (*CSCEFS*, 1:661–62); "The True Lovers" (*CL*, p. 104; *EC*, p. 151); Child 299, "Trooper and Maid" (*CL*, pp. 22–23; *EC*, pp. 57–58); "Valentine's Day" (type 1: *EC*, pp. 192–193; *FD*, p. 101; type 2: *EC*, pp. 193–94; type 3: *CSCEFS*, 1:668–70); Child 100, "Willie o'Winsbury" (*CSCEFS*, 1:121–24; *EC*, pp. 278–79; *WS*, pp. 112–13); "The Worcestershire Wedding" (*FD*, p. 97; *JFSS* 3 [1907]: 119–20); "You Bachelors You Know" (*CSCEFS*, 2:37–38). In my discussion, I do not exemplify every variation that occurs within individual text-types—though those variations can be accounted for by our code. I do exemplify the more striking and established variations, however—hence the occasional designation of subtypes in the above list.

15. A thorough study of this kind of "humorous ballad of adultery" from both Britain and Germany, which treats broadside as well as oral versions, is Klaus Roth, *Ehebruchschwänke in Liedform. Motive*: Freiburger folkloristische Forschungen, vol. 9 (Munich: Wilhelm Fink Verlag, 1977).

16. The appearance of the same song under more than one precept indicates that the maid habitually breaks more than one of the taboos.

17. In one version of "Through the Woods" the maid also breaks precept 9 (*EC*, pp. 186–87). The text is closely related to "Oxford City" (Laws P30).

18. "Jack the Jolly Tar," Laws K40, is actually a little more complex than I have made it out to be, for it exhibits a role-reversal from the norm. From the start it is the male who possesses the feminine trait of lower social status, and it is he who is the *innovative* one and who gains the reward of marriage to a lady. Of all the man/maid songs that do not fall under precepts 6 and 13, "Jack the Jolly Tar" seems to direct its message the most strongly to the male actor. Still, she is the one who undergoes what little ordeal there is in the story, not he.

19. Some of these songs, like "Nutting Girl" and "Spotted Cow," show influence from the metaphorical model's rhetoric; the message of precept 13 is quite consistent with the message of the metaphorical model.

20. She does the same things in type 1 but they do not help her there. Unusual variation of this sort within a text-type indicates ambivalence toward the song's meaning rather than simply weakness of the precept.

21. See *EC*, p. 281, and *WS*, p. 118. A fuller and more clearly metaphorical version, "Roger the Ploughboy," appeared on a nineteenth-century broadside by H. Such of 177 Union Street, London. See Department of Special Collections, University of California, Los Angeles, Accession no. 605, box 4.

22. See Introduction, note 8.

23. In discussing these varieties of metaphorical usage, I shall at the same time account for all those songs of sexual liaisons in our sample that I do not mention in my discussion of each model and in note 3 above, with two exceptions; one exception—"A-Growing" (Laws O35)—I shall examine at some length in the next section of this chapter, the other I discuss in note 24 below.

24. Or perhaps influence from the symbolic code is at work, as there is extensive nature imagery, as well as a tragic consequence for the girl. Compare "The Sprig of May" (*EC*, p. 246), which has an explicit sexual metaphor encountered nowhere else; the man "breaks his finger" to "pleasure" the girl. The song ends with a tragic experience for the lass, which is not in keeping with the traditional metaphorical song message. The hint of the symbolic code (fertile versus infertile ground, heat versus lack of heat) is too weakly represented to make much of. The phrase "sprig of May" could have been a central metaphor (cf. the ambiguous "handful of May" in "As I Walked Through the Meadows" [*CSCEFS*, 1:377–83; *EC*, pp. 213–14; *WS*, p. 96], which I have taken to be non-metaphorical); instead, however, its imagery is distinctly subsidiary to the breaking of the finger. In sum, "The Sprig of May" appears to be an example of a folk composer doing what scholars often do—attempting to make a metaphor out of a symbol. The song has been collected only once, indicating perhaps a moribund status in tradition, one that it fully deserves. The unpleasant metaphor of finger-breaking itself has no analogues in the traditional repertoire.

25. See J. Barre Toelken, " 'Riddles Wisely Expounded,' " *Western Folklore* 25 (1966): 1–16, the finest essay-length interpretive analysis of Anglo-American folk poetry I know of.

26. This stanza is given a different interpretation by A. L. Lloyd, *Folk Song in England*, p. 200, but that interpretation has no parallels in the song repertoire.

27. In dialogue songs two actors take turns of declaration and counter-declaration, or command and reply, or question and answer, as in *débâts*. Dialogue songs are often classed with ballads, but their narrative is invariably so slender and their internal redundancy so high that in most cases "catalogue" is a quite appropriate designation.

28. See Hodgart, *The Ballads*, pp. 21–23.

29. Cf. Buchan, *The Ballad and the Folk*, p. 277.

30. See *JFSS* 2 (1905): 46–47. For texts of "T Stands for Thomas," see *CSCEFS*, 2:596–97; *JFSS* 2 (1906): 152; *JFSS* 5 (1915): 174–75; *WS*, p. 109.

31. Lloyd, *Folk Song in England*, pp. 190–94.

32. Thompson, *Lark Rise to Candleford*, pp. 65–66.

33. Nicholson, *The Folk Speech of East Yorkshire*, pp. 8–9.

34. Though it does differ from the folksong imagery in degree: in the songs, the soundmakers operate in some sort of concert, though indiscriminate, whereas rough music by its very title stresses cacophony and motley. We should not make too much of the bird imagery in this somewhat imaginative account, for rough musicking invariably took place after dark.

35. Brooke and Brooke, *Suffolk Prospect*, p. 122.

36. Thompson, *Lark Rise to Candleford*, p. 241. For Mrs. Macey, see pp. 516–17.

37. Thompson, *Lark Rise to Candleford*, pp. 101–2.

38. The children did not signify as a social category within the paradigms "respectability" and "nonrespectability" (hussiness?). As the quotation indicates, the color or design of their dresses "made no difference"; only utilitarian motives ruled what they wore—in fact they could sport the very same dress in both sacred (church) and profane (May Day) settings.

39. Thompson, *Lark Rise to Candleford*, p. 176.

40. J. Jean Hecht, *The Domestic Servant Class in Eighteenth-Century England* (London: Routledge & Kegan Paul, 1956); Thompson, *Lark Rise to Candleford*, p. 163.

41. Thompson, *Lark Rise to Candleford*, p. 49; Hammond and Hammond, *The Village Labourer*.

42. For a view of gypsies from early in this century see Clifton Johnson, *Among English Hedgerows* (New York: Macmillan, 1925), pp. 98–105. The nongypsy tinker, wrote Richard Jefferies, "notwithstanding his vagrant habits, is sometimes a man of substance . . . when sober and steady, he has a capital trade: his hands are never idle" (*An English Village* [Boston: Little, Brown, 1903], pp. 64–65).

43. Thompson, *Lark Rise to Candleford*, p. 537; also p. 258.

44. Alfred Williams, *A Wiltshire Village* (London: Duckworth, 1912), p. 165.

45. Johnson, *Among English Hedgerows*, pp. 60–62.

46. Thompson, *Lark Rise to Candleford*, p. 386.

47. M. K. Ashby, *Joseph Ashby of Tysoe 1859–1919* (Cambridge: Cambridge University Press, 1961), p. 1.

48. Margaret Llewelyn Davies, ed., *Life as We Have Known It*, by Co-Operative Working Women (London: Leonard and Virginia Woolf at the Hogarth Press, 1931), p. 76.

49. Ford Madox, Ford Hueffer, *The Heart of the Country* (London: Alston Rivers, 1906), p. 112–13: "At nights, lying in the servants' bedroom of Lady Knatchbull's . . . the girls . . . [sang] dismal songs of the murder of trusting girls—with obvious morals for the girls of the servants' room.

. . ." Despite this, his informant ran off at a young age with an itinerant basket-mender. She suffered.

50. Bob Copper, *Songs and Southern Breezes* (London: Heinemann, 1973), pp. 176–78.

51. Thompson, *Lark Rise to Candleford*, p. 47.

52. Thompson, *Lark Rise to Candleford*, p. 48.

53. Copper, *Songs and Southern Breezes*, pp. 139–140.

54. Thompson, *Lark Rise to Candleford*, p. 113.

55. Blythe, *Akenfield*, p. 196.

CHAPTER 3

1. Frank Kidson, *Traditional Tunes* (Oxford: Charles Taphouse, 1891), p. 138.

2. Herbert Halpert, "Vitality of Tradition and Local Songs," *Journal of the International Folk Music Council* 3 (1951): 35–40.

3. George J. Casey, Neil V. Rosenberg, and Wilfred W. Wareham, "Repertoire Categorization and Performance-Audience Relationships: Some Newfoundland Folksong Examples," *Ethnomusicology* 16 (1972): 397–403.

4. Thompson, *Lark Rise to Candleford*, pp. 62–69.

5. For a traditional version of "The Barley Mow," see Karpeles, *Cecil Sharp's Collection of English Folk Songs,* 2: 406–7.

6. This was, perhaps, a version of the song in Greig, *Folk-Song in the North-East,* no. 17.

7. The folklore studies that come closest to this kind of phenomenological perspective on genre are Roger D. Abrahams, "The Complex Relations of Simple Forms," in *Folklore Genres,* ed. Dan Ben-Amos, Publications of the American Folklore Society, Bibliographical and Special Series, vol. 26 (Austin: University of Texas Press, 1976), 193–214, and Gary H. Gossen, "Chamula Genres of Verbal Behavior," *Journal of American Folklore* 84 (1971): 145–67.

8. Most of the sample of fifty local Yorkshire songs that form the database for this study come from the following sources: a quite random search in the archives of the Institute of Dialect and Folk Life Studies at the University of Leeds; local ephemeral publications like magazines, histories, and autobiographies; and a small collection of Yorkshire broadsides made by Frank Kidson and now on deposit in the Leeds Central Library ("Leeds Printed Broadsides"). Upon deciding to undertake a serious study of this material, I added to the collection by searching for all apparently local songs (that is, made by Yorkshire residents themselves on the topic of their own environment) in the following works: Charles F. Forshaw, ed., *Holroyd's Collection of Yorkshire Ballads* (London: George Bell & Sons, 1892); C. J. Davidson Ingledew, *The Ballads and Songs of Yorkshire* (London: Bell & Daldy, 1860); and J. Horsfall Turner, *Yorkshire Anthology: Ballads and Songs—Ancient and Modern* (Idel, Bradford, Yorks.: Printed for the Editor by T. Harrison & Sons, Bingley, 1901).

9. Colin S. Wharton, "Folk Songs from the North Riding" (*M.A.*

thesis, University of Leeds, 1962), pp. 66–68 (Institute of Dialect and Folk Life Studies Archives, University of Leeds, Accession no. 265).

10. Forshaw, *Holroyd's Collection of Yorkshire Ballads*, pp. 77–79.

11. John N. Dransfield, *A History of the Parish of Penistone* (Penistone, Yorks.: James H. Wood, The Don Press, 1906), pp. 398–99.

12. "On a Famous Hunt in the Woodlands," in Dransfield, *A History of the Parish of Penistone*, pp. 437–38.

13. Buttershaw Youth Centre, *The Song of Upper Wharfedale* (Bradford, Yorks.: City of Bradford Educational Services Committee, 1971), pp. 63–64; Florence Foster, "Last Chronicle of Beckermonds," *The Dalesman* 10 (1948): 132–33.

14. W. G. B. Page, *The Life of Thomas Mercer (Commonly Called "Tom Massey"), The Blind Fiddler of Withernwick, East-Riding of Yorkshire* (Hull, Yorks.: M. Harland & Son, 1902), pp. 27–28. A. E. Green brought this pamphlet to my attention and kindly furnished me with a photocopy.

15. Wharton, "Folk Songs from the North Riding," pp. 119–20.

16. Buttershaw Youth Centre, *The Song of Upper Wharfedale*, pp. 7–8, 11–13.

17. *Census of Great Britain, 1851* (London: W. Clowes & Sons, for Her Majesty's Stationery Office, 1852).

18. Forshaw, *Holroyd's Collection of Yorkshire Ballads*, pp. 19–20.

19. *The Universal Songster*, 3 vols. (London: Jones & Co., 1832), 3: 94–95.

20. From a typewritten manuscript, Institute of Dialect and Folk Life Studies Archives, University of Leeds, Accession no. 211. According to the manuscript, the song is by "J. Metcalfe, 1964."

21. The best-known studies are the full length works by Edward D. Ives, *Larry Gorman* and *Lawrence Doyle*.

22. Composed by Norman Harris, Leeds. From the Institute of Dialect and Folk Life Studies Archives, University of Leeds, Accession no. 718.

23. "The Song of the Glaisdale Harriers" (Wharton, "Folk Songs from the North Riding," pp. 72–74).

24. Wharton, "Folk Songs from the North Riding," pp. 52–54.

25. Wharton, "Folk Songs from the North Riding," pp. 121–23.

26. M. C. F. Morris, *Yorkshire Reminiscences (With Others)* (London: Humphrey Milford, Oxford University Press, 1922), pp. 188–89.

27. Page, *Life of Thomas Mercer*, pp. 22–23.

28. Turner, *Yorkshire Anthology*, p. 166.

29. *The Dalesman* 28 (1966), 388.

30. James Parker, *Illustrated Rambles from Hipperholme to Tong* (Bradford, Yorks.: Percy Lund, Humphries & Co., The Country Press, 1904), pp. 119–20.

31. Turner, *Yorkshire Anthology*, pp. 251–52.

32. "Leeds Printed Broadsides."

33. Wharton, "Folk Songs from the North Riding," pp. 47–48, 41.

34. *The Dalesman* 28 (1966): 389.

35. Page, *Life of Thomas Mercer*, p. 19.

36. See Laws Q23 for "Creeping Jane"; English versions may be found in Karpeles, *Cecil Sharp's Collection of English Folk Songs*, 2:255–60.

37. Walter White, *A Month in Yorkshire* (London: Chapman & Hall, 1858), p. 62.

38. Ingledew, *Ballads and Songs of Yorkshire*, pp. 160–61.

39. The story also circulates in prose narrative form; see Richard Blakeborough, *Wit, Character, Folklore and Customs of the North Riding of Yorkshire* (London: Henry Frowde, 1898), p. 64. A further reason for the song's popularity is that its central motif is unusually clever and adaptable to different contexts. For the same motif (K134.7[a]) in American tale tradition, see the references in Ernest W. Baughman, *Type and Motif-Index of the Folktales of England and North America*, Indiana University Folklore Series, no. 20 (The Hague: Mouton, 1966), p. 342.

40. *The Dalesman* 28 (1967): 816–17.

41. For "Beautiful Swaledale," see *The Dalesman* 15 (1953): 102.

42. From a handwritten manuscript in the Institute of Dialect and Folk Life Studies Archives, University of Leeds, Accession no. 2271. Contributed by Mr. G. Metcalfe of Middlemoor.

43. *The Dalesman* 27 (1965): 380.

44. *Transactions of the Yorkshire Dialect Society*, part 53, vol. 9 (1953): 24–25.

45. For "The Sportsman of Leeds," see Buttershaw Youth Centre, *Song of Upper Wharfedale*, pp. 61–62.

46. "Leeds Printed Broadsides."

47. "Leeds Printed Broadsides."

48. "Leeds Printed Broadsides."

49. Tommy Daniel, *Yorkshire Broadsheet* (Batley, Yorks.; typed, mimeographed pamphlet). See Lloyd, *Folk Song in England*, pp. 328–31.

50. "Leeds Printed Broadsides."

51. For a documented account of the tragedy, see Ian Dewhirst, *Gleanings from Victorian Yorkshire* (Driffield, Yorks.: The Ridings Publishing Company, 1972), pp. 95–101.

52. Frank Peel, *The Risings of the Luddites, Chartists and Plug-Drawers*, 4th ed. (New York: Augustus M. Kelley, 1968), p. xiv.

53. Peel, *The Risings of the Luddites*, pp. 47–48.

54. The sledgehammer's cognomen was taken from its manufacturer's name—Enoch and James Taylor of Huddersfield. Ironically, the same firm made the shear-frames; consequently, the epigram was spawned that "Enoch made them and Enoch shall break them." See Taylor Dyson, *The History of Huddersfield and District from the Earliest Times down to 1951*, 2d ed. (Huddersfield, Yorks.: Alfred Jubb & Son, 1951), pp. 339–40; D. F. E. Sykes, *The History of Huddersfield and the Valleys of the Colne, the Holme, and the Dearne* (Huddersfield, Yorks.: "The Worker" Press, n.d.), p. 294.

55. Fred R. Spark, *Memories of My Life* (Leeds: Fred R. Spark & Son, n.d.), p. 144.

56. Spark, *Memories of My Life*, pp. 147–48.

57. "Leeds Printed Broadsides."

58. "Beverley Gaol" is from Frederick Ross, *A Glossary of Words Used in Holderness* (1877), as reproduced in *The Yorkshireman* 6, no. 106 (1878): 56.

59. Institute of Dialect and Folk Life Studies Archives, University of Leeds, Accession no. 2270. The song is a parody of "Island in the Sun," made popular by Harry Belafonte in the 1950s.

60. Ingledew, *Ballads and Songs of Yorkshire*, pp. 308–11.

61. Ingledew, *Ballads and Songs of Yorkshire*, pp. 162–64. Cf. Lloyd, *Folk Song in England*, pp. 238–40.

62. There is theoretically no reason why these same tropes could not be used for *debasement,* the opposite of transcendence; one thinks of the traditional "beggar's litany" ("from Hull and Halifax and Hell, oh Lord, deliver us"), or of the Methodist hymn, "On Bradford likewise look Thou down / Where Satan keeps his seat." But debasement does not appear in our sample.

63. "Leeds Printed Broadsides."

64. MacKerness, *The Journals of George Sturt,* 1:381–82.

65. John Batty, *The History of Rothwell* (Rothwell, Yorks.: Published by the Author, 1877), pp. 65–66.

66. The broadside is reprinted in Turner, *Yorkshire Anthology,* pp. 227–29.

67. The "Bastile" referred to the workhouse, where those on public relief had to reside. It was especially hateful because there were no accommodations for both sexes in the same workhouse, and so families on relief were split up. Oastler's identification with child workers stemmed from his making their conditions his particular concern; he fought especially hard for a ten-hour maximum workday for children. There were other songs current about the reformer; for instance, during a rally in Huddersfield in 1833, "the mass of children sang the song of the Factory Children,

We will have the Ten Hours Bill,
That we will, that we will,
Or the land shall ne'er be still;
We will have the Ten Hours Bill,
For Oastler says we will."

(From W. R. Croft, *The History of the Factory Movement, or, Oastler and His Times* [Huddersfield, Yorks.: George Whitehead & Sons, 1888], pp. 86–87.)

68. *Sketch of the Life and Opinions of Richard Oastler* (Leeds: Printed by Joshua Hobson for Cobbett, 1838), pp. 9–10.

69. Ingledew, *Ballads and Songs of Yorkshire*, pp. 299–300; Forshaw, *Holroyd's Collection of Yorkshire Ballads,* pp. 104–5. (Abraham Holroyd himself was the author of the verses.) For evidence of the song in oral tradition, see *The Dalesman* 28 (1967): 815.

70. H. Ling Roth, *The Yorkshire Coiners 1767–1783. And Notes on Old and Prehistoric Halifax* (Halifax, Yorks.: F. King & Sons, 1906), pp.

216–17. "Bishop Blaze" in stanza three is the legendary patron saint of woolcombers. For his legend and associated ceremony, see Hole, *British Folk Customs,* pp. 175–77 ("St. Blaise's Day").

71. J. Horsfall Turner, *The Annals of Wakefield House of Correction for Three Hundred Years* (Bingley, Yorks.: Privately printed for J. Horsfall Turner by Harrison & Sons, 1904), pp. 231–32.

72. Sturt Bourne, *Change in the Village,* p. 194; *Memoirs of a Surrey Labourer* (London: Duckworth, 1907), p. 110; see also Blythe, *Akenfield,* p. 153.

73. Williams, *A Wiltshire Village,* p. 256.

74. Thompson, *Lark Rise to Candleford,* p. 392.

75. See George A. Miller, *The Psychology of Communication* (Harmondsworth, Middlesex: Penguin Books, 1968), pp. 11–20, 21–50.

76. See the excerpts from contemporary accounts in E. Royston Pike, *"Hard Times": Human Documents of the Industrial Revolution* (New York: Frederick A. Praeger, 1966).

77. For a discussion and evaluation of these opposing views, see E. J. Hobsbawm, *Labouring Men: Studies in the History of Labour* (London: Weidenfeld & Nicolson, 1964), pp. 64–125.

78. For the Luddites see, in addition to Peel, *The Rising of the Luddites,* Malcolm I. Thomis, *The Luddites: Machine-Breaking in Regency England* (New York: Schocken Books, 1972); for the Swing riots see Hobsbawm and Rudé, *Captain Swing.*

79. See Raymond Williams, *The Country and the City* (New York: Oxford University Press, 1973), pp. 85–86; Hammond and Hammond, *The Village Labourer*; Francis George Heath, *The English Peasantry* (London: Frederick Warne, 1874); and W. Hasbach, *A History of the English Agricultural Labourer,* trans. Ruth Kenyon (New York: Augustus M. Kelley, 1966).

80. See Sturt, *Memoirs of a Surrey Labourer,* p. 106, and *Change in the Village,* p. 12; Blythe, *Akenfield,* p. 197; David H. Morgan, "The Place of Harvesters in Nineteenth-Century Village Life," in *Village Life and Labour,* ed. Raphael Samuel (London: Routledge & Kegan Paul, 1975), pp. 36–38.

81. Hammond and Hammond, *The Village Labourer,* pp. 187–88.

82. Hammond and Hammond, *The Village Labourer,* pp. 190–91; see also G. E. Fussell, *The English Rural Labourer* (London: Batchworth, 1949), p. 42.

83. Fussell, *The English Rural Labourer,* pp. 61–62 (see also p. 82); Hasbach, *A History of the English Agricultural Labourer,* p. 409.

84. For a description of the different types of wage systems all over England, see Hobsbawm and Rudé, *Captain Swing,* pp. 37–47. Wages in the northern agricultural sector were also higher than in its southern counterpart because it competed with industry for labor; see E. W. Bovill, *English Country Life 1780–1830* (London: Oxford University Press, 1962), p. 16; Heath, *The English Peasantry,* pp. 231–233.

85. For the older familial paradigm see Laslett, *The World We Have*

Lost, pp. 1–21. For a system similar to Yorkshire's, in the nearby Westmoreland of today, see Williams, *Gosforth,* pp. 34–58. For Yorkshire, see Adam Curle, "Kinship Structure in an English Village," *Man* 52 (1952): 68–69.

86. Perkin, *The Origin of Modern English Society,* pp. 2, 5.

87. John La Page, *The Story of Baildon* (Bradford, Yorks.: Printed by Wm. Byles & Sons, n.d.), p. 117. See also T. W. Hanson, "The Diary of a Grandfather: Cornelius Ashworth, of Waltroyd Wheatley," *Papers, Reports, etc., Read Before the Halifax Antiquarian Society* n.v. (1916): 234.

88. E. P. Thompson, "Time, Work-Discipline and Industrial Capitalism," *Past and Present,* no. 38 (1967): 56–97. For the proverbial phrase "passing the time of day" and its rural usage, see Sturt, *Change in the Village,* p. 38; Thompson, *Lark Rise to Candleford,* p. 310.

89. See Hammond and Hammond, *The Village Labourer,* pp. 163–75.

90. For an Oxfordshire equivalent in Candleford Green, see Thompson, *Lark Rise to Candleford,* pp. 472–73; see also Laslett, *The World We Have Lost,* pp. 305.

91. Thompson, *Lark Rise to Candleford,* p. 310. See also pp. 107, 360.

92. Thompson, *Lark Rise to Candleford,* pp. 207, 239, 32–33.

93. George Ewart Evans, *Tools of Their Trades* (New York: Taplinger, 1971), p. 181.

94. A country proverb, traditional in both north and south, says that "You've got to summer and winter a man before you can pretend to know him" (Thompson, *Lark Rise to Candleford,* p. 600). In Yorkshire's Nidderdale, "Tradition seems to vary as to whether one has to live in the area 21 or 25 years or indeed, whether one's family should be resident for 50 or 100 years to become a 'local'. There is an old saying that they accept no one at face value: 'We summer them, and winter them, and summer them again before we make up our minds'." (Catherine Cook, "A Collection of Folk Tales from Upper Nidderdale" [M.A. thesis, University of Leeds, 1972], p. 21, note 1.)

95. Blythe, *Akenfield,* p. 181.

96. Clement Harris, *Hennage: A Social System in Miniature,* Case Studies in Cultural Anthropology, no. 4 (New York: Holt, Rinehart & Winston, 1974), pp. 11–12, 46. In two instances, villagers were urged to show assertiveness—in organizing a local fête and in visiting their children's school during class hours. Though there was no personal aggrandizement to be gained from either activity, and though the parents showed approval of both endeavors, not a single parent would take the first step in carrying out either activity. Of course, they may also have been reacting against the ethnographer's assertiveness, for he instigated both ideas.

97. Foster, "Peasant Society and the Image of Limited Good."

98. Thus agricultural laborers, for instance, had more ease and freedom of movement; see Williams, *A Wiltshire Village,* pp. 192–93. For village close-mindedness toward outsiders, see Thompson, *Lark Rise to Candleford,* p. 44.

99. Thompson, *Lark Rise to Candleford,* pp. 553–54; Sturt, *Change in the Village,* p. 174.

100. Williams, *Gosforth,* pp. 168–74.

101. Hobsbawm and Rudé, *Captain Swing,* pp. 36–37.

102. Harris, *Hennage,* pp. 22–23, 53. Cf. Sturt, *Memoirs of a Surrey Labourer,* pp. 106–7.

103. See Thomas Wright, A Journeyman Engineer, *Some Habits and Customs of the Working Classes* (London: Tinsley Brothers, 1867), pp. 204–48; see also the pertinent remarks in Mass-Observation, *The Pub and the People* (London: Victor Gollancz, 1943), pp. 336–38.

104. For analogous notions about this function of mummers' activities, see Roger D. Abrahams, "British West Indian Folk Drama and the 'Life Cycle' Problem," *Folklore* 81 (1970): 241–65, and Susan Pattison, "The Antrobus Soulcaking Play: An Alternative Approach to the Mummers' Play," *Folk-Life* 15 (1977): 5–11. For pranks and tricks see Thompson, *Lark Rise to Candleford,* p. 61. For satirical verses see the amusing account in W. Riley and Elisabeth Brockbank, *A Village in Craven* (London: Herbert Jenkins, 1925), pp. 204–12.

105. White, *A Month in Yorkshire,* pp. 60–61. Massey's blindness, poverty, and mobility ensured that his own power as a satirist would not be a threat.

CHAPTER 4

1. B. E. Coates and E. M. Rawstron, *Regional Variations in Great Britain* (London: B. T. Batsford, 1971), pp. 49–55.

2. See T. W. Freeman, *The Conurbations of Great Britain,* 2d rev. ed. (Manchester: Manchester University Press, 1966), pp. 156–79.

3. At the 1961 census. In 1974, Yorkshire's administrative regions were changed significantly in their boundaries and names, with the result that today the ancient West Riding no longer exists as such. Since the data for this study were gathered in 1973, however, I write of the region as it was at that time.

4. Cf. Roger deV. Renwick, "Two Yorkshire Poets: A Comparative Study," *Southern Folklore Quarterly* 40 (1976): 274–75.

5. All texts of Mrs. Bairstow's poems reproduced in this chapter were taken from her two commonplace books. I have adjusted the spelling of the very occasional word.

6. The local weekly newspaper serving a neighboring borough of Mrs. Bairstow's own Morley. Its name was later changed to the *Spenborough Guardian.*

7. "My Will" is the title of a poem by A. C. Benson, the very one that young Martha recited for the Inspector of Schools and on which she modeled her own. See Arthur Christopher Benson, *Selected Poems* (London: John Lane, 1924), pp. 96–97.

8. See J. and R. Fairfax-Blakeborough, *The Spirit of Yorkshire* (London: B. T. Batsford, 1954), p. 35 and passim; Blakeborough, *Wit, Character, Folklore and Customs of the North Riding of Yorkshire.*

9. *Daily Mail* (London), 1 March 1973, p. 3.

Notes

CHAPTER 5

1. From a typewritten MS, Ephraim Mugglestone [Charles Moxon], "A Fair Crack of the Whip: My Life in the Coal Mines and Hospital."

2. See Berger and Luckmann, *The Social Construction of Reality,* pp. 19–46.

3. See Norman Dennis, Fernando Henriques, and Clifford Slaughter, *Coal Is Our Life,* 2d ed. (London: Tavistock, 1969), pp. 15, 27. Public reactions by local civic and religious leaders to the Lofthouse tragedy made frequent reference to this social phenomenon. For instance, the editorial column of the *Dewsbury Reporter,* 30 March 1973, stated that miners are "often apparently regardless of the welfare of others outside their own close-knit community, but possessed of an almost chilling courage when they stride purposefully to the cage to succour their 'own kind' in peril below." And from a letter by six Yorkshire Members of Parliament to the *Wakefield Express,* 30 March 1973: "The ties and comradeship that bind miners and their communities have always been marvelled at."

4. See Dennis, Henriques, and Slaughter, *Coal Is Our Life,* p. 38; E. R. Manley, *Meet the Miner* (Lofthouse, Yorks.: Published by the author, 1947), pp. 69–70.

5. Thus Mr. Willie Long, the mayor-elect of Dewsbury and himself a miner for forty years, wrote a public letter launching an appeal for contributions to the Lofthouse Colliery Disaster Fund: "I believe that numbers of my fellow citizens would wish to show a practical expression of sympathy towards those who are left to mourn." (From the *Dewsbury Reporter,* 6 April 1973.)

6. *Yorkshire Post* (Leeds), 29 May 1973.

7. *Yorkshire Post,* 11 July 1973.

8. *Wakefield Express,* 13 April 1973.

9. An ordinal scale shows only "more than" and "less than" relationships between its points. It is a little more sophisticated than a nominal scale, which simply differentiates points from each other, while it is less sophisticated than an interval scale, which can measure differences between points with a standardized metric, and a ratio scale, which can do all the above as well as relate all points to an absolute zero.

10. The *Express* did not publish the poem, but did run a short news item, "Tribute to the Miners in Verse," which described the poem's contents, prefaced by the comment that "Miners from all over the country have paid their tributes in many different ways to the seven men who perished in the Lofthouse Colliery Disaster." (15 June 1973.) It was this news item that led me to Mr. Wainwright.

11. From the poet's handwritten notebook of poems. I have corrected two minor scribal errors of spelling.

12. *Rotherham Advertiser,* 27 April 1973.

13. From the singing of Walter Greaves at the Royal Hotel, Thornhill Lees, Dewsbury, 26 June 1973. Mr. Greaves set his poem to a traditional Yorkshire lyke-wake air, which he took from *English Dance and Song* 33 (1971): 60.

14. For a short characterization of folk revival activities in the area, see my "Two Yorkshire Poets: A Comparative Study," pp. 245–46.

15. Though stronger in the larger urban than in the smaller provincial regions, and in the 1960s than in the 1970s.

16. *Evening Post* (Leeds), 26 March 1973.

17. A. L. Loyd, *Come All Ye Bold Miners* (London: Lawrence & Wishart, 1952).

18. For "The Ballad of Springhill," by Peggy Seeger and Ewan MacColl, see *The Ewan MacColl–Peggy Seeger Songbook* (New York: Oak Publications, 1963), pp. 20–21. For "The Gresford Disaster" see Lloyd, *Folk Song in England,* pp. 359–60.

19. Lloyd, *Folk Song in England,* p. 360.

20. See Renwick, "Two Yorkshire Poets," pp. 245–46.

21. *Dewsbury Reporter,* 6 April 1973.

22. *Batley News,* 12 April 1973.

23. *Evening Post,* 9 April 1973.

24. British Broadcasting Corporation, "Lofthouse: Aftermath of a Disaster," televised on BBC 1, 24 May 1973.

25. Roger Cross, "Defiant Sid Haigh Says: We Are Winning the Fight," *Yorkshire Post,* 23 March 1973.

26. BBC, "Lofthouse: Aftermath of a Disaster."

27. BBC, "Lofthouse: Aftermath of a Disaster."

BIBLIOGRAPHY

Abrahams, Roger D. "British West Indian Folk Drama and the 'Life Cycle' Problem." *Folklore* 81 (1970): 241–65.

———. The Complex Relations of Simple Forms." In *Folklore Genres*. Edited by Dan Ben-Amos, pp. 193–214. Publications of the American Folklore Society, Bibliographical and Special Series, vol. 26. Austin: University of Texas Press, 1976.

———. "Patterns of Structure and Role Relationships in the Child Ballads in the United States." *Journal of American Folklore* 79 (1966): 448–62.

Ashby, M. K. *The Changing English Village: A History of Bledington, Gloucestershire in Its Setting 1066–1914.* Kineton, Warwick: The Roundwood Press, 1974.

———. *Joseph Ashby of Tysoe 1859–1919: A Study of English Village Life.* Cambridge: Cambridge University Press, 1961.

Baring-Gould, S. *Further Reminiscences: 1864–1894.* New York: E. P. Dutton, 1925.

Barrett, W. A. *English Folk-Songs.* London: Novello, n.d.

Barry, Phillips. " 'Fair Florella.' " *American Speech* 3 (1928): 441–47.

Barthes, Roland. "The Structuralist Activity." *Partisan Review* 34 (1967): 82–88.

Bascom, William R. "Four Functions of Folklore." *Journal of American Folklore* 67 (1954): 333–49.

Bateson, Gregory. *Steps to an Ecology of Mind*. New York: Ballantine Books, 1972.

Batley News (Batley, Yorkshire).

Batty, John. *The History of Rothwell*. Rothwell, Yorks.: Published by the Author, 1877.

Baughman, Ernest W. *Type and Motif-Index of the Folktales of England and North America*. Indiana University Folklore Series, no. 20. The Hague: Mouton, 1966.

Ben-Amos, Dan. "Toward a Definition of Folklore in Context." *Journal of American Folklore* 84 (1971): 3–15.

Benson, Arthur Christopher. *Selected Poems*. London: John Lane, 1924.

Berger, Peter L., and Luckmann, Thomas. *The Social Construction of Reality: A Treatise on the Sociology of Knowledge*. 1966; reprint ed., Garden City, N.Y.: Doubleday Anchor Books, 1967.

Blakeborough, Richard. *Wit, Character, Folklore and Customs of the North Riding of Yorkshire*. London: Henry Frowde, 1898.

Blythe, Roland. *Akenfield*. New York: Pantheon Books, 1969.

Bovill, E. W. *English Country Life 1780–1830*. London: Oxford University Press, 1962.

Briggs, Asa, ed. *How They Lived Volume III: An Anthology of Original Documents Written Between 1700 and 1815*. New York: Barnes & Noble, 1969.

Broadwood, Lucy E., and Maitland, J. A. Fuller, eds. *English County Songs*. London: B. J. Cramer, n.d.

Brocklebank, Joan, and Kindersley, Biddie, eds. *A Dorset Book of Folk Songs*. London: English Folk Dance and Song Society, 1966.

Bronson, Bertrand Harris. *The Traditional Tunes of the Child Ballads with Their Texts, According to the Extant Records of Great Britain and America*. 4 vols. Princeton: Princeton University Press, 1959–72.

Brooke, Justin, and Brooke, Edith. *Suffolk Prospect*. London: Faber & Faber, 1963.

Buchan, David. *The Ballad and the Folk*. London: Routledge & Kegan Paul, 1972.

Burke, Kenneth. *A Grammar of Motives*. Berkeley: University of California Press, 1969.

———. *Permanence and Change: An Anatomy of Purpose*. 2d ed., rev. 1954; reprint ed., Indianapolis: Bobbs-Merrill, 1965.

Burns, Tom. "A Model for Textual Variation in Folksong." *Folklore Forum* 3 (1970): 49–56.

Buttershaw Youth Centre. *The Song of Upper Wharfedale*. Bradford, Yorks.: City of Bradford Educational Services Committee, 1971.

Casey, George J.; Rosenberg, Neil V.; and Wareham, Wilfred W. "Repertoire Categorization and Performance-Audience Relationships: Some Newfoundland Examples." *Ethnomusicology* 16 (1972): 397–403.

Census of Great Britain, 1851. London: W. Clowes & Sons, for Her Majesty's Stationery Office, 1852.

Bibliography

Chambers, J. D. *Laxton: The Last English Open Field Village*. London: Her Majesty's Stationery Office, 1964.

Child, Francis James. *The English and Scottish Popular Ballads*. 5 vols. 1882–98; reprint ed., New York: Dover, 1965.

Coates, B. E., and Rawstron, E. M. *Regional Variations in Great Britain: Studies in Economic and Social Geography*. London: B. T. Batsford, 1971.

Coffin, Tristram Potter. *The British Traditional Ballad in North America*. Rev. ed. With a Supplement by Roger deV. Renwick. Austin: University of Texas Press, 1977.

Collinson, Francis, and Dillon, Francis. *Songs from the Countryside*. London: W. Paxton, 1946.

Colls, Robert. *The Collier's Rant: Song and Culture in the Industrial Village*. Totowa, N.J.: Rowman & Littlefield, 1977.

Cook, Catherine. "A Collection of Folk Tales from Upper Nidderdale." M.A. thesis, University of Leeds, 1972.

Copper, Bob. *A Song for Every Season: A Hundred Years of a Sussex Farming Family*. London: Heinemann, 1971.

————. *Songs and Southern Breezes: Country Folk and Country Ways*. London: Heinemann, 1973.

Cray, Ed. *The Erotic Muse*. New York: Oak Publications, 1968.

Creighton, Helen. *Maritime Folk Songs*. Toronto: Ryerson Press, 1962.

Creighton, Helen, and Senior, Doreen H. *Traditional Songs from Nova Scotia*. Toronto: Ryerson Press, 1950.

Croft, W. R. *The History of the Factory Movement, or, Oastler and His Times*. Huddersfield, Yorks.: George Whitehead & Sons, 1888.

Cross, Roger. "Defiant Sid Haigh Says: We Are Winning the Fight." *Yorkshire Post* (Leeds), 23 March 1973.

Culler, Jonathan. *Structuralist Poetics: Structuralism, Linguistics, and the Study of Literature*. Ithaca: Cornell University Press, 1975.

Curle, Adam. "Kinship Structure in an English Village." *Man* 52 (1952): 68–69.

Daily Mail (London).

The Dalesman (Clapham, Yorkshire).

Davies, Margaret Llewelyn, ed. *Life as We Have Known It*. By Co-Operative Working Women. London: Leonard and Virginia Woolf at the Hogarth Press, 1931.

Davis, Arthur Kyle, Jr., ed. *More Traditional Ballads of Virginia*. Chapel Hill: University of North Carolina Press, 1960.

Dennis, Norman; Henriques, Fernando; and Slaughter, Clifford. *Coal Is Our Life: An Analysis of a Yorkshire Mining Community*. 2d ed. London: Tavistock, 1969.

Dewhirst, Ian. *Gleanings from Victorian Yorkshire*. Driffield, Yorks.: The Ridings Publishing Company, 1972.

Dewsbury Reporter (Dewsbury, Yorkshire).

Dickinson, Bickford H. C. *Sabine Baring-Gould: Squarson, Writer and Folklorist, 1834–1924.* Newton Abbot, Devon: David & Charles, 1970.

Dransfield, John N. *A History of the Parish of Penistone.* Penistone, Yorks.: James H. Wood, The Don Press, 1906.

Dundes, Alan. *The Morphology of North American Indian Folktales.* Folklore Fellows Communications, no. 195. Helsinki: Suomalainen Tiedeakatemia, 1964.

Dyson, Taylor. *The History of Huddersfield and District from the Earliest Times Down to 1951.* 2d ed. Huddersfield, Yorks.: Alfred Jubb & Son, 1951.

English Dance and Song (London).

Evans, George Ewart. *Tools of Their Trade: An Oral History of Men at Work c. 1900.* New York: Taplinger, 1971.

Evening Post (Leeds).

Fairfax-Blakeborough, J., and Fairfax-Blakeborough, R. *The Spirit of Yorkshire.* London: B. T. Batsford, 1954.

Fernandez, James. "The Mission of Metaphor in Expressive Culture." *Current Anthropology* 15 (1974): 119–43.

Flanders, Helen Hartness, and Olney, Marguerite. *Ballads Migrant in New England.* New York: Farrar, Strauss, & Young, 1953.

Folk Music Journal (London).

Ford [Hueffer], Ford Maddox, *The Heart of the Country: A Survey of a Modern Land.* London: Alston Rivers, 1906.

Forshaw, Charles F., ed. *Holroyd's Collection of Yorkshire Ballads.* London: George Bell & Sons, 1892.

Foster, Florence. "Last Chronicle of Beckermonds." *The Dalesman* 10 (1948): 132–35.

Foster, George M. "Peasant Society and the Image of Limited Good." *American Anthropologist* 67 (1965): 293–315.

Freeman, T. W. *The Conurbations of Great Britain,* 2d rev. ed. Manchester: Manchester University Press, 1966.

Fussell, G. E. *The English Rural Labourer: His Home, Furniture, Clothing and Food, from Tudor to Victorian Times.* London: Batchworth, 1949.

Geertz, Clifford. *The Interpretation of Cultures.* New York: Basic Books, 1973.

General Register Office. *Census 1961. England and Wales. County Report: Yorkshire.* London: Her Majesty's Stationery Office, 1963.

Gerould, Gordon Hall. *The Ballad of Tradition.* 1932; reprint ed. New York: Oxford University Press Galaxy Book, 1957.

Gillington, Alice. *Eight Hampshire Folk Songs.* London: J. Curwen & Sons, 1907.

Glassie, Henry; Ives, Edward D.; and Szwed, John F. *Folksongs and Their Makers.* Bowling Green, Ohio: Bowling Green University Popular Press, [1971].

Goldstein, Kenneth. "Monologue Performance in Great Britain." *Southern Folklore Quarterly* 40 (1976): 7–29.

Bibliography

Goldstein, Kenneth S., and Bethke, Robert D., eds. "Monologues and Folk Recitation." Special issue of *Southern Folklore Quarterly* 40, nos. 1–2 (1976).

Gossen, Gary H. "Chamula Genres of Verbal Behavior." *Journal of American Folklore* 84 (1971): 145–67.

Greenleaf, Elisabeth Bristol, and Mansfield, Grace Yarrow. *Ballads and Sea Songs of Newfoundland.* Cambridge: Harvard University Press, 1933.

Greig, Gavin. *Folk-Song of the North-East.* Hatboro, Pa.: Folklore Associates, 1963.

Hagopian, John V. "Symbol and Metaphor in the Transformation of Reality into Art." *Comparative Literature* 20 (1968): 45–54.

Halpert, Herbert. "Vitality of Tradition and Local Songs." *Journal of the International Folk Music Council* 3 (1951); 35–40.

Hamer, Fred. *Garners Gay.* Folk Song Today, no. 2. London: English Folk Dance and Song Society, 1967.

Hammond, J. L. and Hammond, Barbara. *The Village Labourer 1760–1832.* 1911; reprint ed. New York: Harper Torchbooks, 1970.

Hanson, T. W. "The Diary of a Grandfather: Cornelius Ashworth, of Waltroyd Wheatley." *Papers, Reports, etc., Read Before the Halifax Antiquarian Society* n.v. (1916): 233–48.

Harker, David. "Cecil Sharp in Somerset: Some Conclusions." *Folk Music Journal* 3 (1978): 220–40.

Harris, Clement. *Hennage: A Social System in Miniature.* Case Studies in Cultural Anthropology, no. 4. New York: Holt, Rinehart & Winston, 1974.

Hasbach, W. *A History of the English Agricultural Labourer.* Translated by Ruth Kenyon. New York: Augustus M. Kelley, 1966.

Healy, James N., ed. *The Mercier Book of Old Irish Street Ballads.* 3 vols. Cork: Mercier Press, 1967–69.

Heath, Francis George. *The English Peasantry.* London: Frederick Warne, 1874.

Hecht, J. Jean. *The Domestic Servant Class in Eighteenth-Century England.* London: Routledge & Kegan Paul, 1956.

Hirsch, E. D., Jr. *Validity in Interpretation.* New Haven: Yale University Press, 1967.

Hobsbawm, E. J. *Labouring Men: Studies in the History of Labour.* London: Weidenfeld & Nicolson, 1964.

Hobsbawm, E. J., and Rudé, George. *Captain Swing.* New York: Pantheon Books, 1968.

Hodgart, M. J. C. *The Ballads.* 2d ed. London: Hutchinson University Library, 1962.

Hole, Christina. *British Folk Customs.* London: Hutchinson, 1976.

Hoskins, W. G. *The Midland Peasant: The Economic and Social History of a Leicestershire Village.* London: Macmillan, 1952.

Ingledew, C. J. Davidson. *The Ballads and Songs of Yorkshire, Transcribed from Private Manuscripts, Rare Broadsides, and Scarce Publications.* London: Bell & Daldy, 1860.

Ives, Edward D. *Larry Gorman: The Man Who Made the Songs.* Bloomington: Indiana University Press, 1964.

————. *Lawrence Doyle: the Farmer Poet of Prince Edward Island: A Study in Local Songmaking.* University of Maine Studies, no. 92. Orono: University of Maine Press, 1971.

————. "A Man and His Song: Joe Scott and 'The Plain Golden Band.' " In *Folksongs and Their Makers.* By Henry Glassie, Edward D. Ives, and John F. Szwed, pp. 69–146. Bowling Green, Ohio: Bowling Green University Popular Press, [1971].

Jakobson, Roman. "Concluding Statement: Linguistics and Poetics." In *Style in Language.* Edited by Thomas A. Sebeok, pp. 350–77. Cambridge: M.I.T. Press, 1960.

Jefferies, Richard. *An English Village.* Boston: Little, Brown, 1903.

Johnson, Clifton. *Among English Hedgerows.* New York: Macmillan, 1925.

Journal of the English Folk Dance and Song Society (London).

Journal of the Folk-Song Society (London).

Karpeles, Maud. *Cecil Sharp: His Life and Work.* London: Routledge & Kegan Paul, 1967.

————. ed. *Cecil Sharp's Collection of English Folk Songs.* 2 vols. London: Oxford University Press, 1974.

Kennedy, Peter, ed. *Folksongs of Britain and Ireland.* London: Cassell, 1975.

Kidson, Frank. *Traditional Tunes.* Oxford: Charles Taphouse, 1891.

La Page, John. *The Story of Baildon.* Bradford, Yorks.: Printed by Wm. Byles & Sons, n.d.

Laslett, Peter. *The World We Have Lost.* London: Methuen, 1965.

Laslett, Peter, and Oosterveen, Karla. "Long-Term Trends in Bastardy in England: A Study of the Illegitimacy Figures in the Parish Registers and in the Reports of the Registrar General, 1561–1960." *Population Studies* 27 (1973): 255–86.

Laszlo, Ervin. *Introduction to Systems Philosophy: Toward a New Paradigm of Contemporary Thought.* New York: Harper Torchbooks, 1973.

Laws, G. Malcolm, Jr. *American Balladry from British Broadsides: A Guide for Students and Collectors of Traditional Song.* Publications of the American Folklore Society, Bibliographical and Special Series, vol. 8. Philadelphia: American Folklore Society, 1957.

————. *Native American Balladry: A Descriptive Guide and a Bibliographical Syllabus.* Rev. ed. Publications of the American Folklore Society, Bibliographical and Special Series, vol. 1. Philadelphia: American Folklore Society, 1964.

Leach, MacEdward, ed. *The Ballad Book.* New York: A. S. Barnes, 1955.

Legman, G. *The Horn Book: Studies in Erotic Folklore and Bibliography.* New Hyde Park, N.Y.: University Books, 1964.

Lévi-Strauss, Claude. "The Story of Asdiwal." In *The Structural Study of Myth and Totemism.* Edited by Edmund Leach, pp. 1–47. A.S.A. Monographs, no. 5. London: Tavistock, 1967.

————. *Structural Anthropology.* Translated by Claire Jacobson and Brooke Grundfest Schoepf. Garden City, N.Y.: Doubleday Anchor Books, 1967.

Lloyd, A. L. *Come All Ye Bold Miners: Ballads and Songs of the Coalfields.* London: Lawrence & Wishart, 1952.

————. *Folk Song in England.* London: Lawrence & Wishart, 1967.

Long, Eleanor. "Ballad Singers, Ballad Makers, and Ballad Etiology." *Western Folklore* 32 (1973): 225–36.

————. *"The Maid" and "The Hangman": Myth and Tradition in a Popular Ballad.* Folklore Studies, no. 21. Berkeley: University of California Press, 1971.

MacKerness, E. D., ed. *The Journals of George Sturt, 1890–1927.* 2 vols. Cambridge: Cambridge University Press, 1967.

Manley, E. R. *Meet the Miner.* Lofthouse, Yorks.: Published by the Author, 1947.

Marshall, Dorothy. *Industrial England 1776–1851.* London: Routledge & Kegan Paul, 1973.

Marshall, Sybil, ed. *Fenland Chronicle: Recollections of William and Kate Mary Edwards.* Cambridge: Cambridge University Press, 1967.

Mass-Observation. *The Pub and the People: A Worktown Study.* London: Victor Gollancz, 1943.

Miller, George A. *The Psychology of Communication: Seven Essays.* Harmondsworth, Middlesex: Penguin Books, 1968.

Moreau, R. E. *The Departed Village: Berrick Salome at the Turn of the Century.* London: Oxford University Press, 1968.

Morgan, David H. "The Place of Harvesters in Nineteenth-Century Village Life." In *Village Life and Labour.* Edited by Raphael Samuel, pp. 27–72. London: Routledge & Kegan Paul, 1975.

Morris, M. C. F. *Yorkshire Reminiscences (With Others).* London: Humphrey Milford, Oxford University Press, 1922.

Morton, Robin, ed. *Come Day, Go Day, God Send Sunday: The Songs and Life Story, Told in His Own Words, of John Maguire, Traditional Singer and Farmer from Co. Fermanagh.* London: Routledge & Kegan Paul, 1973.

Nettel, Reginald. *Sing a Song of England: A Social History of Traditional Song.* London: Phoenix House, 1954.

Nicholson, John. *The Folk Speech of East Yorkshire.* London: Simpkin, Marshall, 1889; reprint ed., Norwood, Pa.: Norwood Editions, 1977.

Olrik, Axel. "Epic Laws of Folk Narrative." In *The Study of Folklore.* Edited by Alan Dundes, pp. 131–41. Englewood Cliffs, N.J.: Prentice-Hall, 1965.

Page, W. G. B. *The Life of Thomas Mercer (Commonly Called "Tom Massey"), The Blind Fiddler of Witherwick, East-Riding of Yorkshire.* Hull, Yorks.: M. Harland & Son, 1902.

Parker, James. *Illustrated Rambles from Hipperholme to Tong.* Bradford, Yorks.: Humphries & Co., The Country Press, 1904.

Pattison, Susan. "The Antrobus Soulcaking Play: An Alternative Approach to the Mummers' Play." *Folk-Life* 15 (1977): 5–11.

Peacock, Kenneth, ed. *Songs of the Newfoundland Outports.* 3 vols. National Museum of Canada Bulletin, no. 197, Anthropological Series, no. 65. Ottawa: National Museum of Canada, 1965.

Pearce, T. M. "What Is a Folk Poet?" *Western Folklore* 12 (1953): 242–48.

Peel, Frank. *The Risings of the Luddites, Chartists and Plug-Drawers.* 4th ed. New York: Augustus M. Kelley, 1968.

Peel, J. H. B. *Country Talk.* London: Hale, 1970.

Perkin, Harold. *The Origin of Modern English Society 1780–1880.* London: Routledge & Kegan Paul, 1969.

Pike, E. Royston. *"Hard Times": Human Documents of the Industrial Revolution.* New York: Frederick A. Praeger, 1966.

Porter, Enid. *Cambridgeshire Customs and Folklore.* New York: Barnes & Noble, 1969.

Propp, V. *Morphology of the Folktale.* Translated by Laurence Scott, 2d rev. ed. by Louis A. Wagner. Publications of the American Folklore Society, Bibliographical and Special Series, vol. 9; Indiana University Research Center in Anthropology, Folklore, and Linguistics, publication 10. Austin: University of Texas Press, 1968.

Purslow, Frank, ed. *The Constant Lovers: More English Folk Songs from the Hammond and Gardiner Mss.* London: English Folk Dance and Song Society, 1972.

————. *The Foggy Dew: More English Folk Songs from the Hammond and Gardiner Mss.* London: English Folk Dance and Song Society, 1974.

————. *Marrow Bones: English Folk Songs from the Hammond and Gardiner Mss.* London: English Folk Dance and Song Society, 1965.

————. *The Wanton Seed: More English Folk Songs from the Hammond and Gardiner Mss.* London: English Folk Dance and Song Society, 1968.

Reeves, James, ed. *The Everlasting Circle.* London: Heinemann, 1960.

Renwick, Roger deV. "Two Yorkshire Poets: A Comparative Study." *Southern Folklore Quarterly* 40 (1976): 239–81.

Riley, W., and Brockbank, Elisabeth. *A Village in Craven: Character Sketches from the Yorkshire Pennines.* London: Herbert Jenkins, 1925.

Roth, H. Ling. *The Yorkshire Coiners 1767–1783. And Notes on Old and Prehistoric Halifax.* Halifax, Yorks.: F. King & Sons, 1906.

Roth, Klaus. *Ehebruchschwänke in Liedform: Eine Untersuchung zur deutsch-und englischsprachigen Schwankballade.* Motive: Freiburger folkloristische Forschungen, vol. 9. Munich: Wilhelm Fink Verlag, 1977.

Rotherham Advertiser (Rotherham, Yorkshire).

Schutz, Alfred. "Symbol, Reality, and Society." In *Symbols and Society: Fourteenth Symposium of the Conference on Science, Philosophy and Religion.* Edited by Lyman Bryson et al., pp. 135–203. New

York: The Conference on Science, Philosophy and Religion in Their Relationship to the Democratic Way of Life, 1955.

Seeger, Peggy, and MacColl, Ewan. *The Ewan MacColl-Peggy Seeger Songbook.* New York: Oak Publications, 1963.

Sharp, Cecil J. *English Folk Song: Some Conclusions.* London: Simpkin, 1907.

_____. *English Folk Songs.* Selected edition. 2 vols. in one. London: Novello, 1920.

Sing Out! (New York).

Sketch of the Life and Opinions of Richard Oastler. Leeds: Printed by Joshua Hobson for Cobbett, 1838.

Spark, Fred R. *Memories of My Life.* Leeds: Fred R. Spark & Son, n.d.

Stuart [Bourne], George. *Change in the Village.* London: Duckworth, 1912.

_____. *Memoirs of a Surrey Laborer: A Record of the Last Years of Frederick Bettesworth.* London: Duckworth, 1907.

Sykes, D. F. E. *The History of Huddersfield and the Valleys of the Colne, the Holme, and the Dearne.* Huddersfield, Yorks.: "The Worker" Press, n.d.

Szwed, John F. "Paul E. Hall: A Newfoundland Song-Maker and His Community." In *Folksongs and Their Makers.* By Henry Glassie, Edward D. Ives, and John F. Szwed, pp. 147–69. Bowling Green, Ohio: Bowling Green University Popular Press, [1971].

Thomis, Malcolm I. *The Luddites: Machine-Breaking in Regency England.* New York: Schocken Books, 1972.

Thompson, E. P. "Time, Work-Discipline and Industrial Capitalism." *Past and Present,* no. 38 (1967): 56–97.

Thompson, Flora. *Lark Rise to Candleford: A Trilogy.* The World's Classics, no. 542. London: Oxford University Press, 1954.

Toelken J. Barre. "'Riddles Wisely Expounded.'" *Western Folklore* 25 (1966): 1–16.

Transactions of the Yorkshire Dialect Society.

Turner, J. Horsfall. *The Annals of Wakefield House of Correction for Three Hundred Years.* Bingley, Yorks.: Privately Printed for J. Horsfall Turner by Harrison & Sons, 1904.

_____. *Yorkshire Anthology: Ballads and Songs—Ancient and Modern, (With Several Hundred Real Epitaphs,) Covering a Period of a Thousand Years of Yorkshire History in Verse.* Idel, Bradford, Yorks.: Printed for the Editor by T. Harrison & Sons, Bingley, 1901.

Turner, Victor. *The Forest of Symbols: Aspects of Ndembu Ritual.* Ithaca: Cornell University Press, 1967.

_____. "The Syntax of Symbolism in an Ndembu Ritual." In *Structural Analysis of Oral Tradition.* Edited by Pierre and Elli Köngäs Maranda, pp. 125–36. Philadelphia: University of Pennsylvania Press, 1971.

Tyler, Stephen A., ed. *Cognitive Anthropology.* New York: Holt, Rinehart & Winston, 1969.

The Universal Songster. 3 vols. London: Jones & Co., 1832.

Vicinus, Martha. *The Industrial Muse: A Study of Nineteenth Century British Working-Class Literature.* New York: Barnes & Noble, 1974.

Wakefield Express (Wakefield, Yorkshire).

Wharton, Colin S. "Folk Songs from the North Riding." M.A. thesis, University of Leeds, 1962.

White, Walter. *A Month in Yorkshire.* London: Chapman & Hall, 1858.

Whitlock, Ralph. *A Family and a Village.* London: John Baker, 1969.

Wilgus, D. K. *Anglo-American Folksong Scholarship Since 1898.* New Brunswick, N.J.: Rutgers University Press, 1959.

_____. "A Type-Index of Anglo-American Traditional Narrative Songs." *Journal of the Folklore Institute* 7 (1970): 161–77.

Williams, Alfred, ed. *Folk-Songs of the Upper Thames: With an Essay on Folk-Song Activity in the Upper Thames Neighbourhood.* London: Duckworth, 1923; reprint ed., Detroit: Singing Tree Press, 1968.

_____. *Round About the Upper Thames.* London: Duckworth, 1922.

_____. *A Wiltshire Village.* London: Duckworth, 1912.

Williams, Iolo A. *English Folk-Song and Dance.* London: Longmans, Green, 1935.

Williams, Ralph Vaughn, and Lloyd, A. L., eds. *The Penguin Book of English Folk Songs: From the Journal of the Folk Song Society and the Journal of the English Folk Dance and Song Society.* Harmondsworth, Middlesex: Penguin Books, 1959.

Williams, Raymond. *The Country and the City.* New York: Oxford University Press, 1973.

Williams, W. M. *Gosforth: The Sociology of an English Village.* Glencoe, Ill.: The Free Press, 1956.

Wright, Thomas [A Journeyman Engineer]. *Some Habits and Customs of the Working Classes.* London Tinsley Brothers, 1867.

Yorkshire Post (Leeds).

The Yorkshireman (Bradford, Yorkshire).

MISCELLANEOUS SOURCES

"Ballads, English and American." Special Collections, University of California, Los Angeles. Accession no. 605.

British Broadcasting Corporation. *Lofthouse: Aftermath of a Disaster.* Television documentary, broadcast 24 May 1973.

Daniel, Tommy. "Yorkshire Broadsheet." Typed and mimeographed pamphlet. Batley, Yorkshire.

Institute of Dialect and Folk Life Studies Archives, University of Leeds.

"Leeds Printed Broadsides." Compiled by Frank Kidson. Collection in Leeds Central Library.

Mugglestone, Ephraim [Charles Moxon]. "A Fair Crack of the Whip: My Life in the Coal Mines and Hospital." Typewritten manuscript. Langold, Nottinghamshire.

INDEX

POEMS AND SONGS
(cited by title, first line, Child number, or Laws number)

NAMES

SUBJECTS